THE GOLDEN TREASURY OF CHESS

Compiled by

AL HOROWITZ
AND
THE EDITORS OF CHESS REVIEW

CORNERSTONE LIBRARY • NEW YORK

Reprinted 1969

This completely new revised edition is published by arrangement with I. A. Horowitz and Harvey House, Inc.

CORNERSTONE LIBRARY PUBLICATIONS
are distributed by
Simon & Schuster, Inc.
630 Fifth Avenue
New York, New York 10020

Manufactured in the United States of America
under the supervision of
Rolls Offset Printing Co., Inc., N. Y.

Contents

This Book is Dedicated

To the Memory of

HARRY NELSON PILLSBURY

(1872-1906)

PART I

Favorite Games

In the course of the decades which I have devoted to the preparation of this volume, I have had occasion to examine thousands upon thousands of scores. Those that have pleased me most are included in "THE GOLDEN TREASURY OF CHESS." But even among these favorites, there are some which I have enjoyed so much that I have set them aside in order to attract the reader's attention to these games. I will not deny that ten years ago I might have selected other games, and that in the years to come, my tastes will again be modified! Nevertheless, you will be delighted with these games.

1. Warsaw, Nov. 1844

As long as we continue to be charmed by the triumph of mind over matter, such combinations will fascinate us. The idea of readily surrendering the Queen in order to hound the hostile King with the lesser pieces, has been utilized fairly often; but Petroff's sacrifice was one of the first, if not THE first, example of this appealing combinative theme. All honor to his originality!

GIUOCO PIANO

HOFFMAN White	PETROFF Black
1 P—K4	P—K4
2 Kt—KB3	Kt—QB3
3 B—B4	B—B4
4 P—B3	Kt—B3
5 P—Q4	P x P
6 P—K5	Kt—K5
7 B—Q5	Kt x KBP?!
8 K x Kt	P x Pch
9 K—Kt3	P x P
10 B x P	Kt—K2
11 Kt—Kt5	Kt x B
12 Kt x BP	O—O!!
13 Kt x Q	. . . .

And Black mates in eleven moves.

13	B—B7ch
14 K—R3	P—Q3ch
15 P—K6	Kt—B5ch
16 K—Kt4	Kt x KP
17 P—Kt3	Kt x Ktch
18 K—Kt5	R—B4ch
19 K—Kt4	R—B3ch
20 K—R4	R—B5ch
21 K—Kt5	Kt—K3ch
22 K—R5	P—Kt3ch
23 K—R6	R—R5ch
24 P x R	B—K6 mate

---

2. Paris, 1845

It is many years since I first saw this game, but the final position, with Black's Queen trapped by its own far-advanced Pawns, and White's King gaily advancing down the board to assist in the final attack against his colleague, is still good for a chuckle. Imagine Kieseritzky's chagrin as he stares ruefully at the bottled-up Queen! Who says there is no place for humor in chess?!

COCHRANE GAMBIT

MICHELET White	L. KIESERITZKY Black
1 P—K4	P—K4
2 P—KB4	P x P
3 Kt—KB3	P—KKt4
4 B—B4	P—Kt5
5 Kt—K5	Q—R5ch
6 K—B1	P—B6
7 P—Q4	Kt—KB3
8 Kt—B3	B—Kt2
9 P—KKt3	Q—R6ch
10 K—B2	P—Q3
11 Kt x P (B7)	R—B1
12 Kt—KKt5	Q—Kt7ch
13 K—K3	B—R3
14 K—Q3	Kt—B3
15 P—QR3	B x Kt

16 B x B	Kt x KP!?
17 Q—K1	B—B4
18 Kt x Kt	P—B7
19 Q—K3	K—Q2
20 B—Q5	QR—K1
21 QR—KB1	B x Ktch
22 B x B	R—B6
23 Q x R	P x Q
24 B—B5ch	R—K3
25 P—Q5	Kt—K4ch
26 K—Q4	P—KR4
27 P x Rch	K—K1
28 B—B6	P—R5
29 B x Kt	P x Bch
30 K x P	P x KtP
31 K—B6 and wins!	

One of the most astounding endings on record.

3. Paris, Nov. 1846

Poor Kieseritzky! He achieved negative immortality by losing a magnificent game to the great Anderssen, and this feat swallowed up his reputation forever after. That Kieseritzky was a brilliant and able player in his own right, however, is abundantly clear from this game.

BISHOP'S GAMBIT

W. SCHULTEN	L. KIESERITZKY
White	Black
1 P—K4	P—K4
2 P—KB4	P x P
3 B—B4	Q—R5ch
4 K—B1	P—QKt4
5 B x P	Kt—KB3
6 Kt—QB3	Kt—Kt5
7 Kt—R3	Kt—QB3
8 Kt—Q5	Kt—Q5!
9 Kt x Pch	K—Q1
10 Kt x R	P—B6!
11 P—Q3	P—B3
12 B—QB4	P—Q4!
13 B x P	B—Q3
14 Q—K1	P x Pch
15 K x P	Q x Ktch!
16 K x Q	Kt—K6ch
17 K—R4	Kt—B6ch
18 K—R5	B—Kt5 mate

4. Breslau, 1859.

It is difficult to imagine how one could concentrate more brilliancy, more inspired inventiveness, more sparkle into so short a game. Here is the distilled essence of the very best chess of the old masters: one thrill after another!

Sacrificial Orgy

RUY LOPEZ

A. ANDERSSEN	DR. M. LANGE
White	Black
1 P—K4	P—K4
2 Kt—KB3	Kt—QB3
3 B—Kt5	Kt—Q5
4 Kt x Kt	P x Kt
5 B—B4	Kt—B3
6 P—K5	P—Q4
7 B—Kt3	B—KKt5

8	P—KB3	Kt—K5!
9	O—O	P—Q6!
10	P x B	B—B4ch
11	K—R1	Kt—Kt6ch!
12	P x Kt	Q—Kt4
13	R—B5	....

13	....	P—KR4!!
14	KtP x P	Q x R
15	P—Kt4	R x Pch!!
16	P x R	Q—K5!
17	Q—B3	Q—R5ch
18	Q—R3	Q—K8ch
	Resigns	

Bravo!

---

5. Berlin, 1869

You have probably heard that Anderssen was a mighty man with the Evans Gambit, but it is impossible to realize what glorious feats he performed with it, until you have played over such games as this one. Incidentally Zukertort, the great Anderssen's brilliant pupil, knew how to take fitting revenge, as you will see in later games in this volume. These two immortals produced games worthy of their reputation.

A glorious battle

EVANS GAMBIT

	A. Anderssen White	J. H. Zukertort Black
1	P—K4	P—K4
2	Kt—KB3	Kt—QB3
3	B—B4	B—B4
4	P—QKt4	B x P
5	P—B3	B—B4
6	O—O	P—Q3
7	P—Q4	P x P
8	P x P	B—Kt3
9	P—Q5	Kt—R4
10	B—Kt2	Kt—K2
11	B—Q3	O—O
12	Kt—B3	Kt—Kt3
13	Kt—K2	P—QB4
14	R—B1	R—Kt1
15	Q—Q2	P—B3
16	K—R1	B—B2
17	Kt—Kt3	P—Kt4
18	Kt—B5	P—Kt5?
19	R—KKt1	B—Kt3
20	P—Kt4	Kt—K4
21	B x Kt	QP x B
22	R—Kt3	R—B2
23	P—Kt5	B x Kt
24	P x B	Q x P?
25	P x P	R—Q1
26	QR—KKt1	K—R1
27	P x Pch	K—Kt1
28	Q—R6	Q—Q3

White announced mate in five.

29 Q x Pch! — K x Q
30 P—B6ch — K—Kt1
31 B—R7ch! — K x B
32 R—R3ch — K—Kt1
33 R—R8 mate

---

6. St. Petersburg, 1896

There are many attractive settings for a brilliant game; but what is more impressive than an immortal game between two Titans? The man who was able to beat the great Pillsbury in this wonderful game was truly worthy of his title. It is no exaggeration to say that Lasker's combination is one of the greatest feats of the human imagination.

Quadrangular Tourney

QUEEN'S GAMBIT DECLINED

H. N. Pillsbury White	Dr. E. Lasker Black
1 P—Q4	P—Q4
2 P—QB4	P—K3
3 Kt—QB3	Kt—KB3
4 Kt—B3	P—B4
5 B—Kt5	BP x P
6 Q x P	Kt—B3
7 Q—R4?	B—K2
8 O—O—O	Q—R4
9 P—K3	B—Q2
10 K—Kt1	P—KR3
11 P x P	P x P
12 Kt—Q4	O—O
13 B x Kt	B x B
14 Q—R5	Kt x Kt
15 P x Kt	B—K3

The calm before the storm.

16 P—B4 — QR—B1

The charm of the position after Black's 16th move is its surface innocence. Though Pillsbury only half suspects the quicksands, his defense cannot be improved.

17 P—B5 — R x Kt!!

A problem in one half the moves of the entire game, mentally composed and solved in a manner worthy of the champion of the world.

18 P x B — R—QR6!!
19 P x Pch — R x P
20 P x R — Q—Kt3ch
21 B—Kt5 — Q x Bch
22 K—R1 — R—B2

Threatens . . . R—B8ch!

23 R—Q2 — R—B5
24 KR—Q1 — R—B6!
25 Q—B5 — Q—B5
26 K—Kt2 — R x P!

27 Q—K6ch — K—R2
28 K x R — Q—B6ch
29 K—R4 — P—Kt4ch
30 K x P — Q—B5ch
31 K—R5 — B—Q1ch
32 Q—Kt6 — P x Q mate

---

7. Carlsbad, 1911

One of the marks of a great master is the ability to conjure up murderous attacks out of seemingly harmless positions. You will like the way that Spielmann commences an unexpected attack at move 22 and drives it home with sledgehammer blows. Every move tells, and Black's helplessness becomes ever more apparent.

RUY LOPEZ

R. SPIELMANN White	DUS-CHOTIMIRSKI Black
1 P—K4	P—K4
2 Kt—KB3	Kt—QB3
3 B—Kt5	P—QR3
4 B—R4	Kt—B3
5 O—O	B—K2
6 R—K1	P—QKt4
7 B—Kt3	P—Q3
8 P—B3	Kt—QR4
9 B—B2	P—B4
10 P—Q3	O—O
11 QKt—Q2	Q—B2
12 Kt—B1	R—Kt1
13 P—KR3	B—K3
14 Q—K2	P—Kt5
15 Kt(3)—R2	Kt—Q2
16 Kt—Kt3	KR—B1
17 Kt—Kt4	R—Kt2
18 Kt—K3	B—Kt4
19 Kt—Q5	B x Kt
20 P x B	B x B
21 QR x B	Kt—KB3
22 P—Q4!	KP x P
23 Kt—R5!	Kt—Q2
24 Q—Kt4	P—Kt3
25 R—K7	K—B1
26 QR—K1!	Q—Q1
27 Q—Kt5	Kt—K4
28 Q—B6!	Kt(R4)—B5
29 P—B4!	P x Kt
30 P x Kt	Kt x KP
31 R(1) x Kt!	Resigns

8. Iceland, 1931

Reti noted years ago that Alekhine's outstanding quality was his ability to give even the most commonplace positions an unusual turn. This game abounds in such original moves.

FRENCH DEFENSE

A. ALEKHINE White	ASGIERSSEN Black
1 P—K4	P—K3
2 P—Q4	P—Q4
3 Kt—QB3	Kt—KB3
4 B—Kt5	B—K2
5 B x Kt	B x B
6 Kt—B3	O—O
7 B—Q3	R—K1
8 P—K5	B—K2
9 P—KR4	P—QB4
10 B x Pch!	K x B
11 Kt—Kt5ch	B x Kt
12 P x Bch	K—Kt1
13 Q—R5	K—B1
14 O—O—O	P—R3
15 P—Kt6!	K—K2
16 KtP x P	R—B1
17 P x P	Kt—Q2
18 R x P!!	Q—R4
19 Q—Kt5ch	K x P
20 R—R7	R—KKt1
21 R—Q4	Q x BP

22	R x Ktch!	B x R
23	Kt—K4	Q—Kt5
24	Kt—Q6ch	K—B1
25	Q—B6ch!	P x Q
26	R—B7 mate	

---

9. Warsaw, 1935

Anyone who preaches the imminent death of chess ought to take a good look at this game! The striking series of brilliancies initiated by Black's thirteenth move compares favorably, I believe, with any combination ever played over the board.

A Polish "Immortal"

DUTCH DEFENSE

GLUCKSBERG		M. NAJDORF
White		Black
1	P—Q4	P—KB4
2	P—QB4	Kt—KB3
3	Kt—QB3	P—K3
4	Kt—B3	P—Q4
5	P—K3?	P—B3
6	B—Q3	B—Q3
7	O—O	O—O
8	Kt—K2?	QKt—Q2
9	Kt—Kt5?	B x Pch
10	K—R1	Kt—Kt5
11	P—B4	Q—K1

12	P—KKt3	Q—R4
13	K—Kt2	B—Kt8!!
14	Kt x B	Q—R7ch
15	K—B3	P—K4!
16	QP x P	QKt x Pch
17	P x Kt	Kt x Pch
18	K—B4	Kt—Kt3ch
19	K—B3	P—B5!
20	KP x P	B—Kt5ch!
21	K x B	Kt—K4ch!
22	P x Kt	P—R4 mate

PART II

The Pre-Morphy Period

Although chess is a direct descendant of a game played in India in the 7th century, *modern* chess was not initiated until the late 15th century—about the year 1485—when important changes were made in the rules. For a hundred years before this date the game had remained unchanged, the moves of the pieces fixed. Although highly popular, it was a dull game by our standards. The modern chessplayer would regard the chess of the middle ages as a strange and wearisome pastime.

In many respects, of course, the mediaeval game was similar to the chess we play today. The positions of the pieces were the same; the Rooks, Knights and Pawns moved as they move today; Castling had not yet been developed, but the King was allowed to "leap" two squares on its first move.

The main difference lay in the moves of the Queen and Bishop. The Queen was permitted to move only to an adjacent diagonal square. In other words, it moved like our Bishop, but only one square at a time! Instead of being the most powerful piece on the board, it was the weakest. The Bishop of the mediaeval game leaped over the adjacent diagonal square to the square beyond in the diagonal.

When the moves of the Queen and Bishop were changed to those we play today, the entire character of the game was transformed. The old artillery, cavalry and infantry in the form of Rooks, Knights and Pawns, were still in the game, but the devastating power of the new dive-bombing Queen and the speedy attack of the motorized Bishop made it necessary for the chess Generals to develop new strategy and tactics. New and more scientific openings had to be examined and analysed. Pawn play became a primary consideration, now that a promoted pawn could become a powerful Queen. The whole tempo of the game was quickened, the battle shortened and intensified.

Italy was the main center of chess activity when these changes took place and the new game probably originated there. By 1510 the old type of chess was obsolete in most of

Italy and Spain. One of the earliest games of the "new chess" to be recorded appears in a late 15th century manuscript in which a poem describes the courtship of Venus by Mars by means of a game of chess. Francisco de Castellvi takes the part of Mars, Narciso Vinoles that of Venus. Historically important, the game is also interesting because it was undoubtedly played over the board by actual chessplayers of reasonable proficiency for the period.

Analysis was the ruling motive in the literature of the period. Openings known today as the Ruy Lopez, Giuoco Piano, Petroff Defense, Philidor Defense, Bishop's Opening and Queen's Gambit Accepted, were first outlined in a late 15th century manuscript (in the Gottingen University Library.) *

The first "best-seller" was a book written by Damiano and printed in Rome in 1512. Eight editions were published in the 16th Century and it was also translated and published in French, English and German. All that is known of the author is that he was an apothecary and a native of Portugal. To judge from his analysis, he was also a mediocre chessplayer.

The famous name of Ruy Lopez first appears in 1559 when this Spanish priest visited Italy and defeated all the Roman players. Although he did not invent the opening which bears his name, Ruy Lopez was the leading player of Spain for over 20 years and noted for his skill at blindfold chess. He played often at the court of his patron, Philip II of Spain. In 1561 Lopez published a book on chess containing a code of laws, general advice to players (including the suggestion that you "place your opponent with the sun in his eyes") and a miscellaneous collection of openings. He deals with a wider range of openings than his predecessors but his analysis is considered weak. Interesting is the fact that this book gave international currency to the term "gambit," a slang term which Lopez had learned in Italy. According to Lopez, "it is derived from the Italian *gamba*, a leg, and *gambitare* means to set traps, from which a gambit game means a game of traps and snares."

Among the leading Italian players of the period 1560 to 1630 were Paolo Boi, Giovanni Leonardo da Cutri, Giulio Cesare Polerio and Gioachino Greco. As a youth, Leonardo had been trounced by Ruy Lopez in Rome but he had his re-

---

*The names by which we call openings today usually have little or nothing to do with their origins and seldom commemorate the names of the earliest authorities to discover the openings.

venge in 1575 when he visited Spain and defeated the aging Lopez in a match held in the presence of Philip II.

Although existing text-books had become obsolete, the strong players of the early part of this period did not publish their findings. The high stakes for which they played made them secretive. However, a patron could always obtain a copy of the player's notes on openings for a consideration and many of these manuscripts have survived, particularly those of Polerio.

The manuscripts of Polerio, considered the leading player of Rome in 1606, again widen the range of the openings and include the Queen's Gambit Declined (by 2 . . . P-QB3 only), the Fianchetto Defenses, the Caro-Kann, the Sicilian, most of the known variations of the King's Gambit, the Center Gambit, the Greco Counter Gambit, the Two Knights' Defense and the Four Knights' Game. There are also some printed books from this period, including three works published by Dr. Alessandro Salvio, one of the leading Neapolitan players. For his time, Salvio was an analyst of great ability.

Greco was one of the last great Italian players. Although a man of poor parentage and no education, he made and left his mark on the pages of chess history. About 1619 he began to keep a manuscript collection of games and gave extracts to wealthy patrons. In the early days of his career he lived in Rome but about 1620 he travelled abroad, sojourning in France, England and Spain. In 1624 he re-arranged his collection of games and many years later, in 1669, a French translation of this re-arrangement was published in Paris. Forty-one editions have since been published in many languages.

After Greco's death in 1634, Italy produced no outstanding players for over a hundred years. In England, France and Germany, however, the popularity of chess had steadily increased and in the 18th century the coffee-houses of London and Paris were the leading centers of chess activity. The name of Andre D. Philidor dominates the history of this period. Equally famous as a chessplayer and as a musician, Philidor defeated all the strongest players at the Cafe de la Regence in Paris and Slaughter's Coffee House in London. After 1775 Philidor spent the Spring of each year in London and the rest of the year in Paris. The English gentry flocked to Parsloe's Club in London where Philidor then played. This great player set forth his theories of chess in lucid fashion in his "Analyze du Jeu des Echecs," written when he was only 23 years old. He was the first to define and explain the principles of chess strategy and tactics. Since his death in 1795, his book has often been reprinted. It was an important milestone in the progress of chess.

In the time of Philidor, Italy again produced some gifted players, including Ponziani, E. del Rio and G. Lolli. French contemporaries of Philidor before the Revolution were Verdoni, Leger, Carlier and Bernard.

In the first half of the 19th century the firmament of chess is studded with many chess stars whose names are familiar to the modern player. In England we hear of the exploits of J. H. Sarratt; William Lewis; John Cochrane; Captain W. D. Evans (who discovered his gambit in 1824, the same year in which the London-Edinburgh postal match was played, giving us the name "Scotch Game"); William Lewis (who published his "Progressive Lessons" in 1831 and laid the foundations for much later work on the openings); Alexander MacDonnell and the great Howard Staunton.

In France, the leading players were Alexander Deschapelles; Pierre de Saint-Amant (who captained the victorious French team in the 1831 postal match with London which gave us the name "French Defense"); De La Bourdonnais (who vanquished MacDonnell in the match of 1834). Many notable players also arose in Central Europe including Johann Allgaier (who originated the idea of tabulating openings in an original and important treatise, first published in 1795); Von Bilguer (whose famous "Handbuch" was published in 1843); L. E. Bledow (who started the magazine *Schachzeitung* in 1846); B. Horwitz; K. Schorn; von der Lasa; W. Hanstein and C. Mayet. Other masters of the period were the Russian Petroff, the Livonian Kieseritzky, the Viennese Hampe and the Hungarians Szen and Lowenthal.

In 1843 Staunton established himself as the first player of Europe by defeating Saint-Amant in a match. Staunton's "Chessplayers Handbook," published in 1847, became the leading English text-book. In this book, and in the German "Handbuch," the names we now use for most openings were systematically arranged.

The year 1851 stands out as the beginning of a new age in chess. It was in this year that the first International Chess Tournament was held. The site was London and 16 competitors took part in the main tournament. Adolph Anderssen of Berlin took first prize. A brilliant player, Anderssen later demonstrated that the luck of the pairings in this "knock-out" tournament was not responsible for his success.

In subsequent tournaments, the "round-robin" system was adopted and Anderssen won first prize in 7 of the 12 events in which he competed.

With the establishment of tournament competition and the advent of Paul Morphy, the brilliant young American master who defeated Anderssen and all other European experts, the truly modern era of chess was ushered in. From a purely technical point of view, the games played in the 350-odd years from the early beginnings of modern chess to the 19th century are not of vital importance to the present-day chessplayer. The selections presented in this chapter comprise a mere handful of historical and representative games from this long, formative epoch.

If chess has gained much since the passing of this period, it has also lost much. We have gained a great deal in experience, in theory, in knowledge, in systematic analysis of the openings, in the assembling of a fine literature and the experience of many great players. And yet there are times when one wonders whether all these gains compensate for the disappearance of the spirit of freshness, of eternal adventure, of naivete.

It is a development which we see present in all the arts and sciences. Of course, our great contemporary players have originality and imagination, but they also have a tremendous backlog of study and acquired knowledge based on the heritage of their predecessors. The games of the pre-Morphy period, whatever their faults may be, are the productions of players who were self-reliant, who had to find their way through uncharted country, who had to perform brilliant feats of improvisation. Remember also, when you play over these games, that many of them were played for pure amusement, not as part of a gruelling contest and not for the record; in that way you can savor their charm, their sociable and leisurely character.

10. Late 15th Century.

This is one of the earliest recorded games of modern chess. It was played shortly after 1485, when the mediaeval moves of the Queen and Bishop were changed. Score is from a poem in a Catalan manuscript.

CENTER COUNTER GAME

FRANCISCO DE CASTELLVI
NARCISO VINOLES

	White	Black
1	P—K4	P—Q4
2	P x P	Q x P
3	Kt—QB3	Q—Q1
4	B—B4	Kt—KB3
5	Kt—B3	B—Kt5
6	P—KR3	B x Kt
7	Q x B	P—K3
8	Q x P	QKt—Q2
9	Kt—Kt5	R—B1
10	Kt x RP	Kt—Kt3
11	Kt x R	Kt x Kt
12	P—Q4	Kt—Q3
13	B—Kt5ch	Kt x B
14	Q x Ktch	Kt—Q2
15	P—Q5	P x P
16	B—K3	B—Q3
17	R—Q1	Q—B3
18	R x P	Q—Kt3
19	B—B4	B x B
20	Q x Ktch	K—B1
21	Q—Q8 mate	

---

11. Rome, 1560.

Played when Lopez visited Rome in 1559-60. His youthful opponent later became a famous player.

DAMIANO'S DEFENSE

RUY LOPEZ LEONARDO DA CUTRI

	White	Black
1	P—K4	P—K4
2	Kt—KB3	P—KB3
3	Kt x P	P x Kt?
4	Q—R5ch	P—Kt3
5	Q x KPch	Q—K2
6	Q x R	Kt—KB3
7	P—Q4	K—B2
8	B—B4ch	P—Q4
9	B x Pch	Kt x B

and White eventually won.

---

12. Madrid, 1561.

Ruy Lopez analyzes the Ruy Lopez. A sample from the collection of openings in the book by Lopez.

RUY LOPEZ

	White	Black
1	P—K4	P—K4
2	Kt—KB3	Kt—QB3
3	B—Kt5	B—B4
4	P—B3	P—Q3
5	P—Q4	P x P
6	P x P	B—Kt5ch
7	Kt—B3	B—Q2
8	B—Kt5	Kt—B3
9	Q—Q3	B x Ktch
10	P x B	

"with better game."

---

13. Madrid, 1575.

This game is believed to have been played in the match between Lopez and Leonardo, won by the latter.

KING'S GAMBIT DECLINED

RUY LOPEZ LEONARDO DA CUTRI

	White	Black
1	P—K4	P—K4
2	P—KB4	P—Q3
3	B—B4	P—QB3
4	Kt—KB3	B—Kt5?
5	P x P	P x P

6 B x Pch	K x B
7 Kt x Pch	K—K1
8 Q x B	Kt—B3?
9 Q—K6ch	Q—K2
10 Q—B8ch	Q—Q1
11 Q x Qch	K x Q
12 Kt—B7ch	Resigns

Other games from this match are recorded in a manuscript by Polerio. A game won by Leonardo (White) went as follows: 1 P—K4, P—K4; 2 Kt—KB3, Kt—QB3; 3 B—B4, B—B4; 4 P—B3, Q—K2; 5 P—QKt4, B—Kt3; 6 P—QR4, P—QR3; 7 B—R3, P—Q3; 8 P—Q3, Kt—B3; 9 Q—K2, B—Kt5; 10 QKt—Q2 and White eventually won.

---

14. Rome, about 1580.

One of the earliest examples of the Fegatello or "Fried Liver" Attack.

TWO KNIGHTS' DEFENSE

POLERIO	DOMENICO
White	Black
1 P—K4	P—K4
2 Kt—KB3	Kt—QB3
3 B—B4	Kt—B3
4 Kt—Kt5	P—Q4
5 P x P	Kt x P
6 Kt x BP	K x Kt
7 Q—B3ch	K—K3
8 Kt—B3	Kt—K2
9 P—Q4	P—B3
10 B—KKt5	P—KR3
11 B x Kt	B x B
12 O—O—O	R—B1
13 Q—K4	R x P
14 P x P	B—Kt4ch
15 K—Kt1	R—Q7
16 P—KR4	R x Rch
17 R x R	B x P
18 Kt x Kt	P x Kt
19 R x P	Q—Kt4
20 R—Q6ch	K—K2
21 R—KKt6	Resigns

15.

GIUOCO PIANO

A specimen from Greco's collection of games which he began to keep in 1619. Greco was the last great Italian player of this early period. He died before 1634.

White	Black
1 P—K4	P—K4
2 Kt—KB3	Kt—QB3
3 B—B4	B—B4
4 P—B3	Q—K2
5 O—O	P—Q3
6 P—Q4	B—Kt3
7 B—KKt5	P—B3
8 B—R4	P—Kt4?
9 Kt x KtP!	P x Kt
10 Q—R5ch	K—Q2
11 B x P	Q—Kt2
12 B—K6ch	K x B
13 Q—K8ch	KKt—K2
14 P—Q5 mate	

---

16. Paris, 1680.

A brevity by two of the leading Parisian players of this period.

KING'S GAMBIT

MORANT	ABBE DE FEUQUIERES
White	Black
1 P—K4	P—K4
2 P—KB4	P x P
3 Kt—KB3	Kt—K2
4 P—Q4	P—KKt4
5 Kt x P	Kt—Kt3
6 P—KR4	B—Kt2
7 B—B4	O—O
8 Q—R5	P—KR3
9 Q x Kt	P x Kt
10 P x P	R—K1
11 Q x P mate.	

17. London, March 13, 1790.

Philidor in Action

KING'S BISHOP OPENING

CAPT. SMITH White	PHILIDOR Black
1 P—K4	P—K4
2 B—B4	Kt—KB3
3 P—Q3	P—B3
4 B—KKt5	P—KR3
5 B x Kt	Q x B
6 Kt—QB3	P—QKt4
7 B—Kt3	P—QR4
8 P—QR3	B—B4
9 Kt—B3	P—Q3
10 Q—Q2	B—K3
11 B x B	P x B
12 O—O	P—Kt4
13 P—R3	Kt—Q2
14 KKt—R2	P—R4
15 P—KKt3	K—K2
16 K—Kt2	P—Q4
17 P—B3	Kt—B1
18 Kt—K2	Kt—Kt3
19 P—B3	QR—KKt1
20 P—Q4	B—Kt3

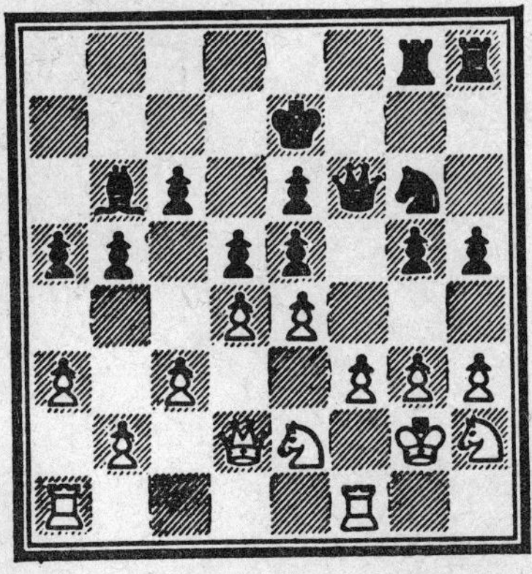

21 QP x P	Q x P
22 Kt—Q4	K—Q2
23 QR—K1	P—KR5
24 Q—KB2	B—B2!
25 Kt—K2	RP x P
26 Q x P	Q x Qch
27 Kt x Q	Kt—B5ch
28 K—R1	R x P
29 R—KKt1	R x Ktch
30 K x R	R—R1ch
31 Kt—R5	R x Ktch
32 K—Kt3	Kt—R6ch
33 K—Kt4	R—R5 mate

---

18. London, Dec. 29, 1796.

White's ingenious sacrifices leave his opponent in a helpless state.

PHILIDOR DEFENSE

ATWOOD White	WILSON Black
1 P—K4	P—K4
2 Kt—KB3	P—Q3
3 P—Q4	P—KB4
4 QP x P	BP x P
5 Kt—Kt5	P—Q4
6 P—K6	Kt—KR3
7 Kt—QB3	P—B3
8 KKt x KP	P x Kt
9 Q—R5ch	P—Kt3
10 Q—K5	R—Kt1
11 B x Kt	B x B
12 R—Q1	Q—K2
13 B—B4	P—QKt4
14 B—Kt3	P—R4
15 Kt x KP	P—R5
16 Kt—B6ch	K—B1
17 Kt x R	K x Kt
18 R—Q8ch!	Q x R
19 P—K7ch	Q—Q4
20 P—K8 (Q) ch	B—B1
21 Q—R8ch	K x Q
22 Q x Bch	Q—Kt1
23 Q x Q mate	

19

From Allgaier's Collection

KING'S BISHOP'S OPENING

——	ALLGAIER
White	Black
1 P—K4	P—K4
2 B—B4	P—KB4
3 B x Kt	R x B
4 P x P	P—Q4
5 Q—R5ch	P—Kt3
6 P x P	R x P
7 P—KR3	Q—B3
8 Kt—KB3	Kt—B3
9 Kt—R4	B—QB4
10 Kt x R	P x Kt
11 Q—B3	B—B4
12 P—KKt4	Kt—Q5
13 Q x P	Kt x Pch
14 K—Q1	R—Q1!
15 Q x B	B—K5
16 R—K1	Q—B6ch
17 R—K2	Q—R8ch
18 R—K1	Q x R mate

---

20. London, 1820.

The following game was played by Mouret, while conducting the Automaton Chess player in London, 1820. Out of 300 games in the course of a few months, giving odds of KBP and move to every comer, the French master lost only six games, and these to Cochrane, Brand and Mercier.

(Remove Black's KBP)

J. COCHRANE	AUTOMATON (Mouret)
White	Black
1 P—K4	P—K3
2 P—Q4	P—B3?
3 P—KB4	P—Q4
4 P—K5	P—B4
5 Kt—KB3	Kt—QB3
6 P—B3	Kt—R3
7 B—K2	Q—Kt3
8 Q—Kt3	Q—B2
9 O—O	B—K2
10 Q—B2	P x P
11 P x P	Q—Kt3
12 R—Q1	Kt—B4
13 Q—Q3	QKt x QP!
14 Kt x Kt	Kt x Kt
15 K—R1	Kt x B
16 Q x Kt	O—O
17 Kt—B3	B—Q2
18 B—K3	B—B4
19 B x B	Q x B
20 Q—Kt4	R—B2?
21 Kt x P	P x Kt
22 P—K6	B x P
23 Q x B	P—Q5?
24 QR—B1	Q—Kt5?
25 R—B7	R—KB1
26 R x R	R x R
27 R—QB1	P—KR3
28 R—B7	Q—B1
29 R—B8	Q x R
30 Q x Qch and wins	

---

21. London, about 1830.

This game is of historic interest, as Capt. Evans here shows his gambit for the first time.

EVANS GAMBIT

CAPT. EVANS	A. MACDONNELL
White	Black
1 P—K4	P—K4
2 Kt—KB3	Kt—QB3
3 B—B4	B—B4
4 O—O	P—Q3

5 P—QKt4	B x P
6 P—B3	B—R4
7 P—Q4	B—KKt5
8 Q—Kt3	Q—Q2
9 Kt—Kt5	Kt—Q1
10 P x P	P x P
11 B—R3	Kt—R3
12 P—B3	B—Kt3ch
13 K—R1	B—KR4
14 R—Q1	Q—B1
15 R x Ktch	Q x R
16 Kt x BP!	Q—R5
17 Q—Kt5ch	P—B3

White mates in three.

18 Q x KPch	K—Q2
19 Q—K6ch	K—B2
20 B—Q6 mate	

---

22. London, 1830.

Critics consider this the most brilliant EVANS GAMBIT ever played at odds of QKt.

(Remove White's QKt)

EVANS GAMBIT

A. MACDONNELL	AMATEUR
White	Black
1 P—K4	P—K4
2 Kt—KB3	Kt—QB3
3 B—B4	B—B4
4 P—QKt4	B x P
5 P—B3	B—R4
6 O—O	Kt—B3
7 Q—B2	O—O
8 B—R3	R—K1
9 P—Q4	P—Q4?
10 KP x P	KKt x P
11 P x P	Kt x BP
12 QR—Q1!	Kt x R
13 R x Kt	B—Q2
14 B x Pch!	K x B
15 R x Bch!	Q x R
16 Kt—Kt5ch	K—Kt1
17 Q x P mate	

---

23. Westminster, London, June, 1834

This 16th game is one of the prettiest of the entire series of 85 match games played.

QUEEN'S GAMBIT ACCEPTED

C. DE LABOURDONNAIS	A. MACDONNELL
White	Black
1 P—Q4	P—Q4
2 P—QB4	P x P
3 P—K3	P—K4
4 B x P	P x P
5 P x P	Kt—KB3
6 Kt—QB3	B—K2
7 Kt—B3	O—O
8 B—K3	P—B3
9 P—KR3	QKt—Q2
10 B—Kt3	Kt—Kt3
11 O—O	KKt—Q4
12 P—QR4	P—QR4
13 Kt—K5	B—K3
14 B—B2	P—KB4??
15 Q—K2	P—B5?
16 B—Q2	Q—K1
17 QR—K1	B—B2
18 Q—K4	P—Kt3
19 B x P!	Kt x B
20 Q x Kt	B—B5
21 Q—R6	B x R
22 B x P!	P x B
23 Kt x KtP	Kt—B1
24 Q—R8ch	K—B2
25 Q—R7ch	K—B3
26 Kt—B4	B—Q6
27 R—K6ch	K—Kt4
28 Q—R6ch	K—B4
29 P—Kt4 mate	

---

24. Played at London, Aug. 1834.
The Immortal 50th battle.

Connoisseurs hold that the annals of Chess produce no higher flights of genius than the play of M'Donnell in this game.

QUEEN'S GAMBIT

DE LABOURDONNAIS — MACDONNELL

	White	Black
1	P—Q4	P—Q4
2	P—QB4	P x P
3	P—K4	P—K4
4	P—Q5	P—KB4
5	Kt—QB3	Kt—KB3
6	B x P	B—B4
7	Kt—B3	Q—K2
8	B—Kt5?	B x Pch
9	K—B1	B—Kt3
10	Q—K2	P—B5
11	R—Q1	B—Kt5
12	P—Q6	. . . .
12	. . . .	P x P
13	Kt—Q5	Kt x Kt!!

Two minor pieces will be more than a match for the Queen!

14	B x Q	Kt—K6ch
15	K—K1	K x B

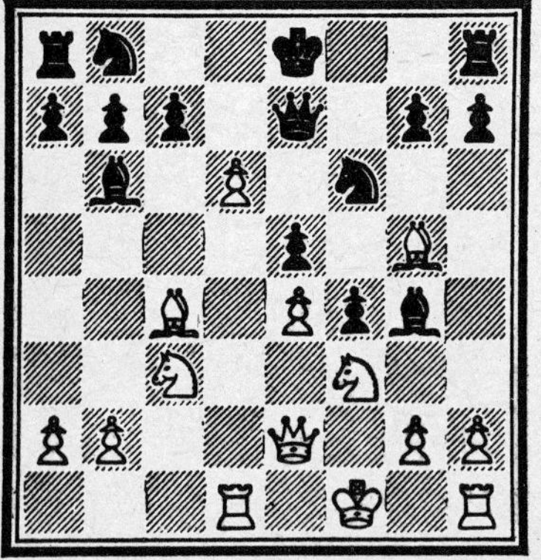

16	Q—Q3	R—Q1!
17	R—Q2	Kt—B3
18	P—QKt3	B—QR4
19	P—QR3	QR—B1
20	R—Kt1	P—QKt4!
21	B x P	B x Kt
22	P x B	Kt—Q5
23	B—B4	Kt x Pch
24	K—B2	Kt x R (Q7)
25	R x Pch	K—B3
26	R—B7ch	K—Kt3
27	R—Kt7	Kt (Q7) x B
28	P x Kt	R x P
29	Q—Kt1	B—Kt3!
30	K—B3	R—B6
31	Q—R2	Kt—B5ch
32	K—Kt4	R—KKt1
33	R x B	P x R
34	K—R4	K—B3
35	Q—K2	R—Kt3
36	Q—R5	Kt—K6
	Resigns	

One of the most magnificent chess masterpieces on record.

---

25. Berlin, Dec. 29, 1837.
"Crime and Punishment"

GIUOCO PIANO

B. HORWITZ — L. BLEDOW

	White	Black
1	P—K4	P—K4
2	Kt—KB3	Kt—QB3
3	B—B4	B—B4
4	P—B3	B—Kt3
5	P—Q4	Q—K2
6	P—Q5	Kt—Q1
7	B—K2?	P—Q3
8	P—KR3?	P—KB4
9	B—Kt5	Kt—KB3
10	QKt—Q2	O—O
11	Kt—R4?	P x P
12	Kt x P	Kt x Kt!
13	B x Q	B x Pch
14	K—B1	Kt—Kt6 mate

26.

De Labourdonnais plays blindfold against M. Jouy, about 1838.

SALVIO GAMBIT

M. JOUY   C. DE LABOURDONNAIS

	White	Black
1	P—K4	P—K4
2	P—KB4	P x P
3	Kt—KB3	P—KKt4
4	B—B4	P—Kt5
5	Kt—K5	Q—R5ch
6	K—B1	P—B6
7	Kt x P (B7)	Kt—QB3
8	P—Q4	B—Kt2
9	P—B3	Kt—B3
10	Kt x R	P—Q4!
11	P x QP	Kt—K5
12	Q—K1	P—Kt6
13	B—Q3	P x Pch
14	K x P	B—R6ch
15	K—Kt1	Kt x P!
16	Q x Ktch	Q x Q
17	B x Q	Kt—K7 mate

---

27. Berlin, 1839 (?)

Masterly combinative play.

SCOTCH GAMBIT

P. VON BILGUER
T. VON DER LASA

	White	Black
1	P—K4	P—K4
2	Kt—KB3	Kt—QB3
3	P—Q4	P x P
4	B—QB4	B—Kt5ch
5	P—B3	P x P
6	O—O	P x P
7	B x P	P—B3
8	Q—Kt3	Kt—R3
9	P—K5!	P x P
10	Kt x P	Q—K2
11	Kt x Kt	
12	B x P!	
13	Q x B	
14	R—K1ch	
15	Kt—B3!	B—R6
16	P—Kt3	P x B
17	QR—Q1ch	B—Q2
18	Q—Kt7	QR—B1
19	Q x BP	R—K1

20	R x Bch!	Q x R
21	Q—B6ch	R—K2
22	Kt—Q5!	Kt—Kt1
23	Q—Kt5	Q—K1
24	R—Q1!	Resigns

---

28. New Orleans, June 22, 1849

Paul's First Blindfold Game

GIUOCO PIANO

PAUL MORPHY (aged 12)   ERNEST MORPHY (Uncle)

	White	Black
1	P—K4	P—K4
2	Kt—KB3	Kt—QB3
3	B—B4	B—B4
4	P—B3	Kt—B3
5	P—Q4	P x P
6	O—O	P—Q3

P x P	B—Kt3
8 P—KR3	P—KR3
9 Kt—B3	O—O
10 B—K3	R—K1
11 P—Q5	B x B
12 P x Kt	B—Kt3
13 P—K5	QP x P
14 Q—Kt3	R—K2
15 B x Pch	R x B
16 Kt x P	Q—K1
17 P x P	B x KtP
18 QR—K1	B—R3
19 Kt—Kt6	Q—Q1
20 R—K7	Resigns (b)

(b) This game occurred on Paul's 12th birthday, and Dr. Ford and others present carried the youthful victor away in triumph.

For this victory, he received a fine set of chessmen.

(Paul played blindfold, but his uncle did NOT.*)*

---

29. New Orleans, May 25, 1850.

Paul, at the age of thirteen, defeats the great Hungarian master. (2 to 0 and 1 draw.)

SICILIAN DEFENSE

PAUL MORPHY (aged 13)	J. LOEWENTHAL
White	**Black**
1 P—K4	P—QB4
2 P—KB4	P—K3
3 Kt—KB3	P—Q4
4 P x P	P x P
5 P—Q4	B—Kt5
6 B—K2	B x Kt
7 B x B	Kt—KB3
8 O—O	B—K2
9 B—K3	P x P
10 QB x P	O—O
11 Kt—B3	Kt—B3
12 B x Kt	B x B
13 Kt x P	B x P
14 R—Kt1	B—Q5ch
15 K—R1	R—Kt1
16 P—B3	B—B4
17 P—B5!	Q—R5
18 P—Kt3	Q—Kt4
19 P—B6	Kt—K4
20 P x P	KR—Q1
21 B—K4	Q x P(Kt2)
22 Q—R5!	R—Q3
23 B x Pch	K—B1
24 B—K4	R—KR3
25 Q—B5	Q x P
26 R—Kt2	R—K1
27 Kt—B6	R—K3
28 R—Kt2?	Q x Rch
29 B x Q	KR x Kt
30 Q x KR	R x Q
31 R x R	Kt—Kt5
32 R—B5	P—Kt3
33 B—Q5	Kt—R3
34 R—B6	K—Kt2
35 R—B6	P—R4
36 R—B7	K—Kt3
37 K—Kt2	P—B3
38 K—B3	Kt—B4
39 B—K4	K—Kt4
40 B x Kt	K x B
41 P—KR4	K—Kt3
42 R—B6	K—R4
43 K—Kt3	P—B4
44 R—B6	P—B5ch
45 K x P!	B—B7
46 K—K4	B—B4
47 R—B5ch	K x P
48 R x B	P x R
49 K—Q5	Resigns

---

30. Berlin, January 1851.

A choice example of this opening.

EVANS GAMBIT

KOSSAK — J. DUFRESNE

White	Black
1 P—K4	P—K4
2 Kt—KB3	Kt—QB3
3 B—B4	B—B4
4 P—QKt4	B x P
5 P—B3	B—R4
6 O—O	Kt—B3
7 P—Q4	O—O
8 P x P	KKt x P
9 B—Q5	Kt x QBP
10 Kt x Kt	B x Kt
11 Kt—Kt5!	Kt x P
12 Q—R5	P—KR3
13 P—B4	B x R
14 P x Kt	Q—K2
15 Kt x P	Q—B4ch
16 K—R1	Q x KB
17 Kt x Pch	K—R1
18 Kt—B5ch	K—Kt1
19 Kt—K7 mate	

---

31. Berlin, 1851.

Falkbeer's Immortal.

VIENNA OPENING

E. FALKBEER — A. ANDERSSEN

White	Black
1 P—K4	P—K4
2 Kt—QB3	P—KB4
3 P x P	Kt—KB3
4 P—KKt4	B—B4
5 P—Kt5	O—O?!
6 P x Kt	Q x P
7 Q—B3	B—Kt3
8 P—Q3	P—B3
9 Kt—K4	Q—K2
10 B—Q2	P—Q4
11 P—B6	Q—QB2
12 O—O—O!?	P x Kt
13 QP x P	R x P
14 B—B4ch	K—R1
15 Q—R5	Kt—Q2
16 P—B4	R—B1
17 Kt—B3	Kt—B3
18 Q—R4	B—Kt5
19 Kt x P	B—KR4
20 B—B3	B—K6ch
21 K—Kt1	B x P
22 Q x KB	Kt—Q4

23 R x Kt!?	R x Q
24 R—Q7	Q—B1
25 Kt—Kt6ch	P x Kt
26 R x KKtP	R—B6? (. . . Q—R6!)
27 B—K5	Q—B1
28 R—KB7ch	K—Kt1
29 R x Rch	K—R2
30 R x Q	Resigns

---

32. Berlin, 1851.

An absorbing struggle all the way.

FALKBEER COUNTER GAMBIT (in effect)

E. FALKBEER — A. ANDERSSEN

White	Black
1 P—K4	P—K4
2 B—B4	Kt—KB3

3	P—B4	P—Q4
4	KP x P	P—K5
5	Kt—QB3	B—QB4
6	P—Q3	P x P
7	P x P	O—O
8	P—Q4	B—Kt3
9	Kt—B3	P—B3
10	Q—Kt3	B—Kt5
11	O—O	B x Kt
12	R x B	B x Pch
13	K—R1	B x Kt
14	Q x B	P x P
15	B—Q3	Kt—K5
16	Q—B2	Kt—QB3
17	B—K3	R—K1!
18	P—QR3	QR—B1
19	Q—R4	P—Q5
20	B—KKt1	P—QR3
21	P—QKt4?	Kt—R2
22	Q—Q1	Q—Q2
23	R—R3	R—B6!
24	Q—R5	P—R3
25	R—Q1	Kt—KB3
26	Q—R4	Kt—Kt4?
27	P—R4?	Kt—Q3!
28	B x QP	Kt—B4!!
29	B x R	Kt x Q
30	B—R7ch	K x B
31	R x Q	Kt x R
32	R x Kt	R—K6!
33	R—R3	R x R
34	P x R	Kt—Kt3!
35	P—R5	Kt—Q4
36	B—Q2	K—Kt3
37	K—Kt2	K—B4
38	K—B3	P—R4
39	P—R4	P—B3
40	P—R3	P—KKt3
	Resigns	

---

33. Simpson's Divan, London, 1851.

The Immortal Game.

Most authorities agree that this "partie" is the most brilliant game of which there is any record.

KING'S BISHOP GAMBIT

	A. ANDERSSEN White	L. KIESERITZKY Black
1	P—K4	P—K4
2	P—KB4	P x P
3	B—B4	P—QKt4
4	B x P	Q—R5ch
5	K—B1	Kt—KB3
6	Kt—KB3	Q—R3
7	P—Q3	Kt—R4
8	Kt—R4	P—QB3
9	Kt—B5	Q—Kt4
10	P—KKt4	Kt—B3
11	R—KKt1	P x B
12	P—KR4	Q—Kt3
13	P—R5	Q—Kt4
14	Q—B3	Kt—Kt1
15	B x P	Q—B3
16	Kt—B3	B—B4
17	Kt—Q5!	Q x P

18	B—Q6!	B x R
19	P—K5!	Q x Rch
20	K—K2	Kt—QR3
21	Kt x Pch	K—Q1
22	Q—B6ch!	Kt x Q
23	B—K7 mate	

"In this game occurs almost a continuity of brilliancies, every one of

which bears the stamp of intuitive genius, that could have been little assisted by calculations, as the combination-point arises only at the very end of the game with a final sacrifice of the Queen after Anderssen had already given up two Rooks and a Bishop."—STEINITZ.

---

34. Berlin, 1852.

Magnificently timed Attack

DUTCH DEFENSE

A. ANDERSSEN White	J. DUFRESNE Black
1 P—Q4	P—KB4
2 P—K4	P x P
3 Kt—QB3	Kt—KB3
4 B—KKt5	P—Q4?
5 B x Kt	KP x B
6 Q—R5ch	P—Kt3
7 Q x QP	B—R3
8 Kt x P!	Q—K2
9 B—K2	Kt—Q2
10 Kt—QB3	P—KB4
11 Kt—B3	P—B3
12 Q—Kt3	Kt—Kt3
13 O—O	B—K3
14 P—Q5!	Kt x P
15 B—B4	O—O—O
16 KR—K1	Q—B3
17 QR—Q1	K—Kt1
18 Kt—Q4	B—B2
19 B x Kt!	P x B
20 R—K7!	P—Kt3
21 Q—R4	P—R4
22 Kt—B6ch	K—B1
23 Kt—Kt5	R—Q2
24 Kt(5)—R7ch	K—B2
25 R x Rch	K x R
26 R—K1!	Resigns

---

35. Berlin, 1853.

Drastic Punishment

GIUOCO PIANO

DR. MAX LANGE White	C. MAYET Black
1 P—K4	P—K4
2 Kt—KB3	Kt—QB3
3 B—B4	B—B4
4 O—O	P—Q3
5 P—QKt4	Kt x P
6 P—B3	Kt—QB3
7 P—Q4	P x P
8 P x P	B—Kt3
9 P—KR3	Kt—R4
10 B—Q3	P—Q4?
11 P x P	Q x P
12 Kt—B3	Q—R4
13 R—K1ch	K—Q1
14 Kt—KKt5!	Q x Q
15 Kt x Pch	K—Q2
16 B—B5ch	K—B3
17 Kt—Q8ch	K—Q3
18 B—B4 mate	

---

36. Berlin, 1853.

Anderssen's Immortal

The 2nd of Anderssen's two immortal games, is considered the most brilliant Evans Gambit ever played.

EVANS GAMBIT

A. ANDERSSEN White	J. DUFRESNE Black
1. P—K4	P—K4
2 Kt—KB3	Kt—QB3
3 B—B4	B—B4
4 P—QKt4	B x P
5 P—B3	B—R4
6 P—Q4	P x P
7 O—O	P—Q6

8 Q—Kt3	Q—B3
9 P—K5	Q—Kt3
10 R—K1	KKt—K2
11 B—R3	P—Kt4
12 Q x P	R—QKt1
13 Q—R4	B—Kt3
14 QKt—Q2	B—Kt2
15 Kt—K4	Q—B4
16 B x P	Q—R4
17 Kt—B6ch	P x Kt
18 P x P	R—Kt1
19 QR—Q1	. . . .

Lasker declares this to be one of the most subtle moves on record, and the 21st to be simply grand. .

19	Q x Kt
20 R x Ktch	**Kt x R**
21 Q x Pch!!	K x Q
22 B—B5ch	K—K1
23 B—Q7ch	K—Q1
24 B x Kt mate!	

---

37. Berlin, 1853.

Old-fashioned but effective

QUEEN'S GAMBIT DECLINED

C. MAYET	A. ANDERSSEN
White	Black
1 P—Q4	P—Q4
2 P—QB4	P—K3
3 P—QR3?	P—QB4
4 QP x P	B x P
5 Kt—KB3	P—QR4
6 P—K3	Kt—QB3
7 P x P	P x P
8 B—Kt5	Kt—B3
9 Kt—K5	O—O!
10 Kt x Kt	P x Kt
11 B x P	B—R3!
12 B x R	Q x B
13 Q—B3	Kt—Q2!
14 Kt—B3	Kt—K4!
15 Q x P	Kt—Q6ch
16 K—Q1	Q—B1!
17 K—B2	R—Q1
18 Q—R5	Kt—B5!!
Resigns	

---

38. First published in 1857.

"The Desperate Journey"

SCOTCH GAMBIT

MAX LANGE	VON SCHIERSTEDT
White	Black
1 P—K4	P—K4
2 Kt—KB3	Kt—QB3
3 P—Q4	P x P
4 B—QKt5	B—B4
5 O—O	KKt—K2
6 QKt—Q2	P—Q4
7 P x P	Q x P
8 B—B4	Q—Q1
9 Kt—Kt5	Kt—K4
10 Kt x BP	Kt x Kt
11 B x Ktch	K x B
12 Q—R5ch	P—Kt3
13 Q x B	Kt—B3
14 Kt—B3	R—K1
15 B—R6!	B—B4
16 QR—K1	Q—Q2
17 Q—B4ch	B—K3
18 Kt—Kt5ch	K—B3

19	Q—K2!	B—Kt5
20	P—KB3!!	R x Q
21	P x Bch	K—K4
22	R x Rch	K—Q4
23	Kt—K4	K—B5
24	P—QR4	Q x P
25	P—Kt3ch	K—Kt5
26	B—Q2ch	K—R6
27	Kt—B3!	P x Kt
28	B x P	Kt—Kt5

White announced mate in six.

29 R—R1ch, Kt—R7; 30 R x Kt ch, K x R; 31 R—K1, Q—Q5ch; 32 B x Q, K—R6; 33 B—B3, any; 34 R—R1 mate.

PART III

The Morphy Period

Those who worship Morphy as the great master of the brilliant combination, must remember that it was he who introduced the innovation which proved to be a death-knell of that type of chess in which brilliancy was the be-all and end-all of every game.

Before Morphy's influence came to be felt, sacrifices were made willy-nilly without rhyme or reason, generally with very little regard for their soundness or objective effectiveness. Lest this be taken as a harsh criticism of the earlier players, it must be remembered that the relative absence of organized competition made for a kind of style which ignored the whole idea of playing a game in such a way as to make sure of winning it.

We realize how radical an innovator Morphy was when we study his games and see how scrupulously conceived and executed are his combinations, for all their complexity and variegated character. It is interesting that while Morphy has always been admired as the most brilliant of all chess players, his games are equally notable for the correctness of his moves. How truly great he was, is seen in the fact that he united superb sacrificial effects with severe elegance, unfailing good taste, and a very high percentage of accuracy. Yes, he was a very great artist, for he fused the intuitive with the logical as only the great artist can. I have offered you what I consider the cream of his games and I am sure you will enjoy them.

Note how quickly Morphy made converts. Steinitz, Kolisch, Bird, Blackburne and many others were so deeply impressed by his games that each one, while still retaining his own individuality, began to reflect the influence of Morphy in a very marked manner. Another great player, almost as great as Morphy, and in the opinion of some capable judges even superior to him, was Adolph Anderssen. It is hard to know just where to place him. Although he had made his mark about ten years before Morphy's appearance, Anderssen too, was famous for the simultaneous brilliancy and accuracy of his combinations. It therefore seems proper to group these two immortals in the same section.

39. First American Chess Congress, New York, 1857

Morphy's most famous sacrifice

FOUR KNIGHTS' GAME

L. PAULSEN White	P. MORPHY Black
1 P—K4	P—K4
2 Kt—KB3	Kt—QB3
3 Kt—B3	Kt—B3
4 B—Kt5	B—B4
5 O—O	O—O?!
6 Kt x P	R—K1
7 Kt x Kt	QP x Kt
8 B—B4	P—QKt4
9 B—K2	Kt x P
10 Kt x Kt	R x Kt
11 B—B3	R—K3
12 P—B3?	Q—Q6!
13 P—QKt4	B—Kt3
14 P—QR4	P x P
15 Q x P	B—Q2
16 R—R2	QR—K1
17 Q—R6?	. . . .

17	Q x B!!
18 P x Q	R—Kt3ch
19 K—R1	B—R6
20 R—Q1	B—Kt7ch
21 K—Kt1	QB x Pch
22 K—B1	B—Kt7ch
23 K—Kt1	B—R6ch
24 K—R1	B x P
25 Q—B1	B x Q
26 R x B	R—K7
27 R—R1	R—R3
28 P—Q4	B—K6
Resigns	

---

40. New York, 1857.

A beautiful specimen of blindfold chess.

KING KNIGHTS' GAMBIT

PAUL MORPHY (blindfold) White	T. LICHTENHEIM Black
1 P—K4	P—K4
2 P—KB4	P x P
3 Kt—KB3	P—Q4
4 P x P	B—K2
5 B—Kt5ch	P—B3
6 P x P	P x P
7 B—B4	B—R5ch
8 P—Kt3?!	P x P
9 O—O	P x Pch
10 K—R1	B—B3
11 Kt—K5	Kt—KR3
12 P—Q4	B x Kt
13 Q—R5	Q x P
14 B x Pch	Kt x B
15 Q x Ktch	K—Q1
16 B—Kt5ch!	B—B3
17 Kt—B3	B—Q2?

17 . . . B x B! was better.

18 R x B	K—B2
19 B—B4ch	K—Kt2
20 R—Q6	Q—B4
21 Kt—K4!	Q x P
22 R x Bch	Kt x R
23 Q x Ktch	K—R3
24 Kt—Q6	KR—Q1
25 Q—Kt7ch	K—R4
26 B—Q2ch	Q x B

27 Kt—B4ch	K—R5
28 P—Kt3 mate!	

---

41. New York, 1857.

Counterattack with a Punch.

EVANS GAMBIT

N. MARACHE White	P. MORPHY Black
1 P—K4	P—K4
2 Kt—KB3	Kt—QB3
3 B—B4	B—B4
4 P—QKt4	B x P
5 P—B3	B—R4
6 P—Q4	P x P
7 P—K5?	P—Q4
8 P x P e.p.	Q x P
9 O—O	KKt—K2
10 Kt—Kt5?	O—O
11 B—Q3	B—B4!
12 B x B	Kt x B
13 B—R3	Q—Kt3!
14 B x R	Q x Kt
15 B—R3	P x P
16 B—B1	Q—Kt3
17 B—B4	R—Q1
18 Q—B2	Kt(B3)—Q5!
19 Q—K4?	. . . .

19	Kt—KKt6
20 Q x Q	Kt(Q5)—K7 mate!

42. New York, 1858.

A Flash of Genius.

FALKBEER COUNTER GAMBIT

J. SCHULTEN White	P. MORPHY Black
1 P—K4	P—K4
2 P—KB4	P—Q4
3 P x QP	P—K5
4 Kt—QB3	Kt—KB3
5 P—Q3	B—QKt5
6 B—Q2	P—K6!
7 B x P	O—O
8 B—Q2	B x Kt
9 P x B	R—K1ch
10 B—K2	B—Kt5
11 P—B4	P—B3
12 P x P	Kt x P
13 K—B1	R x B!
14 Kt x R	Kt—Q5
15 Q—Kt1	B x Ktch
16 K—B2	Kt—Kt5ch
17 K—Kt1	. . . .

Black now forces mate in seven.

17	Kt—B6ch
18 P x Kt	Q—Q5ch
19 K—Kt2	Q—B7ch
20 K—R3	Q x BPch
21 K—R4	Kt—K6

22	Q—Kt1	Kt—B4ch
23	K—Kt5	Q—R4 mate!

---

43. London, July 1858.

The most brilliant of Morphy's masterpieces.

PHILIDOR DEFENSE

	H. E. BIRD	P. MORPHY
	White	Black
1	P—K4	P—K4
2	Kt—KB3	P—Q3
3	P—Q4	P—KB4
4	Kt—B3	P x KP
5	QKt x P	P—Q4
6	Kt—Kt3	P—K5
7	Kt—K5	Kt—KB3
8	B—KKt5	B—Q3
9	Kt—R5	O—O
10	Q—Q2	Q—K1
11	P—KKt4?	Kt x P
12	Kt x Kt	Q x Kt
13	Kt—K5	Kt—B3
14	B—K2	Q—R6
15	Kt x Kt	P x Kt
16	B—K3	. . . .

16	. . . .	R—Kt1
17	O—O—O	R x BP!!

The beginning of a beautiful combination.

18	B x R	Q—R6!
19	P—B3	Q x P
20	P—Kt4	Q—R8ch
21	K—B2	Q—R5ch
22	K—Kt2?	B x KtP
23	P x B	R x Pch
24	Q x R	Q x Qch
25	K—B2	P—K6!
26	B x P	B—B4ch
27	R—Q3	Q—B5ch
28	K—Q2	Q—R7ch
29	K—Q1	Q—Kt8ch
	Resigns	

---

44. London, July 1858.

This game is interesting because of the fact that it is the first of two games which took place on the only occasions that the great English and American masters met in friendly contest. Both were won by Morphy.

PHILIDOR DEFENSE

	H. STAUNTON REV. J. OWEN	P. MORPHY T. BARNES
	White	Black
1	P—K4	P—K4
2	Kt—KB3	P—Q3
3	P—Q4	P—KB4
4	QP x P	BP x P
5	Kt—Kt5	P—Q4
6	P—K6	Kt—KR3
7	Kt—QB3	P—B3
8	KKt x KP	P x Kt
9	Q—R5ch	P—Kt3
10	Q—K5	R—Kt1
11	B x Kt	B x B
12	QR—Q1	Q—Kt4
13	Q—B7	B x P

14	Q x KtP	P—K6!
15	P—B3	Q—K2
16	Q x R	K—B2
17	Kt—K4	B—KB5
18	B—K2	K—Kt2
19	O—O	Q—QB2
20	Kt—B5	B x Pch
21	K—R1	B—B1
22	R—Q4	B—Kt6
23	R—K4	K—R1
24	R—Q1	Q—KKt2
25	R—KR4	B x R
26	Q x Kt	B—R3
27	Q—R2?	B x B
28	R—Q7	Q—R3
29	Kt—K4	B—B5
30	Kt—B6	P—K7
31	R—K7	Q—B8ch
32	Q—Kt1	Q x Qch
33	K x Q	P—K8 (Q) ch
34	R x Q	B x R
	Resigns	

---

45. Paris, Sept. 1858.
4th game of match

Black is outplayed all the way

PHILIDOR DEFENSE

	P. MORPHY	D. HARRWITZ
	White	Black
1	P—K4	P—K4
2	Kt—KB3	P—Q3
3	P—Q4	P x P
4	Q x P	Kt—QB3
5	B—QKt5	B—Q2
6	B x Kt	B x B
7	B—Kt5	P—B3
8	B—R4	Kt—R3
9	Kt—B3	Q—Q2
10	O—O	B—K2
11	QR—Q1	O—O
12	Q—B4ch	R—B2
13	Kt—Q4	Kt—Kt5
14	P—KR3	Kt—K4
15	Q—K2	P—KKt4
16	B—Kt3	R—Kt2
17	Kt—B5	R—Kt3
18	P—B4	P x P
19	KR x P	K—R1
20	R—R4	B—B1
21	B x Kt	BP x B
22	R—KB1	Q—K3
23	Kt—Kt5	Q—Kt1
24	R—B2	P—QR3
25	Kt x BP	R—B1
26	Kt—Q5	B x Kt
27	P x B	R—B2
28	P—B4	B—K2
29	R—R5	Q—K1
30	P—B5!	R x P
31	R x Pch!	K x R
32	Q—R5ch	K—Kt1
33	Kt x Bch!	K—Kt2
34	Kt—B5ch	K—Kt1
35	Kt x P!	Resigns

---

46. Cafe de la Regence,
Paris, Sept. 27, 1858.

One of eight blindfold games.

PETROFF DEFENSE

	P. MORPHY	POTIER
	White	Black
1	P—K4	P—K4
2	Kt—KB3	Kt—KB3
3	B—B4	Kt x P
4	Kt—B3	Kt—KB3
5	Kt x P	P—Q4
6	B—Kt3	B—K2
7	P—Q4	P—B3
8	O—O	QKt—Q2
9	P—B4	Kt—Kt3
10	Q—B3	P—KR4
11	P—B5	Q—B2
12	B—KB4	B—Q3
13	QR—K1	K—B1
14	Q—Kt3	P—R5
15	Kt—Kt6ch!	K—Kt1
16	B x B	P x Q
17	B x Q	P x Kt

18	BP x P	P x Pch
19	K—R1	B—Kt5
20	R—K7	QKt—Q2
21	B—K5	K—B1
22	R—B7ch	K—Kt1
23	Kt x P!	P x Kt
24	B x P	Kt—Kt3
25	B—QKt3	Resigns

---

47. Paris, Sept. 1858.

Morphy's Most Famous Game. Played during the performance of "Barber of Seville."

PHILIDOR DEFENSE

P. MORPHY — DUKE OF BRUNSWICK, COUNT ISOUARD

	White	Black
1	P—K4	P—K4
2	Kt—KB3	P—Q3
3	P—Q4	B—Kt5?
4	P x P	B x Kt
5	Q x B	P x P
6	B—QB4	Kt—KB3
7	Q—QKt3	Q—K2
8	Kt—B3	P—B3
9	B—KKt5	P—Kt4
10	Kt x P	P x Kt
11	B x KtPch	QKt—Q2
12	O—O—O!	R—Q1
13	R x Kt	R x R
14	R—Q1	Q—K3
15	B x Rch	Kt x B
16	Q—Kt8ch!	Kt x Q
17	R—Q8 mate!	

"A very fine finish to a most elegant game.—STEINITZ.

---

48. Paris, Dec. 27, 1858.
9th game of match

Black never gets started

SICILIAN DEFENSE

P. MORPHY — A. ANDERSSEN

	White	Black
1	P—K4	P—QB4
2	P—Q4	P x P
3	Kt—KB3	Kt—QB3
4	Kt x P	P—K3
5	Kt—Kt5	P—Q3
6	B—KB4	P—K4
7	B—K3	P—B4
8	QKt—B3	P—B5
9	Kt—Q5!	P x B?
10	Kt(Kt5)—B7ch	K—B2
11	Q—B3ch	Kt—B3
12	B—B4	Kt—Q5
13	Kt x Ktch	P—Q4
14	B x Pch	K—Kt3
15	Q—R5ch	K x Kt
16	P x P	Kt x Pch
17	K—K2	Resigns

---

49. Paris, 1858.

"My King likes to go for a walk."

SCOTCH GAMBIT

A. ANDERSSEN — A. DE RIVIERE

	White	Black
1	P—K4	P—K4
2	Kt—KB3	Kt—QB3
3	P—Q4	P x P
4	B—B4	Kt—B3
5	Kt—Kt5	Kt—K4
6	B—Kt3	P—KR3
7	P—KB4	P x Kt
8	P x Kt	Kt x P
9	O—O	P—Q4
10	P x P e.p.	P—KB4
11	Kt—Q2	Q x P
12	Kt x Kt	Q x Pch
13	K—B2	P x Kt
14	Q x P	B—K2
15	Q x KP	B—B4?
16	B—B7ch	K x B
17	Q x QBch	K—Kt1

	White	Black
18	Q—Q5ch	K—R2
19	Q—K4ch	K—R3
20	B—K3!	KR—B1ch
21	K—K2	Q—R4ch
22	P—Kt4!!	Q—R7ch
23	R—B2	R x Rch
24	B x R	R—KB1
25	R—R1!	R x Bch
26	K—Q3	R—Q7ch
27	K—B4	R x Pch
28	K—Q5	B—B3
29	K—K6!	B x P
30	K—B7	R—B7ch
31	K—Kt8	P—KKt3
32	Q—K7	Resigns

---

50. Paris, 1859.

This elegant game, played at Paris, 1859, is a clever specimen of the smothered mate.

TWO KNIGHTS' DEFENSE

	P. MORPHY White	AMATEUR Black
1	P—K4	P—K4
2	Kt—KB3	Kt—QB3
3	B—B4	Kt—B3
4	P—Q4	P x P
5	O—O	Kt x P
6	R—K1	P—Q4
7	B x P	Q x B
8	Kt—B3	Q—KR4
9	Kt x Kt	B—K3
10	QKt—Kt5	B—Kt5
11	R x Bch	P x R
12	Kt x KP	Q—B2
13	KKt—Kt5	Q—K2
14	Q—K2	B—Q3
15	Kt x KtPch	K—Q2
16	Q—Kt4ch	K—Q1
17	Kt—B7ch!	Q x Kt
18	B—Kt5ch	B—K2
19	Kt—K6ch	K—B1
20	Kt—B5ch	K—Kt1

White mates in four.

21	Kt—Q7ch	K—B1
22	Kt—Kt6ch	K—Kt1
23	Q—B8ch	R x Q
24	Kt—Q7 mate	

---

51. Vienna, 1859.

The "Austrian Morphy"

VIENNA OPENING

	L. HAMPPE White	W. STEINITZ Black
1	P—K4	P—K4
2	Kt—QB3	Kt—KB3
3	P—B4	P—Q4
4	KP x P	Kt x P
5	P x P	Kt x Kt
6	KtP x Kt	Q—R5ch
7	K—K2	B—Kt5ch
8	Kt—B3	Kt—B3
9	P—Q4	O—O—O
10	B—Q2	B x Ktch
11	P x B	Kt x P!?
12	P x Kt	B—B4
13	Q—K1	Q—B5ch
14	K—Q1	Q x BP
15	QR—Kt1	Q x KBPch

16 Q—K2? (B—K2!)	
	R x Bch!
17 K x R	R—Q1ch
18 K—B1	B—R6ch
19 R—Kt2	Q—B6
20 B—R3ch	K—Kt1
21 Q—Kt5	Q—Q7ch
22 K—Kt1	Q—Q8ch
23 R x Q	R x R mate

---

52. Philadelphia, 1860.

Knights without armor

GIUOCO PIANO

AMATEUR White	DERRICKSON Black
1 P—K4	P—K4
2 B—B4	Kt—KB3
3 Kt—KB3	Kt—B3
4 O—O	B—B4
5 P—Q3	P—Q3
6 B—KKt5	B—KKt5
7 P—KR3	P—KR4!!
8 P x B?	P x P
9 Kt—R2	P—Kt6
10 KKt—B3	KKt—Kt5!
11 B x Q	B x Pch
12 R x B	P x Rch
13 K—B1	R—R8ch
14 K—K2	R x Q
15 KKt—Q2	Kt—Q5ch!
16 K x R	Kt—K6ch
17 K—B1	Kt—K7 mate

---

53. London, 1861.

Spirited play by Kolisch

GIUOCO PIANO

I. KOLISCH White	LOUIS PAULSEN Black
1 P—K4	P—K4
2 Kt—KB3	Kt—QB3
3 B—B4	B—B4
4 O—O	Kt—B3
5 P—QKt4	B x P
6 P—B3	B—K2
7 P—Q4	P x P
8 P x P	KKt x P
9 P—Q5	Kt—R4
10 B—Q3	Kt—B4
11 B—R3	Kt x B
12 Q x Kt	O—O
13 P—Q6!	P x P
14 Kt—B3	P—QKt3
15 Kt—Q5	Kt—Kt2
16 B—Kt2	Kt—B4
17 Q—K3	Kt—K3
18 Kt—Q4!	B—B3
19 Kt—B6!!	P x Kt
20 Kt x Bch	P x Kt
21 Q—R6	P—Q4
22 B x P	Q—Q3
23 P—B4	R—K1
24 R—B3	Resigns

---

54. Naples, 1861.

An Historic Game

This fine game was played by correspondence more than four score years ago.

It was published in Naples in 1861, and reproduced in "Newcastle Chronicle" August 16, 1890.

PONZIANI OPENING

NEWCASTLE White	GLASGOW Black
1 P—K4	P—K4
2 Kt—KB3	Kt—QB3
3 P—B3	Kt—B3
4 P—Q4	Kt x KP
5 P x P	P—Q4
6 B—QKt5	B—QB4
7 Kt—Q4	O—O
8 B x Kt	P x B

9 O—O B—Q2
10 P—B3 Kt—Kt4
11 K—R1 P—B3
12 B x Kt P x B
13 Kt—Q2 R—K1
14 R—K1 B—Kt3
15 P—K6 B—B1
16 Q—R4 P—B4
17 Q—B6 B—Kt2
18 Q x QB P x Kt
19 P—QB4 B—R4
20 P—K7 Q—Q3
21 P—B5! Q—Q2
22 P—QKt4! QR—Kt1
23 P—B6! Q—Q3
24 P x B R x Q
25 P x R P—B4
26 QR—Kt1 Q—Kt1
27 P—R6 P—B5
28 R—Kt5 P—Q6
29 R x P P—B6
30 R x QP! P x Kt
31 R x P K—B2
32 R—Q7 Q—B5
33 P—QR3 P—R4
34 R—Q8 P—Kt5
35 P x P Q—B7
36 R—QKt1 R x P
37 R(Q8)—Q1! Q—K7
38 P—Kt8(Q) Resigns

---

55. London, Nov. 12, 1861.

The English lovers of chess were so enthused over the brilliant outcome of this game, that they styled it the "Kohinoor" of chess.

EVANS GAMBIT DECLINED

REV. G. A. MACDONNELL BODEN

White Black

1 P—K4 P—K4
2 Kt—KB3 Kt—QB3
3 B—B4 B—B4
4 P—QKt4 B—Kt3
5 O—O P—Q3
6 P—KR3 Kt—B3
7 P—Q3 O—O
8 Kt—B3 P—KR3
9 B—K3 Kt x KtP
10 Kt—K2 Kt—B3
11 Kt—Kt3 P—Q4
12 B—QKt5 P x P
13 B x Kt P x B
14 Kt(B3) x P P x P
15 P x P Q—K1
16 B x B RP x B
17 P—B4 Kt—Q4
18 Q—R5 P—B3
19 Kt—Kt6 Q—K6ch
20 K—R2 R—Q1
21 KR—K1 Q x QP
22 QR—Q1 Q—B7
23 Kt—K7ch K—R1
24 Q—B7 B x P

The spectators, among them several very strong players, declared that after Black's 24th move, White's game was hopelessly lost. MacDonnell quietly assured them that he had in reality a winning position and proved it to the astonishment of all, by a few brilliant moves.

25 R—K2! Q x QR
26 Kt—R5 R—KKt1

27 Kt x R	R x Kt
28 R—K8	Resigns

Mate cannot be averted by Black.

---

56. London, July 1861.

Another dashing Kolisch attack

EVANS GAMBIT

I. KOLISCH	A. ANDERSSEN
White	Black
1 P—K4	P—K4
2 Kt—KB3	Kt—QB3
3 B—B4	B—B4
4 P—QKt4	B x P
5 P—B3	B—R4
6 P—Q4	P x P
7 O—O	P x P
8 Q—Kt3	Q—B3
9 P—K5	Q—Kt3
10 Kt x P	P—Kt4
11 Kt x P	R—Kt1
12 Q—K3	KKt—K2
13 Q—K2	Q—R4
14 B—R3	B—Kt2
15 QR—Q1	Kt—B4?

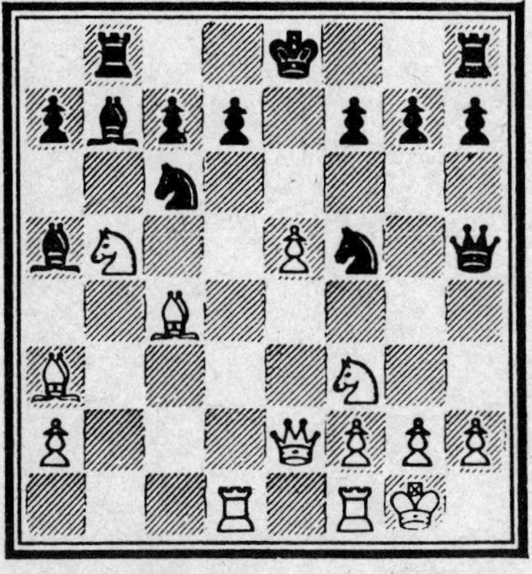

16 R x P!!	K x R
17 P—K6ch!	K—B1
18 P x P	B—R1
19 Kt x Pch!	Kt x Kt
20 Q—K6ch	K—Q1
21 R—Q1ch	Kt—Q3
22 R x Ktch!	P x R
23 Q x Pch	K—B1
24 B—K6ch	K—Kt2
25 B—Q5ch	Q x B
26 Q x Qch	K—R3
27 Q—B4ch	K—Kt2
28 Q—K4ch	Kt—B3
29 Kt—K5	K—R3
30 Q—B4ch	K—R2
31 B—B5ch	R—Kt3
32 B x Rch	B x B
33 Kt x Ktch	B x Kt
34 Q x B	Resigns

---

57. London, June, 1862.

"The Most Beautiful Game of the Tournament."—ANDERSSEN.

CENTER COUNTER GAME

W. STEINITZ	A. MONGREDIEN
White	Black
1 P—K4	P—Q4
2 P x P	Q x P
3 Kt—QB3	Q—Q1
4 P—Q4	P—K3?
5 Kt—B3	Kt—KB3
6 B—Q3	B—K2
7 O—O	O—O
8 B—K3	P—QKt3
9 Kt—K5	B—Kt2
10 P—B4	QKt—Q2
11 Q—K2	Kt—Q4?
12 Kt x Kt	P x Kt
13 R—B3	P—KB4
14 R—R3	P—Kt3
15 P—KKt4	P x P

(see diagram next page)

16 R x P!!	Kt x Kt
17 BP x Kt	K x R
18 Q x P	KR—Kt1
19 Q—R5ch	K—Kt2

20	Q—R6ch	K—B2
21	Q—R7ch	K—K3
22	Q—R3ch	K—B2
23	R—B1ch	K—K1
24	Q—K6	R—Kt2
25	B—Kt5	Q—Q2
26	B x Pch	R x B
27	Q x Rch	K—Q1
28	R—B8ch	Q—K1
29	Q x Q mate	

---

58. London, 1862.

Compare this with game No. 75!

GIUOCO PIANO

S. DUBOIS		W. STEINITZ
White		Black
1	P—K4	P—K4
2	Kt—KB3	Kt—QB3
3	B—B4	B—B4
4	O—O	Kt—B3
5	P—Q3	P—Q3
6	B—KKt5	P—KR3
7	B—R4?	P—KKt4!
8	B—Kt3	P—KR4!
9	P—KR4	B—KKt5
10	P—B3	Q—Q2
11	P—Q4	P x P
12	P—K5	P(3) x P
13	B x P	Kt x B
14	Kt x Kt	Q—B4
15	Kt x B	P x Kt
16	B—Q3	Q—Q4
17	P—Kt4	O—O—O!
18	P—QB4	Q—B3
19	P x B	R x P
20	P—B3	QR—R1
21	P x P	Q—K1!
22	Q—K1	Q—K6ch
23	Q x Q	P x Q
24	P—Kt3	R—R8ch
25	K—Kt2	R(1)—R7ch
26	K—B3	R x Rch
27	B x R	R—B7ch
28	K x P	R x B
29	P—R4	K—Q2
30	K—Q3	Kt x P
31	K—B3	Kt—K6
32	R—R2	R x Kt
33	R—Q2ch	K—B3
		and wins

---

59. Paris, 1863.

Black's greediness is punished

DANISH GAMBIT

LINDEHN		MACZUSKI
White		Black
1	P—K4	P—K4
2	P—Q4	P x P
3	P—QB3	P x P
4	B—QB4	P x P
5	B x P	B—Kt5ch
6	Kt—B3	Kt—KB3
7	Kt—K2	Kt x P
8	O—O	Kt x Kt
9	Kt x Kt	B x Kt
10	B x B	Q—Kt4
11	R—K1ch	K—Q1
12	P—B4	Q x P
13	B x KtP	R—Kt1
14	Q—Kt4!	Q—Q3
15	B—B6ch	Q x B
16	Q x R mate	

60. Breslau, 1863.

Extraordinarily ingenious and pretty.

KIESERITZKY GAMBIT

J. ROSANES	A. ANDERSSEN
White	Black
1 P—K4	P—K4
2 P—KB4	P x P
3 Kt—KB3	P—KKt4
4 P—KR4	P—Kt5
5 Kt—K5	Kt—KB3
6 B—B4	P—Q4
7 P x P	B—Q3
8 P—Q4	Kt—R4
9 B—Kt5ch	P—B3
10 P x P	P x P
11 Kt x QBP	Kt x Kt
12 B x Ktch	K—B1
13 B x R	Kt—Kt6!
14 R—R2	B—KB4
15 B—Q5	K—Kt2!
16 Kt—B3	R—K1ch
17 K—B2	Q—Kt3
18 Kt—R4	Q—R3!
19 Kt—B3	B—K4!

20 P—R4	Q—B8ch!!
21 Q x Q	B x Pch
22 B—K3	R x B
23 K—Kt1	R—K8 mate

61. Berlin, 1864.

The proverbial two Bishops!

FALKBEER COUNTER GAMBIT

A. ANDERSSEN	E. SCHALLOPP
White	Black
1 P—K4	P—K4
2 P—KB4	P—Q4
3 Kt—KB3	QP x P
4 Kt x P	B—Q3
5 B—B4	B x Kt
6 P x B	Q—Q5
7 Q—K2	Q x KP
8 P—Q4!	Q x QP
9 Kt—B3	Kt—KB3
10 B—K3	Q—Q1
11 O—O	P—KR3
12 B—B5	QKt—Q2?
13 Q x Pch!	Resigns

---

62. Cafe National, Leipsig, Jan., 1864.

One of four blindfold games.

EVANS GAMBIT

L. PAULSEN	H. SCHNEIDER
White	Black
1 P—K4	P—K4
2 Kt—KB3	Kt—QB3
3 B—B4	B—B4
4 P—QKt4	B x P
5 P—B3	B—B4
6 O—O	Kt—B3
7 P—Q4	P x P
8 P x P	B—Kt3
9 P—K5	P—Q4
10 P x Kt	P x B
11 P—Q5	Q x BP
12 P x Kt	Q x R

(see diagram next page)

To the astonishment of all, White announced mate in eleven.

13 R—K1ch	B—K3
14 Q—Q7ch	K—B1
15 R x B	B x Pch

16 K—R1	P—KR3
17 P x P	P—Kt4
18 P x R(Q)ch	K—Kt2
19 Q—K4	Q—B3
20 R x Q	R—KB1
21 Q(7)—K7	B—B4
22 R x P	K x R
23 Q x P mate	

---

63. Paris, 1864.

A game that has had echoes!

SCOTCH GAME

MACZUSKI	I. KOLISCH
White	Black
1 P—K4	P—K4
2 Kt—KB3	Kt—QB3
3 P—Q4	P x P
4 Kt x P	Q—R5
5 Kt—QB3	B—Kt5
6 Q—Q3	Kt—B3
7 Kt x Kt	QP x Kt
8 B—Q2	B x Kt
9 B x B	Kt x P
10 Q—Q4	Q—K2
11 O—O—O	Q—Kt4ch
12 P—B4!	Q x Pch
13 B—Q2	Q—Kt5
14 Q—Q8ch!	K x Q
15 B—Kt5ch	K—K1
16 R—Q8 mate!	

---

64. Berlin, 1865.

Was a great master ever mated in such short order?!

RUY LOPEZ

J. H. ZUKERTORT	A. ANDERSSEN
White	Black
1 P—K4	P—K4
2 Kt—KB3	Kt—QB3
3 B—Kt5	KKt—K2
4 P—B3	P—Q3
5 P—Q4	B—Q2
6 O—O	Kt—Kt3
7 Kt—Kt5	P—KR3
8 Kt x P!	K x Kt
9 B—B4ch	K—K2
10 Q—R5	Q—K1
11 Q—Kt5ch!	P x Q
12 B x P mate	

---

65. Berlin, 1865.

Another fine win from the celebrated master.

SICILIAN DEFENSE

J. H. ZUKERTORT	A. ANDERSSEN
White	Black
1 P—K4	P—QB4
2 Kt—KB3	P—K3
3 P—Q4	P x P
4 Kt x P	Kt—KB3
5 Kt—QB3	B—Kt5

6	B—Q3	Kt—B3
7	B—K3	P—Q4
8	P x P	Kt x P
9	O—O!	KKt x Kt
10	P x Kt	B x P
11	Kt x Kt	P x Kt
12	R—Kt1	O—O
13	R—Kt3!	B—R4
14	B—QB5	R—K1

15	B x Pch!	K x B
16	R—R3ch	K—Kt1
17	Q—R5	P—B4
18	R—Q1!	B—Q2
19	Q—R7ch	K—B2
20	R—Kt3	B—B6
21	Q—Kt6ch!	K—Kt1
22	R x B (B3)	P—B5
23	R—KR3	R—K2
24	Q—R7ch	K—B2
25	Q—R5ch	K—Kt1
26	B x R	Q x B
27	Q—R8ch	K—B2
28	Q x R	Resigns

---

66. London, Sept., 1867.

A lapse of Steinitz's famous defensive skill!

RUY LOPEZ

H. E. BIRD WM. STEINITZ

	White	Black
1	P—K4	P—K4
2	Kt—KB3	Kt—QB3
3	B—Kt5	Kt—B3
4	P—Q4	P x P
5	P—K5	Kt—K5
6	Kt x P	B—K2
7	O—O	Kt x Kt
8	Q x Kt	Kt—B4
9	P—KB4	P—QKt3
10	P—B5!	Kt—Kt6
11	Q—K4	Kt x R
12	P—B6!	B—B4ch
13	K—R1	R—QKt1
14	P—K6!	R—Kt1
15	Q x P*	R—B1
16	P x Pch	R x P
17	R—K1ch	B—K2
18	Q—Kt8ch	R—B1
19	P—B7 mate!	

**White misses mate in 3!*

---

67. About 1868.

"Brilliantissimo!" Deserves to be perpetuated.

KING'S GAMBIT

THOMPSON G. H. MACKENZIE

	White	Black
1	P—K4	P—K4
2	P—KB4	P x P
3	Kt—KB3	P—KKt4
4	P—Q4	P—Kt5
5	Kt—K5	Q—R5ch
6	K—Q2	Q—B7ch
7	K—B3	Kt—QB3
8	P—QR3?	P—Q3
9	Kt x Kt	P x Kt
10	B—Q3	R—Kt1
11	R—B1?	Q x QPch!
12	K x Q	B—Kt2ch
13	P—K5	B x Pch
14	K—K4	Kt—B3 mate

---

68. London, April, 1869.

One of Boden's Best.
Full of fine points and interest

KING'S BISHOP OPENING

	S. BODEN White	H. E. BIRD Black
1	P—K4	P—K4
2	B—B4	Kt—KB3
3	P—Q4	P x P
4	Q x P	Kt—B3
5	Q—K3	P—QKt3
6	QKt—B3	B—B4
7	Q—Kt3	O—O
8	B—KKt5	R—K1
9	O—O—O	QKt—R4
10	B—K2	B—K2
11	P—B4	B—Kt2
12	B—B3	K—R1
13	P—KR4	P—B4
14	KKt—K2	QR—B1
15	P—K5	Kt—Kt1
16	KB x B	Kt x B
17	P—B5	P—B3
18	P—K6	P—Q3

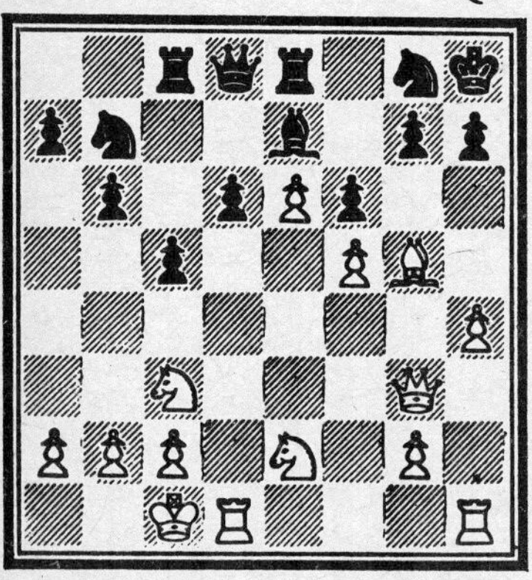

19	Kt—B4!!	P x B
20	Kt—Kt6ch	P x Kt
21	P x Pch	Kt—R3
22	P x Kt	B—Kt4ch
23	K—Kt1	B x P
24	Q x KtP	R—K2
25	P—B6	Q—K1
26	P—B7	Q—B1
27	R x Bch	P x R
28	R—R1	R x KP
29	Q x R	K—R2
30	Kt—K4	R—B2
31	Kt—Kt5ch	K—R1
32	R x Pch	Q x R
33	Q x Q mate	

---

69. London, 1869.

A Cherished Antique.

KIESERITZKY GAMBIT

	MATCHEGO White	E. FALKBEER Black
1	P—K4	P—K4
2	P—KB4	P x P
3	Kt—KB3	P—KKt4
4	P—KR4	P—Kt5
5	Kt—K5	Kt—KB3
6	Kt—QB3?	P—Q3
7	Kt—B4	B—K2
8	P—Q4	Kt—R4
9	B—K2	B x Pch
10	K—Q2	Q—Kt4
11	K—Q3	Kt—QB3
12	P—QR3	B—B7
13	Kt—Q5	B x P
14	Kt x BPch	K—Q1
15	Kt—Q5	P—B4
16	Kt x QP	P x Pch
17	K—B4	. . . .

(see diagram next page)

Black now gives mate in 9 moves.

17	. . . .	Q x Ktch
18	K x Q	Kt—B3ch
19	K—B4	B—K3ch
20	K—Kt5	P—R3ch
21	K—R4	P—Kt4ch
22	Kt x P	P x Ktch
23	K x P	R—R4ch
24	K x Kt	B—Q4ch
25	K—Q6	Kt—K1 mate

A most brilliant and remarkable ending.

18	R—B2	Q—R6
19	P—Q4	Kt—Kt6ch
20	K—Kt1	Q—Kt7ch!
21	R x Q	Kt—R6 mate

---

70. Norwich, 1871.

A gamelet with one of the most exquisitely beautiful endings in the annals of chess.

GIUOCO PIANO

	AMATEUR White	J. H. BLACKBURNE Black
1	P—K4	P—K4
2	Kt—KB3	Kt—QB3
3	B—B4	B—B4
4	O—O	Kt—B3
5	P—Q3	P—Q3
6	P—KR3	Kt—K2
7	B—Kt5	P—B3
8	B—K3	B—Kt3
9	Kt—B3	Kt—Kt3
10	Q—Q2	B—K3
11	B—Kt3	O—O
12	QR—Q1	Q—Q2
13	Kt—R2	B x P!
14	B x B	B x P!
15	K x B	Kt—B5ch
16	K—R1	P x B
17	P—B3	Kt(3)—R4

71. London Chess Club, 1871.

Finest game Blackburne ever played blindfold.

One of ten games played simultaneously.

SCOTCH GAMBIT

	J. H. BLACKBURNE White	DR. BALLARD Black
1	P—K4	P—K4
2	Kt—KB3	Kt—QB3
3	P—Q4	P x P
4	B—QB4	B—B4
5	Kt—Kt5	Kt—R3
6	Q—R5	Q—K2
7	O—O	Kt—K4
8	B—Kt3	P—Q3
9	P—KR3	Kt—Kt1
10	P—KB4	P—Q6ch
11	K—R2	Kt—KB3
12	Q—Q1	QKt—Kt5ch
13	P x Kt	Kt x Pch
14	K—Kt3!	P—KR4! (a)
15	P—B5	B—K6

16 B x Pch	K—B1
17 Q x Kt!!	P x Q
18 B x B	Q—K4ch
19 B—B4	Q x KtP
20 Kt—Q2	P x P
21 Kt—B4	. . . .

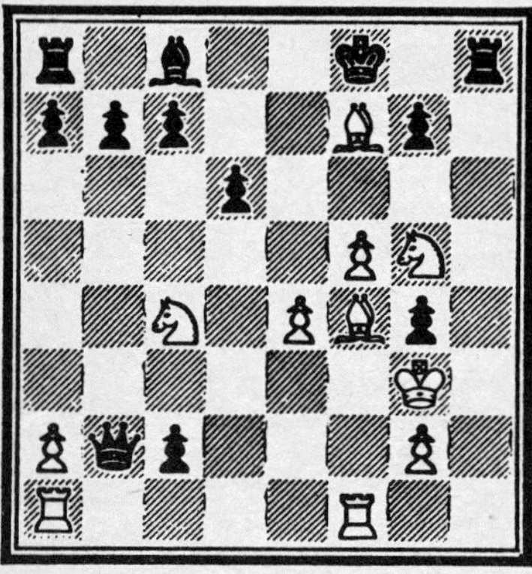

21	Q—B6ch
22 Kt—K3	B—Q2
23 K x P	B—R5
24 Kt—Q5	Q—Q6
25 B—Kt6	R—R3!
26 Kt—K6ch	K—Kt1
27 Kt—K7ch	K—R1
28 R—R1	Q—Q8ch
29 QR x Q	P x R(Q) ch
30 R x Q	B x Rch
31 K—Kt3	R—R8
32 B—Q2!	B—R4
33 B—B3	R—KKt1
34 P—B6	B x B
35 Kt x Bch	K—R2
36 P—B7 and wins	

(a) At this stage the game was adjourned and most of the spectators held that white had a lost position; yet not only did he actually win, but exhaustive analysis proved that he could do so in every variation.

---

72. Vienna, 1872.

Perhaps the most extraordinary game ever played.

VIENNA OPENING

L. HAMPPE White	J. MEITNER Black
1 P—K4	P—K4
2 Kt—QB3	B—B4
3 Kt—R4	B x Pch!?
4 K x B	Q—R5ch
5 K—K3	Q—B5ch
6 K—Q3	P—Q4
7 K—B3	Q x KP
8 K—Kt3	Kt—QR3
9 P—QR3	Q x Ktch!!
10 K x Q	Kt—B4ch
11 K—Kt4	P—R4ch!
12 K x Kt	Kt—K2
13 B—Kt5ch!	K—Q1
14 B—B6	P—Kt3ch
15 K—Kt5	Kt x B!
16 K x Kt!	B—Kt2ch!!
17 K—Kt5!	B—R3ch
18 K—B6!	B—Kt2ch

Drawn!!!

---

73. Played by correspondence in 1875.

How women played chess three score years ago.

RUY LOPEZ

MRS. J. W. GILBERT White	W. J. BERRY Black
1 P—K4	P—K4
2 Kt—KB3	Kt—QB3
3 B—Kt5	P—QR3
4 B—R4	Kt—B3
5 O—O	Kt x P
6 R—K1	Kt—B4
7 B x Kt	QP x B

8 P—Q4	Kt—K3
9 P x P	Q—K2?
10 Kt—B3	B—Q2
11 P—QR4	O—O—O
12 P—QKt3	P—B3
13 Q—K2	Q—B2
14 Kt—K4	R—Kt1
15 P—B3	P—R3
16 P—QKt4	P—KB4
17 Kt—Kt3	P—KKt4
18 Kt—Q4	Kt x Kt
19 P x Kt	R—K1
20 P—Kt5!	BP x P
21 P x P	B x P
22 P—K6!	Q—Kt3
23 Q x B	P—B5

White announced mate in 18.

24 R x P	P x R
25 Q x Pch	K—Kt1
26 Q—Kt5ch	K—B1
27 Q—Q7ch	K—Kt1
28 B x P	P x B
29 Q—Kt5ch	K—B1
30 R—R1	B—R6
31 R x B	Q—Kt8ch
32 Q x Q	R x P
33 R—R7	K—Q2
34 Q—Kt5ch	R—B3
35 P—Q5	R—Kt3
36 P x Rch	R x P
37 Kt—K4	P—B6
38 Q—Q5ch	R—Q3
39 Q x Rch	K—K1
40 Q x BP	Any move
41 R—R8 mate	

---

74. Played in Perugia, about 1875.

The following game, played by Joachim Cardinal Pecci (afterwards Pope Leo XIII) was obtained during my visit at Vatican city in 1925-26, from my old colleague Rev. Maurice de la Taille, S. J., Professor of professors at the Gregorian University, Rome Italy, and author of "Mysterium Fidie."—F.J.W.

GIUOCO PIANO

REV. FR. GUILA

JOACHIM CARDINAL PECCI

White	Black
1 P—K4	P—K4
2 Kt—KB3	Kt—QB3
3 B—B4	B—B4
4 P—B3	Kt—B3
5 P—Q4	P x P
6 P—K5	P—Q4
7 P x Kt	P x B
8 Q—K2ch	B—K3
9 P x KtP	R—KKt1
10 P x P	Kt x P

11 Kt x Kt	B x Kt
12 Q—R5	Q—B3
13 O—O	R x P
14 Q—Kt5ch	P—B3
15 Q x KtP	. . . .
15	R x Pch!
16 K x R	Q—Kt3ch
17 K—R1	B—Q4ch
18 P—B3	B x Pch
19 R x B	Q—Kt8 mate

---

75. New York Tournament, 1876.

For the beautiful and well sustained conduct of this game, Bird was awarded a silver cup as brilliancy prize.

FRENCH DEFENSE

H. E. Bird White	James Mason Black
1 P—K4	P—K3
2 P—Q4	P—Q4
3 Kt—QB3	Kt—KB3
4 P x P	P x P
5 Kt—B3	B—Q3
6 B—Q3	O—O
7 O—O	P—KR3
8 R—K1	Kt—B3
9 Kt—QKt5	B—QKt5
10 P—B3	B—R4?
11 Kt—R3	B—KKt5
12 Kt—B2	Q—Q2
13 P—Kt4	B—Kt3
14 P—KR3	B—KR4
15 Kt—K3	KR—K1
16 P—Kt5	Kt—K2
17 P—Kt4	B—Kt3
18 Kt—K5	Q—B1
19 P—QR4	P—B3
20 P x P	P x P
21 B—R3	Kt—K5
22 Q—B2	Kt—Kt4
23 B x Kt	R x B
24 B x B	P x B
25 Q x P	Kt x Pch
26 K—R2	Kt—B5
27 Q—B5	Kt—K3
28 Kt—Kt2	Q—B2
29 P—R5!!	B x RP
30 R x B	R—KB1
31 R—R6!	R x Q
32 P x R	Kt—Q1
33 Kt—B4	Q—B1
34 Kt(B4)—Kt6	R—K1
35 Kt x P!	Q—B2ch
36 Kt(B6)—K5	Q x P
37 R—K3	Q—Q7
38 K—Kt2	Q x P
39 P—B6!	P x P
40 R x BP	Kt—K3
41 R—KKt3	Kt—Kt4
42 Kt—Kt4	K—Kt2
43 Kt—B4!!	Q—K5ch
44 K—R2	Kt—R2
45 Kt—R5ch	K—R1
46 R x P	Q—B7
47 Kt(R5)—B6	R—K2
48 K—Kt2	P—Q5
49 Kt—K5!	Q—B1
50 Kt—Kt6ch	Resigns

---

76. Leipzig, December, 1877.

The Queen's Sacrifice Rejected.

RUY LOPEZ

A. Anderssen White	L. Paulsen Black
1 P—K4	P—K4
2 Kt—KB3	Kt—QB3
3 B—Kt5	P—QR3
4 B—R4	P—QKt4
5 B—Kt3	B—Kt2
6 O—O	P—Kt3
7 P—Q3	B—Kt2
8 P—QR4	KKt—K2
9 Kt—B3	Kt—Q5
10 B—R2	P—Kt5
11 Kt x Kt	P x Kt
12 Kt—K2	P—Q4

13	P—KB3	O—O
14	Q—K1	P—QB4
15	Q—Kt3	P—B5
16	B—Kt5	P—Kt6?
17	BP x P	P x QP
18	Kt—B4	P x KP
19	P x P	B x P
20	Q—K1!	P—B4
21	P—Kt4ch	R—B2
22	Kt—K6	Q—Q3
23	Kt x B	K x Kt

24	Q x B!	QR—KB1
25	Q—R4	Kt—B3
26	R—B3	

and wins

---

77. Paris Tournament, July 15, 1878.

Mackenzie's Immortal.

FRENCH DEFENSE

G. H. MACKENZIE		JAMES MASON
White		Black
1	P—K4	P—K3
2	P—Q4	P—Q4
3	Kt—QB3	Kt—KB3
4	P x P	P x P
5	Kt—B3	B—Q3
6	B—Q3	O—O
7	O—O	Kt—B3
8	B—KKt5	Kt—K2
9	B x Kt	P x B
10	Kt—KR4	K—Kt2
11	Q—R5	R—R1
12	P—B4	P—B3
13	R—B3	Kt—Kt3
14	QR—KB1	Q—B2
15	Kt—K2	B—Q2
16	Kt—Kt3	QR—KKt1

17	Q—R6ch!!	K x Q
18	Kt(4)—B5ch	B x Kt
19	Kt x Bch	K—R4
20	P—Kt4ch	K x P
21	R—Kt3ch	K—R4
22	B—K2 mate	

Morphy nor Anderssen ever played more brilliantly.

---

78. Match, 1880.

Tchigorin at his best

SCOTCH GAME

M. TCHIGORIN		E. SCHIFFERS
White		Black
1	P—K4	P—K4
2	Kt—KB3	Kt—QB3
3	P—Q4	P x P

4	Kt x P	B—B4
5	B—K3	Q—B3
6	P—QB3	KKt—K2
7	B—QB4	P—Q3
8	P—B4	Q—Kt3
9	O—O	Q x P
10	R—K1	Q—Kt3
11	Kt x Kt	B x Bch
12	R x B	P x Kt
13	Q—K2	Q—B3
14	Kt—Q2	P—Q4
15	B—Q3	B—K3
16	R—KB1!	P—Kt3
17	Kt—Kt3	O—O
18	P—Kt4!	QR—K1
19	Kt—B5	P—Q5
20	P—Kt5	Q—R1
21	R x B	P x R
22	Q x Pch	K—Kt2
23	R—K1!	P x P
24	Q x Ktch!	R x Q
25	R x Rch	Resigns

PART IV

The Age of Steinitz

Few masters in the history of chess have been so maligned as has been Wilhelm Steinitz. To most players he has been known as "the man who destroyed brilliancy in chess." But this is simply not true; just play over the twentieth century games in this volume, and you will readily see that Steinitz's influence on the game was definitely not pernicious. Remember also that Steinitz himself was a strikingly brilliant player, not only as a mettlesome youngster, but even as a feeble old man. See for example Game No. 173.

Game No. 73 shows us how Steinitz played at the beginning of his career. We all know that very shortly thereafter he experienced a thoroughgoing conversion. At first an enthusiastic disciple of the attacking school, he became obsessed with the deeply-rooted carelessness, flashiness and frequent unsoundness of that school. Equally impressive, but in a favorable sense, must have been the enchanting combinations of Morphy, with their natural development, logical preparation and accurate execution. As a man of genius, Steinitz at once drew the conclusion which was to become clear to lesser men much later. A pervasive interest in the defense became his life-time passion; he was fascinated by the idea of refuting an unsound attack, of demonstrating to the opponent that one cannot lightly toss away Pawns, not to mention pieces, without retribution, that hit-or-miss and helter-skelter attacks should not be permitted to achieve their goal.

As we know, these theories had a lasting effect on the chess world. It is common knowledge that all the great masters, beginning with Steinitz's contemporaries, whether they have agreed with him or agreed to disagree, have absorbed the fundamentals of his theories into their own styles. This is just as apparent today as it was in the games of Steinitz's greatest rivals, such poets of the chessboard as Zukertort, Tchigorin and Blackburne. The combinations of these masters were not discouraged by Steinitz; on the contrary, their attacking play was purified and raised to finer artistic levels by Steinitz's probing and fruitful criticism.

79. Dresden, 1880.

Black's Queen-sacrifice upsets the apple-cart.

BISHOP'S GAMBIT

DR. SCHMID	WAYTE
White	Black
1 P—K4	P—K4
2 P—KB4	P x P
3 B—B4	Kt—KB3
4 Kt—QB3	Kt—B3
5 Kt—B3	B—Kt5
6 P—K5	P—Q4
7 B—Kt5	Kt—K5
8 O—O	O—O
9 Kt—K2	B—Kt5
10 P—Q3	B—B4ch
11 P—Q4	B—Kt3
12 B x P	P—B3
13 P—B3	P x P
14 B x Kt	KtP x B
15 Kt x P	B x Kt
16 Q x B	P—B4
17 B—K3	P x P
18 R x Rch	Q x R
19 R—KB1	. . . .

19	P x B!
20 R x Qch	R x R
21 Kt—B3	P—Kt4
22 P—KR3	Kt—Kt6
23 Q—K1	P—K7ch
24 K—R2	Kt—B8ch
25 K—R1	B—K6!
26 Q—Kt1	R x Kt!
27 P x R	B—B7
28 Q—Q3	Kt—Kt6ch
29 K—Kt2	P—K8 (Kt) ch

This pretty move crowns the end of this beautiful game.

30 K x B	Kt x Qch
31 K x Kt	Kt x P
Resigns	

---

80. Played about 1880.

A charming gamelet.

TWO KNIGHTS' DEFENSE

L. HOFFER	AMATEUR
White	Black
1 P—K4	P—K4
2 Kt—KB3	Kt—QB3
3 B—B4	Kt—B3
4 Kt—Kt5	P—Q4
5 P x P	Kt—QR4
6 B—Kt5ch	P—B3
7 P x P	P x P
8 Q—B3	Q—Kt3
9 Kt—B3	B—K2
10 P—Q3	P—KR3
11 B—K3	Q—B2
12 Kt—Q5!	Kt x Kt
13 Q x Pch	K—Q1
14 Q x Ktch!	P x Q
15 Kt—B7 mate!	

---

81. London, about 1880.

Magna Carta:
King John and the Barons.

STEINITZ GAMBIT

W. STEINITZ	ALLIES
White	Black
1 P—K4	P—K4
2 Kt—QB3	Kt—QB3
3 P—B4	P x P
4 P—Q4	Q—R5ch
5 K—K2	P—Q4
6 P x P	B—Kt5ch
7 Kt—B3	O—O—O!?
8 P x Kt	B—QB4
9 P x Pch	K—Kt1
10 Kt—Kt5	Kt—B3
11 K—Q3	Q—R4
12 K—B3	P—QR3
13 K—Kt3	P x Kt
14 P—B3	. . . .

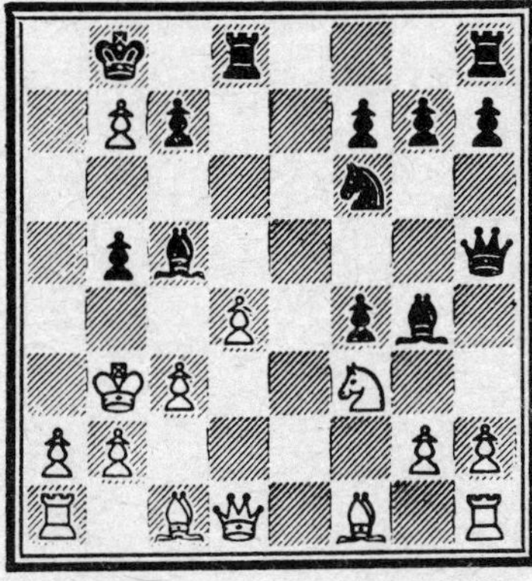

14	R x P!
15 P x R	Q—Q4ch
16 K—B2	B—B4ch
17 K—Q2	B—Kt5ch
18 K—K2	Kt—Kt5
Resigns	

The march of the White King was curious; out of a total of eighteen moves, seven were made by the King.

---

82. Berlin Tournament, 1881.

Blackburne's Masterpiece.

FRENCH DEFENSE

J. H. BLACKBURNE	J. SCHWARZ
White	Black
1 P—K4	P—K3
2 P—Q4	P—Q4
3 Kt—QB3	Kt—KB3
4 P x P	P x P
5 Kt—B3	B—Q3
6 B—Q3	P—B3
7 O—O	O—O
8 Kt—K2	B—KKt5
9 Kt—Kt3	Q—B2
10 B—K3	QKt—Q2
11 Q—Q2	KR—K1
12 QR—K1	Kt—K5
13 Q—B1	QB x Kt
14 P x B	Kt x Kt
15 RP x Kt	B x P

Black here proposed a draw.

16 K—Kt2	B—Q3
17 R—R1	Kt—B1
18 R—R3	P—KKt3
19 QR—R1	QR—Q1
20 B—KKt5	R—Q2
21 P—QB4	P x P
22 B x BP	P—KR4
23 R—R4	P—Kt4
24 B—Kt3	Kt—K3

25	B—B6	Kt—B5ch
26	Q x Kt!	B x Q

"White's design especially from 21st move in combination with the brilliant finish, belongs to the finest efforts of chess genius in modern match play."—(STEINITZ)

27	R x P	P x R
28	R x P	Resigns

83.

An exquisite mating combination

PETROFF DEFENSE

	G. H. MACKENZIE	HAMMOND
	White	Black
1	P—K4	P—K4
2	Kt—KB3	Kt—KB3
3	Kt x P	P—Q3
4	Kt—KB3	Kt x P
5	P—Q4	P—Q4
6	B—Q3	B—Q3
7	O—O	O—O
8	P—B4	P—QB3
9	P x P	P x P
10	Kt—B3	Kt x Kt
11	P x Kt	B—KKt5
12	R—Kt1	Q—B2
13	P—KR3	B—R4?
14	B x Pch	K x B
15	Kt—Kt5ch	K—Kt3
16	P—Kt4	B—B5
17	R x P!	Q x R
18	B x B	R—KR1
19	Q—Q3ch	K—B3
20	R—K1!	B—Kt3
21	Kt—R7ch!	R x Kt
22	P—Kt5 mate.	

---

84. Vienna, June 18, 1882.

Mason conjures up a masterly combination out of a harmless-looking position.

GIUOCO PIANO

	JAMES MASON	S. WINAWER
	White	Black
1	P—K4	P—K4
2	Kt—KB3	Kt—QB3
3	B—B4	B—B4
4	P—Q3	P—Q3
5	B—K3	B—Kt3
6	QKt—Q2	P—KR3
7	Kt—B1	Kt—B3
8	P—KR3	Kt—K2
9	Kt—Kt3	P—B3
10	B—Kt3	B x B
11	P x B	Q—Kt3
12	Q—Q2	P—QR4
13	P—B3	P—R5
14	B—Q1	B—K3
15	O—O	Q—B2
16	Kt—R4	P—QKt4
17	B—B2	P—B4
18	Kt(3)—B5	B x Kt
19	Kt x B	Kt x Kt
20	R x Kt	Kt—Q2
21	QR—KB1	P—B3
22	B—Q1	P—R6
23	B—R5ch	K—K2
24	P—QKt3	KR—KB1
25	R(5)—B3	Kt—Kt3
26	R—Kt3	K—Q1
27	B—Kt4	Q—K2
28	B—K2	K—B2
29	P—Q4!	P—B5
30	R—Kt1	P—Kt4
31	KtP x P!	KtP x P
32	QR—Kt4	Q—K3
33	P—Q5!	Q—B1
34	B x P	Kt—R5
35	B—Kt5	Kt—B4
36	Q—K2!	P—B4
37	P x P	P—K5
38	B—B6	QR—Kt1
39	Q—R5	R—B3
40	R x KtP!	P x R
41	Q—R7ch	Kt—Q2
42	B x Kt	Q—Kt1

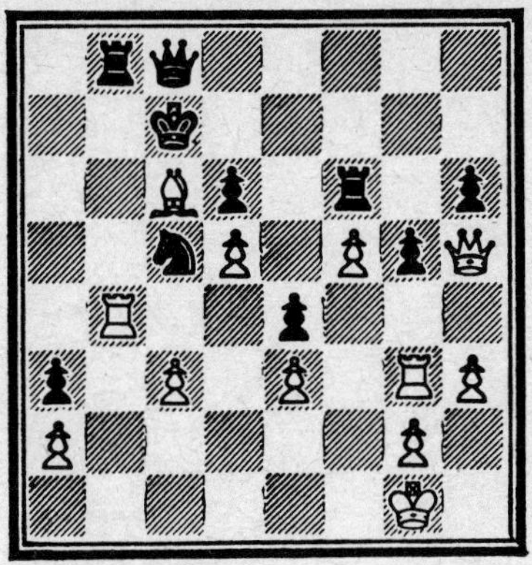

43 R—Kt7ch!!	K x R
44 B—B8ch	K—R1
45 Q x Q	R x P
46 Q—Q8	R x P
47 Q—Q7	R—Kt8ch
48 K—R2	R—Q7
49 Q—B6ch	K—Kt1
50 Q x P	QR—Kt7
51 B—K6 and wins	

---

85. London, Played in 1882.

Mephisto's Mate

TWO KNIGHTS' DEFENSE

MEPHISTO* S. TINSLEY

White	Black
1 P—K4	P—K4
2 Kt—KB3	Kt—QB3
3 B—B4	Kt—B3
4 Kt—Kt5	P—Q4
5 P x P	Kt x P
6 Kt x BP?!	K x Kt
7 Q—B3ch	K—K3
8 Kt—B3	Kt—Kt5
9 Q—K4	P—QKt4
10 B—Kt3	B—Kt2
11 P—Q4	B—Q3
12 P x P	B—B4
13 Q—Kt4ch	K—B2
14 B—Kt5	Q—K1
15 O—O—O	Q—K3
16 Q—B3ch	K—K1
17 Kt x Kt	Kt x Kt
18 R x Kt	Q—KKt3
19 P—K6	R—KB1
20 Q—B7ch!!	R x Q
21 P x Rch	K—B1
22 R x B	P—KR3
23 B—Q2	Q x KtP
24 R—K1	Q x BP
25 R x BP	Q x Rch
26 B x Q	P—Kt3
27 B—Kt4ch	K—Kt2
28 P—B8(Q) mate!	

*Gunsberg?

---

86. London Tournament, May 5, 1883.

Zukertort's Immortal.

"One of the most brilliant games on record."—(STEINITZ).

QUEEN'S GAMBIT DECLINED (in effect)

J. H. ZUKERTORT J. H. BLACKBURNE

White	Black
1 P—QB4	P—K3
2 P—K3	Kt—KB3
3 Kt—KB3	P—QKt3
4 B—K2	B—Kt2
5 O—O	P—Q4
6 P—Q4	B—Q3
7 Kt—B3	O—O
8 P—QKt3	QKt—Q2
9 B—Kt2	Q—K2
10 Kt—QKt5	Kt—K5
11 Kt x B	P x Kt
12 Kt—Q2	QKt—B3
13 P—B3	Kt x Kt
14 Q x Kt	P x P
15 B x P	P—Q4
16 B—Q3	KR—B1
17 QR—K1!	R—B2

18 P—K4	QR—QB1
19 P—K5	Kt—K1
20 P—B4	P—Kt3
21 R—K3!	P—B4
22 P x P e.p.	Kt x P
23 P—B5!	Kt—K5
24 B x Kt	P x B
25 P x KtP!!	R—B7
26 P x Pch	K—R1
27 P—Q5ch	P—K4
28 Q—Kt4!!	....

28	R(B1)—B4
29 R—B8ch	K x P

In conjunction with White's previous play, this forms one of the most noble combinations ever conceived over the chess board.

30 Q x Pch	K—Kt2
31 B x Pch	K x R
32 B—Kt7ch	K—Kt1
33 Q x Q	Resigns

---

87. London Tournament, 1883.

Dashing demolition of a World Champion.

THREE KNIGHTS' OPENING

J. H. Blackburne	W. Steinitz
White	Black
1 P—K4	P—K4
2 Kt—KB3	Kt—QB3
3 Kt—B3	P—KKt3
4 P—Q4	P x P
5 Kt x P	B—Kt2
6 B—K3	Kt—B3
7 B—K2	O—O
8 O—O	Kt—K2
9 B—B3	P—Q3
10 Q—Q2	Kt—Q2
11 B—R6	Kt—K4
12 B x B	K x B
13 B—K2	P—KB3
14 P—B4	Kt—B2
15 QR—Q1	P—B3
16 B—B4	B—Q2
17 B x Kt	R x B
18 P—B5	Kt—B1
19 P—K5	BP x P
20 Kt—K6ch	B x Kt
21 P x B	R—K2
22 Q—Kt5	Q—K1
23 R—Q3!	R x P
24 R—R3!	Q—K2
25 Q—R6ch	K—Kt1
26 R—B8ch	Q x R
27 Q x RP mate	

---

88. Manhattan Chess Club, New York, March 3, 1883.

Steinitz' Best Game?!

(One of 28 simultaneous games.)

KIESERITZKY GAMBIT

W. Steinitz	Dr. Simonson
White	Black
1 P—K4	P—K4
2 P—KB4	P x P
3 Kt—KB3	P—KKt4
4 P—KR4	P—Kt5
5 Kt—K5	P—KR4
6 B—B4	Kt—KR3
7 P—Q4	P—Q3
8 Kt—Q3	P—B6

9 P x P	B—K2
10 B—K3	B x Pch
11 K—Q2	P x P
12 Q x P	B—Kt5
13 Q—B4	Kt—B3
14 Kt—B3	Kt—K2
15 QR—B1	R—R2
16 R x B	Kt—Kt3
17 R x B!	Kt x Q
18 R(4) x Kt	P—QB3
19 R—B6	Kt—Kt5
20 B x Pch	K—Q2
21 B—K6ch	K—B2
22 R—B7ch	R x R
23 R x Rch	K—Kt3
24 B x Kt	P x B
25 P—Q5ch	P—B4
26 P—K5	K—R3
27 B x P!	P x B
28 Kt x Pch	K—Kt3
29 R x Pch!	K x Kt

30 K—Q3!!	Q—R4
31 P—Kt4ch	Q x P
32 Kt—K4ch and wins	

This game is considered the finest which Steinitz played in America.

---

89. London Congress, 1883.

How Bird was robbed of his prey.

GIUOCO PIANO

H. E. BIRD	B. ENGLISCH
White	Black
1 P—K4	P—K4
2 Kt—KB3	Kt—QB3
3 B—B4	B—B4
4 P—B3	Kt—B3
5 P—QKt4	B—Kt3
6 P—Q3	P—Q3
7 O—O	O—O
8 B—KKt5	B—K3
9 QKt—Q2	Q—K2
10 P—QR4	P—QR3
11 P—R5	B—R2
12 K—R1	P—R3
13 B—R4	QR—Q1
14 P—Kt5	B x B
15 Kt x B	P x P
16 Kt—K3	B x Kt
17 P x B	Q—K3
18 Q—Kt1!	P—Kt4
19 B—Kt3	Kt—QR2
20 P—B4!	P—B3
21 P—B5!	Kt—R4
22 P—R6!	P x RP
23 R x P	Q—Q2
24 P—Q4!	Kt x Bch
25 P x Kt	Kt—B1
26 P x QP	P—B3
27 R—B1	Kt x P
28 KR x P	Kt—K1
29 Q x P	P—Kt5

30 Kt—R4	P x P
31 P x P	Q x P
32 Kt—B5	Q x P
33 R—K6	R—Q8ch
34 K—R2	Q—Kt8
35 Q x Q	R x Q
36 R—R7	R—Kt4
37 Kt x Pch	K—R1
38 Kt x P	R—Kt4
39 R x Kt	R—R4ch
40 K—Kt1	R x R
41 Kt x P	R—R8ch!
42 K x R	R—K8ch
43 K—R2	R—R8ch
44 K x R	Stalemate!

---

90. Riga, May, 1884.

A Gem.

EVANS GAMBIT

GLOBUS White	GROSS Black
1 P—K4	P—K4
2 Kt—KB3	Kt—QB3
3 B—B4	B—B4
4 P—QKt4	B x P
5 P—B3	B—R4
6 P—Q4	P x P
7 O—O	P—Q3
8 P x P	P—KR3
9 Q—Kt3	Q—K2
10 Kt—B3	B x Kt
11 Q x B	B—Q2
12 P—K5	P x P
13 B—R3	P x P
14 Kt x P	Q—B3
15 QR—K1ch	KKt—K2
16 Kt x Kt!	Q x Q
17 R x Ktch	K—B1
18 R x Pch	K—Kt1
19 Kt—K7ch	K—R2
20 B—Kt2!!	B—K1

Mate in two.

---

91. Paris, July 17, 1884.

Black's attack makes use of problem moves!

KING'S GAMBIT

A. CLERC White	BARON ALBERT ROTHSCHILD Black
1 P—K4	P—K4
2 P—KB4	P x P
3 Kt—KB3	P—KKt4
4 B—B4	B—Kt2
5 P—Q4	P—Q3
6 O—O	P—KR3
7 P—B3	Kt—QB3
8 P—KR4	P—Kt5
9 Kt—R2	P—B6
10 P x P	P—Kt6
11 Kt—Kt4	Q x P
12 K—Kt2	B x Kt
13 R—R1	Q—B3
14 P x B	Q—B7ch
15 K—R3	P—Kt7
16 R—Kt1	P—KR4
17 P—Kt5	Kt—R3!!
18 P x Kt	B—B3
19 Q x P?	Q x R
20 Q x Pch	K—Q1
21 Q x Bch	Kt—K2
22 B—K3	R x Pch!
23 Q x R	Q—R8ch
24 K—Kt3	Q x Q
25 B x Q	P—Kt8 (Q) ch
Resigns	

---

92. Philadelphia, 1885.

A Zukertort Masterpiece.

EVANS GAMBIT DECLINED

J. H. ZUKERTORT White	C. S. MARTINEZ Black
1 P—K4	P—K4
2 Kt—KB3	Kt—QB3

3	B—B4	B—B4
4	P—QKt4	B—Kt3
5	P—QR4	P—QR3
6	P—B3	P—Q3
7	P—R5	B—R2
8	P—Q3	Q—K2
9	QKt—Q2	Kt—B3
10	Kt—B1	P—KR3
11	Kt—Kt3	Kt—Q1
12	O—O	B—K3
13	B—R2	O—O
14	Kt—R4	K—R2
15	Kt(4)—B5	Q—Q2
16	K—R1	P—Q4
17	P—KB4	KP x P
18	QB x P	P x P
19	Kt x KtP!!	B x B
20	R x B	Q—Q4
21	Kt(7)—R5	Kt x Kt
22	Kt x Kt	P—KB4
23	R—Q2	P—K6
24	R—K2	Q—B2
25	B x KP	Q x Kt
26	B x B	R—B2
27	B—Q4	Kt—B3
28	R—K7!	Q—Kt3
29	R x Rch	Q x R
30	B—K3	Kt—K4
31	P—Q4	Kt—B5
32	B—B4	R—KKt1
33	Q—Q3	Q—Q4
34	Q—R3	R—Kt3
35	B x BP	Kt—K6
36	Q—B3	Q—R7
37	R—KKt1	Kt—Q4
38	B—K5	P—B5
39	B x P	Q—B5
40	B—K5	Kt x BP
41	P—Q5	Resigns

"Herr Zukertort considers this the best game he played in America."

---

93. First Game of Match Played at Manhattan Chess Club, *How to smash a crowded position.* Oct. 4, 1886.

RUY LOPEZ

	G. H. MACKENZIE White	S. LIPSCHUETZ Black
1	P—K4	P—K4
2	Kt—KB3	Kt—QB3
3	B—Kt5	Kt—B3
4	O—O	P—Q3
5	P—Q4	B—Q2
6	Kt—B3	B—K2
7	P—Q5	Kt—QKt1
8	B—Q3	B—Kt5
9	Kt—K2	QKt—Q2
10	Kt—Kt3	Kt—B1
11	P—KR3	B—Q2
12	Kt—R2	Kt—Kt3
13	P—KB4	P x P
14	B x P	O—O
15	Q—Q2	Kt—K1
16	Kt—B3	B—KB3
17	P—B3	Kt x B
18	Q x Kt	P—KKt3
19	QR—K1	Kt—Kt2
20	P—K5	B—K2
21	Q—R6!	P x P
22	R x P	P—KB3
23	Kt—R5!!	Kt x Kt
24	R x Kt	B—B4ch
25	K—R1	Q—K2
26	B x P	Q—Kt2
27	B x Pch	K—R1
28	B—B5ch	Resigns

---

94. New York, December, 1886.

Exemplifying Judd's brilliant and forceful style.

FRENCH DEFENSE

MAX JUDD	J. M. HANHAM
White	Black

1	P—K4	P—K3
2	P—Q4	P—Q4
3	Kt—QB3	Kt—KB3
4	P—K5	KKt—Q2
5	QKt—K2	P—QB4
6	P—QB3	Kt—QB3
7	P—KB4	P—QKt3
8	Kt—B3	B—Kt2
9	B—K3	B—K2
10	Kt—Kt3	P—Kt3
11	R—B1	R—QB1
12	B—Q3	P—QR3
13	O—O	O—O
14	Kt—Kt5	B x Kt
15	P x B	P—Kt4
16	Kt—R5!!	P x P
17	P x P	Q—Kt3
18	R x Kt!	B x R
19	Kt—B6ch	K—Kt2
20	Q—K1	R—KR1
21	Q—R4	K—B1
22	Kt x Ktch	B x Kt
23	B x KKtP	B—K1
24	B x BP!	B x B
25	P—Kt6	R—B2
26	Q—Q8ch	Resigns

---

95. Frankfort, 1887.

A grand old-time favorite.

GIUOCO PIANO

E. SCHIFFERS		M. HARMONIST
	White	Black
1	P—K4	P—K4
2	Kt—KB3	Kt—QB3
3	B—B4	B—B4
4	P—B3	Kt—B3
5	P—Q4	P x P
6	P x P	B—Kt5ch
7	B—Q2	B x Bch
8	QKt x B	P—Q4
9	P x P	KKt x P
10	Q—Kt3	QKt—K2
11	O—O	O—O
12	KR—K1	P—QB3
13	P—QR4	Q—B2
14	QR—B1	Kt—B5
15	Kt—Kt5	Kt (K2)—Kt3
16	R—K8!!	R x R
17	B x Pch	K—R1
18	B x R	Kt—K7ch
19	K—R1	Kt x R
20	Kt—B7ch	K—Kt1
21	Kt—R6ch	K—B1
22	Q—Kt8ch	K—K2
23	B x Kt	P x B
24	Q x Pch	K—Q1
25	Q—B8ch	K—Q2
26	Kt—K4	Q—Q1
27	Q—Q6ch	K—K1
28	Kt—B6ch	Resigns

---

96. Frankfort Tournament, July 23, 1887.

"A Genuine Masterpiece"
—(STEINITZ)

GIUOCO PIANO

I. GUNSBERG		M. HARMONIST
	White	Black
1	P—K4	P—K4
2	Kt—KB3	Kt—QB3
3	B—B4	B—B4
4	P—Q3	P—Q3
5	B—K3	B—Kt3
6	QKt—Q2	Kt—B3
7	Kt—B1	P—Q4
8	P x P	Kt x P
9	Q—Q2	P—KR3
10	O—O—O	B—K3
11	B—QKt5	Q—Q3
12	Kt—Kt3	P—B4
13	B x B	RP x B
14	Kt x KP	Q x Kt
15	QR—K1	R x P!
16	P—QB4	O—O!
17	B x Kt	. . . .

17	.. . . .	Q—Q5
18	B x Kt	B x B
19	P x B	R—R8ch
20	K—B2	Q—R5ch
21	K—B3	Q—R4ch
22	P—Kt4	R—R6ch
23	K—Q4	P—B4ch
24	K—K5	Q—R1!
25	K—B4	Q—Q1
26	Q—Kt2	R x P
	Resigns	

---

97. Sixth American Congress, N. Y., March 30, 1889.

An abrupt finish!

Special Prize for best game

GIUOCO PIANO

J. MASON		I. GUNSBERG
White		Black
1	P—K4	P—K4
2	Kt—KB3	Kt—QB3
3	B—B4	B—B4
4	P—Q3	P—Q3
5	B—K3	B—Kt3
6	P—B3	Kt—B3
7	QKt—Q2	Q—K2
8	P—QR4	B—K3
9	B—QKt5	B x B
10	P x B	P—QR3
11	B x Ktch	P x B
12	P—QKt4	O—O
13	O—O	Kt—Kt5
14	Q—K2	P—KB4
15	P x P	B x P
16	P—K4	B—Q2
17	Kt—B4	Kt—B3
18	Kt—K3	P—Kt3
19	P—B4	Kt—R4
20	P—Kt3	B—R6
21	R—B2	Kt—Kt2
22	Q—Kt2	Kt—K3
23	R—K1	R—B2
24	QR—K2	QR—KB1
25	Kt—K1	Kt—Q5
26	R—Q2	Q—Kt4
27	Kt(K3)—Kt2	B x Kt
28	K x B	Q—K6
29	K—B1	Kt—Kt6!
	Resigns	

A master coup of extraordinary depth and beauty.

---

98. Sixth American Chess Congress, New York, March, 1889.

Submitted for Brilliancy Prize

SCOTCH GAME

J. W. SHOWALTER		G. GOSSIP
White		Black
1	P—K4	P—K4
2	Kt—KB3	Kt—QB3
3	P—Q4	P x P
4	Kt x P	Kt—B3
5	Kt x Kt	KtP x Kt
6	B—Q3	P—Q4
7	P—K5	Kt—Kt5
8	O—O	B—QB4
9	B—KB4	P—Kt4
10	B—Q2	Kt x KP
11	R—K1	Q—K2
12	Kt—B3	B—Q2
13	Q—R5	O—O—O

14	QB x P	P—B3
15	B—R4	Q—Kt2
16	B—R6ch	K—Kt1
17	B—Kt3	KR—Kt1
18	Q—Q1	Kt—Kt5
19	B—KB1	Kt—K4
20	P—Kt4	B—Kt5
21	Q—Kt1	B—Q5
22	Q—Kt3	P—KR4
23	QR—Kt1	P—R5

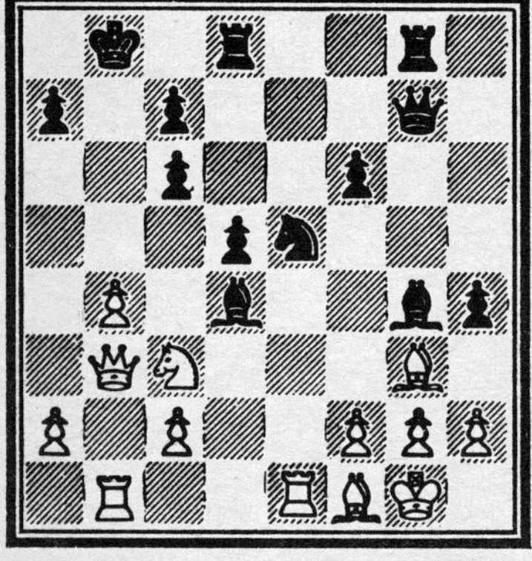

24	B x P	Kt—B6ch!
25	P x Kt	QB x Pch
26	B—Kt3	Q x Bch!
27.	P x Q	R x Pch
28	K—R2	B x P
29	B—R3	R x Bch!
	Resigns	

Much gossip had been going around because this game had not been awarded the special prize over the game won by Gunsberg over Mason!
Hence, both games are included, so the public of today can judge for itself.

---

99. Sixth American Chess Congress, New York, May 11, 1889

Pollock wins the Brilliancy Prize, and how!!

RUY LOPEZ

MAX WEISS — W. H. K. POLLOCK

	White	Black
1	P—K4	P—K4
2	Kt—KB3	Kt—QB3
3	B—Kt5	P—QR3
4	B—R4	Kt—B3
5	P—Q3	P—QKt4
6	B—Kt3	B—B4
7	P—B3	P—Q4!
8	P x P	Kt x P
9	Q—K2	O—O
10	Q—K4	B—K3!
11	Kt x P	Kt x Kt
12	Q x Kt	Kt—Kt5?!
13	O—O	Kt x QP
14	Q—R5	B x B
15	P x B	R—K1
16	Kt—Q2	Q—K2
17	P—QKt4	B x Pch!
18	K—R1	Q—K8!
19	P—R3	Kt x B!!
20	R x Q	R x Rch
21	K—R2	B—Kt8ch
22	K—Kt3	R—K6ch
23	K—Kt4!	Kt—K7

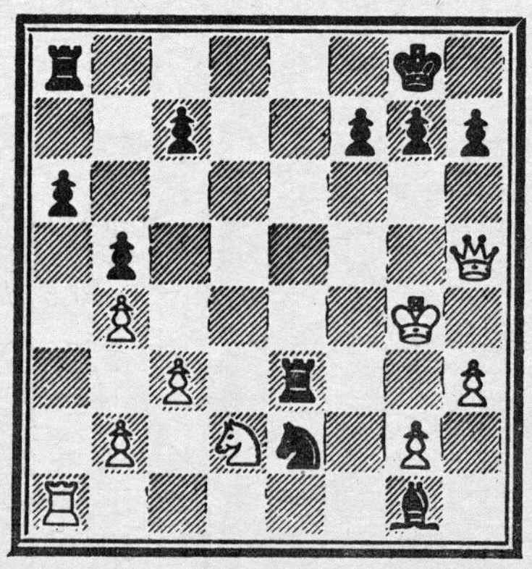

24	Kt—B1!	P—Kt3
25	Q—Q5	P—R4ch
26	K—Kt5	K—Kt2!!

27 Kt x R	....

Black now mates in three, e. g.:

27	P—B3ch
28 K—R4	B—B7ch
29 P—Kt3	B x P mate

---

100. Sixth American Congress, 1889.

A finely executed attack.

PETROFF DEFENSE

I. GUNSBERG	M. WEISS
White	Black
1 P—K4	P—K4
2 Kt—KB3	Kt—KB3
3 Kt x P	P—Q3
4 Kt—KB3	Kt x P
5 P—Q4	P—Q4
6 B—Q3	Kt—QB3
7 O—O	B—K2
8 R—K1	B—KKt5
9 P—B3	P—B4
10 QKt—Q2	O—O
11 Q—Kt3	K—R1
12 Q x KtP	R—B3
13 Q—Kt3	R—Kt1
14 Q—B2	R—KKt3
15 P—QKt3	B—Q3
16 B—K2	B—KR6
17 B—B1	Q—B3
18 P—Kt3	B x B
19 K x B	R—KB1
20 Kt x Kt	BP x Kt
21 Kt—R4	R x P!!
22 P x R	B x P
23 K—Kt2	B x Kt
24 B—K3	Q—B6ch
25 K—R2	B—K2
26 K—Kt1	R—B3
27 K—B1	Q—Kt5
28 Q—Q1	R—B6
29 R—B1	Q—R6ch
Resigns	

If 30 K—K2, R x Bch.

---

101. Amsterdam Tournament, 1889

A Thing of Beauty

One of the most famous victories ever won by Dr. Lasker was his magnificent combination at Amsterdam in 1889 when he was only 21. The power of the two Bishops has never been shown to greater advantage.

BIRD'S OPENING

E. LASKER	J. H. BAUER
White	Black
1 P—KB4	P—Q4
2 Kt—KB3	P—K3
3 P—K3	Kt—KB3
4 P—QKt3	B—K2
5 B—Kt2	P—QKt3
6 B—Q3	B—Kt2
7 Kt—B3	O—O
8 O—O	QKt—Q2
9 Kt—K2	P—B4
10 Kt—Kt3	Q—B2
11 Kt—K5	Kt x Kt
12 B x Kt	Q—B3
13 Q—K2	P—QR3
14 Kt—R5!	Kt x Kt

(see diagram next page)

15 B x Pch!	K x B

The beginning of a most profound and elegant combination.

16 Q x Ktch	K—Kt1
17 B x P!	K x B
18 Q—Kt4ch	K—R2
19 R—B3	P—K4
20 R—R3ch	Q—R3
21 R x Qch	K x R
22 Q—Q7	B—KB3
23 Q x B	K—Kt2
24 R—KB1	QR—Kt1
25 Q—Q7	KR—Q1
26 Q—Kt4ch	K—B1
27 P x P	B—Kt2
28 P—K6	R—Kt2

29 Q—Kt6	P—B3
30 R x Pch	B x R
31 Q x Bch	K—K1
32 Q—R8ch	K—K2
33 Q—Kt7ch	K x P
34 Q x R and wins	

---

102. Prague, Austria, Sept., 1889.

A very instructive and beautifully terminated game.

STEINITZ GAMBIT

H. NEUSTADL	O. VALENTA
White	Black
1 P—K4	P—K4
2 Kt—QB3	Kt—QB3
3 P—B4	P x P
4 P—Q4	Q—R5ch
5 K—K2	P—Q4
6 P x P	B—Kt5ch
7 Kt—B3	O—O—O
8 P x Kt	B—QB4
9 P x Pch	K—Kt1
10 Kt—Kt5	P—QR3
11 P—B3	P x Kt
12 K—Q3	B—B4ch
13 K—Q2	Q—Kt5
14 K—K2	Kt—B3
15 K—B2	Kt—K5ch
16 K—Kt1	Kt—Kt4
17 KB x P?	R x P!!
18 P x R	B x Pch
19 K—B1	. . . .

(see diagram next column)

19	Q x Pch!!

It is doubtful whether a finer two-

move combination in actual play, has ever been seen.
If 20 K—K1, Q—B7 mate. And if K x Q, B—R6 mate.

Resigns

---

103. Franklin Chess Club, Oct. 31, 1889.

An example of inspired combination play.

SCOTCH GAME

W. P. SHIPLEY	C. S. MARTINEZ, JR.
White	Black
1 P—K4	P—K4
2 Kt—KB3	Kt—QB3
3 P—Q4	P x P
4 Kt x P	Kt—B3
5 Kt x Kt	KtP x Kt
6 B—Q3	B—B4

7	P—K5	Kt—Q4
8	Q—Kt4	Kt—K2
9	Q x P	KR—Kt1
10	Q—B6	P—Q3
11	B x P	R x P
12	B—Kt5	B x Pch
13	K—B1	B—R6
14	Q—R8ch	K—Q2
15	B—B5ch	Kt x B!
16	P—K6ch	K x P

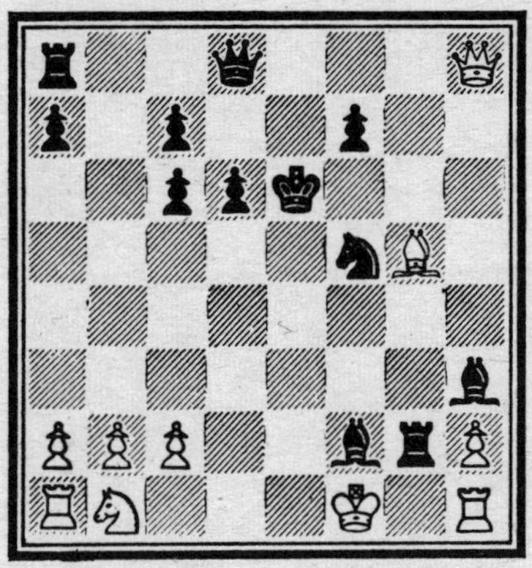

17	B x Q	Kt—K6ch
18	K—K2	B—Kt8ch
19	K—Q3	B—B4ch
20	K—B3	R x Pch
21	K—Kt3	R—Kt1ch
22	K—R3	Kt—B5ch
23	K—R4	Kt—Kt3ch!
24	K—R5	R—B4ch
25	K—R6	B—Q6ch
26	K x P	R—R1ch
27	K—Kt7	B—R3ch
28	K x P	Kt—Q4 mate

---

104. Match game played at Boston, 1889.

Barry's Masterpiece

RUY LOPEZ

JOHN F. BARRY	H. N. PILLSBURY
White	Black

1	P—K4	P—K4
2	Kt—KB3	Kt—QB3
3	B—Kt5	Kt—B3
4	P—Q4	Kt x KP
5	P—Q5	Kt—Q3
6	Kt—B3	P—K5
7	Kt—Kt5	Kt—K4
8	Q—Q4	P—KB3
9	KKt x KP	Kt x B
10	Kt x Kt	P—QR3
11	Q—R4	R—QKt1
12	Kt—Q4	B—K2
13	Q—Kt3	P—Q3
14	P—KB4	P—KB4
15	Kt—Kt3	Kt—Kt5
16	O—O	O—O
17	Kt—B6	P x Kt
18	Q x R	P x P
19	Q—Kt3	P—B3
20	B—Q2	Q—B2
21	QR—K1	B—B3
22	P—KR3	B—Q5ch
23	K—R1	Kt—B7ch
24	K—R2	Kt—K5
25	Kt x Kt	BP x Kt
26	R x P	B x KtP
27	P—B3!	B—R6
28	KR—K1	B—QB4
29	R—K7	Q—Kt3
30	Q—Q1	B—B4
31	Q—R5	P—R3

White now calls mate in 13 moves.

32 R x Pch	K x R
33 R—K7ch	K—Kt1
34 Q x P	B—Kt8ch
35 K—R1	B—Q5
36 P x B	Q x P
37 Q—Kt5ch	K—R1
38 Q—R4ch	K—Kt1
39 Q—Kt3ch	K—R1
40 B—B3	Q x B
41 Q x Qch	P—Q5
42 Q x Pch	R—B3
43 Q x Rch	K—Kt1
44 Q mates	

105.

An Immortal Evans Gambit

So classed by E. Schiffers in St. Petersburg Zeitung, about 1890.

EVANS GAMBIT

H. CLEMENS White	F. EISENSCHMIDT Black
1 P—K4	P—K4
2 Kt—KB3	Kt—QB3
3 B—B4	B—B4
4 P—QKt4	B x P
5 P—B3	B—B4
6 P—Q4	P x P
7 P x P	B—Kt3
8 O—O	P—Q3
9 Kt—B3	B—Q2?
10 P—K5	P x P
11 R—K1	KKt—K2
12 Kt—KKt5	B—K3
13 B x B	P x B
14 Kt x KP	Q—Q3
15 Kt x KtPch	K—B1
16 Q—Kt4	B x P
17 Kt—K4	Q—Kt5
18 Kt—K6ch	K—K1
19 Kt—B6ch	K—B2
20 Kt—Kt5ch	K—B1
21 B—R3!!	. . . .

(see diagram)

21	Q x B
22 Q—K6	Kt—Q1

23 Q—B7ch!	Kt x Q
24 Kt—K6 mate	

PART V

Modern Chess

Hereabouts we arrive at the era of what is called, occasionally in rather a disdainful tone, "modern chess." It is the age of the great Lasker and Tarrasch, of Schlechter and Maroczy, of the attacking geniuses Pillsbury and Marshall and Janowski. As the number of grandmasters increases, as it becomes more difficult to bowl over one's opponent in short order, we find that positional chess begins to be pre-eminent; before the opponent can be finished off with a brilliant combination, it is generally necessary to outplay him positionally, in order to create favorable conditions for sacrificial play. That is why Emanuel Lasker once wrote: "If you play well positionally, the combinations will come of themselves."

While I am fond of the finest games of all these masters, I love above all the beautiful games of the immortal Harry Nelson Pillsbury. I am sure that the reader, as he plays over these marvellous games, will share my admiration for this immortal, whose beautiful productions, I am sorry to say, do not seem to be adequately appreciated nowadays. During his lifetime his uncanny skill in blindfold play was particularly admired, and that is why I have carefully assembled the cream of his efforts in this field. Happy the man who plays over these games for the first time! And as for old-timers like myself, they will relish the opportunity to renew their acquaintance with these gracious companions of their youth!

106. Manchester Tournament, 1890

Briton meets Briton

GIUOCO PIANO

E. THOROLD — J. H. BLACKBURNE

	White	Black
1	P—K4	P—K4
2	Kt—KB3	Kt—QB3
3	B—B4	B—B4
4	P—Q3	Kt—B3
5	B—K3	B—Kt3
6	B x B	RP x B
7	QKt—Q2	O—O
8	P—B3	P—Q4
9	B—Kt3	P x P
10	P x P	Q—K2
11	Q—K2	P—Kt3
12	P—Kt3	Kt—Q2
13	P—KR4	Kt—B4
14	B—B2	P—R4
15	Q—K3	R—Q1
16	P—QKt4	Kt—Q2
17	B—Kt3	Kt—B1
18	Kt—Kt5	B—K3
19	Kt x B	Kt x Kt
20	P—KB4	Q—B3
21	P—B5!	Kt—B1
22	P x P	Q x P
23	O—O	R—Q2
24	R—B5	Kt—KR2
25	QR—KB1	R—KB1
26	Kt—B4	P—Kt4
27	Kt x P	Kt x Kt
28	R x Kt	K—R1
29	Q—B4	R—KKt1
30	R—B3	Q—Kt3ch
31	K—Kt2	R—Kt5
32	R—K8ch	K—Kt2
33	Q—K5ch	K—R3
34	R—B5	R—Q7ch
35	K—B1	Q—Kt3
36	R—KKt8!	. . . .

(see diagram next column)

36	. . . .	Q x R
37	R x Pch	K—Kt3
38	Q—B5ch	K—Kt2
39	Q x Rch	K—R1
40	Q—B4	Q—Q1
41	B—Q5	R—QKt7
42	Q x KBP	Resigns

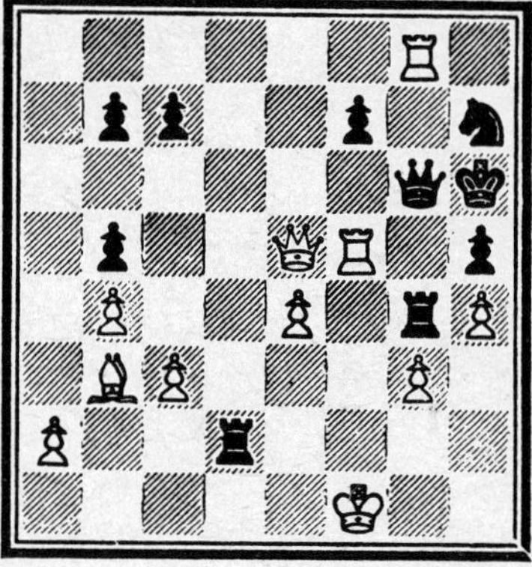

---

107. Nuremberg, about 1891.

An attack carried out with admirable verve.

VIENNA GAME

M. KUERCHNER — DR. S. TARRASCH

	White	Black
1	P—K4	P—K4
2	Kt—QB3	Kt—QB3
3	P—KKt3	Kt—B3
4	B—Kt2	B—B4
5	P—Q3	P—QR3
6	P—B4	P—Q3
7	P—B5	P—KKt3
8	P—KKt4	P—KR4
9	B—Kt5	Kt—Q5
10	Kt—Q5	Kt x Kt!!
11	B x Q	Kt—K6
12	Q—Q2	QKt x Pch

13 K—K2	Kt—Q5ch
14 K—B2	Kt x Pch
15 K—Kt3	P x P
16 Q—Kt5	P—R5ch
17 Q x P	P—B5ch
18 K—R3	Kt—B7 mate

---

108. Havana, January, 1892.

For World Supremacy in Chess This is the fourth game of the second match and is also one of the most beautiful games ever played in a similar contest.

RUY LOPEZ

W. STEINITZ	M. TCHIGORIN
White	Black
1 P—K4	P—K4
2 Kt—KB3	Kt—QB3
3 B—Kt5	Kt—B3
4 P—Q3	P—Q3
5 P—B3	P—KKt3
6 QKt—Q2	B—Kt2
7 Kt—B1	O—O
8 B—R4	Kt—Q2
9 Kt—K3	Kt—B4
10 B—B2	Kt—K3
11 P—KR4	Kt—K2
12 P—R5	P—Q4
13 RP x P	BP x P?
14 P x P	Kt x P
15 Kt x Kt	Q x Kt
16 B—Kt3	Q—B3
17 Q—K2	B—Q2
18 B—K3	K—R1
19 O—O—O	QR—K1
20 Q—B1!	P—QR4
21 P—Q4	P x P
22 Kt x P	B x Kt
23 R x B!	Kt x R
24 R x Pch!	K x R
25 Q—R1ch	K—Kt2
26 B—R6ch!	K—B3

27 Q—R4ch	K—K4
28 Q x Ktch	K—B4
29 Q—B4 mate	

---

109. Dresden Tournament, 1892.

First edition of a famous trap!

RUY LOPEZ

DR. S. TARRASCH	G. MARCO
White	Black
1 P—K4	P—K4
2 Kt—KB3	Kt—QB3
3 B—Kt5	P—Q3
4 P—Q4	B—Q2
5 Kt—B3	Kt—B3
6 O—O	B—K2
7 R—K1	O—O?
8 B x Kt!	B x B

From this point Black's moves are all forced.

9 P x P	P x P
10 Q x Q	QR x Q
11 Kt x P	B x P
12 Kt x B	Kt x Kt
13 Kt—Q3!	P—KB4
14 P—KB3	B—B4ch
15 Kt x B	Kt x Kt
16 B—Kt5	R—Q4
17 B—K7	Resigns

---

110. New York, 1892.

Outplaying a future world champion.

RUY LOPEZ

DR. E. LASKER	A. B. HODGES
White	Black
1 P—K4	P—K4
2 Kt—KB3	Kt—QB3
3 B—Kt5	P—Q3
4 Kt—B3	B—Q2
5 O—O	KKt—K2
6 P—Q3	Kt—Kt3
7 B—K3	B—K2
8 P—Q4	O—O
9 B—QB4	B—Kt5
10 P—Q5	Kt—Kt1
11 P—KR3	B x Kt
12 Q x B	P—KB4
13 P x P	Kt—R5
14 Q—Kt4	Kt x P
15 B—Q2	Kt—Q2
16 B—Q3	P—KKt3
17 Kt—K4	R—B2
18 QR—K1	Q—KB1
19 Kt—B3	P—QR3
20 Kt—Q1	Q—Kt2
21 B—B3	QR—KB1
22 P—Kt4	B—Q1
23 B—Kt2	Kt—B3
24 Q—QB4	Kt—R4!
25 P—B4	P—QKt4
26 Q—B6	Kt—K2
27 Q x RP	Kt x BP
28 Q x KtP	Q—R3
29 Kt—B2	Q—Kt4
30 B—K4	Kt—B4
31 Q—B4	Kt—Kt6
32 B—KB3	Kt x R
33 R x Kt	Q—R5
34 Q—K4	Kt x Pch
35 Kt x Kt	Q x Q
36 B x Q	R x Rch
37 K—R2	R—K8
38 B—Q3	P—K5
39 B—B4	B—B3
40 B x B	R x B
41 K—Kt3	P—K6
42 Kt—Kt5	R—B7
43 B—Q3	R—KKt8
Resigns	

---

111. Played at Zugzidi, in spring of 1892.

Most Brilliant of Dadian's Combinations.

TWO KNIGHTS' DEFENSE

PRINCE DADIAN (of Mingrelia)	M. BITCHAM
White	Black
1 P—K4	P—K4
2 Kt—KB3	Kt—QB3
3 B—B4	Kt—B3
4 P—Q4	P x P
5 O—O	Kt x P
6 R—K1	P—Q4
7 B x P	Q x B
8 Kt—B3	Q—B5
9 R x Ktch	B—K3
10 B—Kt5	B—B4
11 Kt—Q2	Q—R3
12 Kt—Kt3	B—Kt3
13 Kt—Q5	P—KR3
14 Kt—B5	. . . .

14	....	Q—Kt4
15	R x Bch!	K—B1
16	Kt—Q7ch	K—Kt1
17	Q—Kt4	P—KR4
18	Kt(Q5)—B6ch!	P x Kt
19	B—R6ch!	Q—Kt4
20	Kt x P mate	

112. Boston, Nov. 8, 1892.

Caught in the Web

DANISH GAMBIT

F. K. YOUNG		L. DORE
White		Black
1	P—K4	P—K4
2	P—Q4	P x P
3	P—QB3	P x P
4	B—QB4	Kt—KB3
5	Kt—KB3	Kt x P
6	O—O	Kt—Q3
7	Kt x P	Kt x B
8	R—K1ch	B—K2
9	Kt—Q5	Kt—B3
10	B—Kt5	P—B3
11	R—QB1	P—Kt4
12	R x Kt	P x R
13	Kt—K5!	....

13	....	P x B
14	Q—R5ch	P—Kt3
15	Kt—B6ch!	B x Kt
16	Kt x KtPch	Q—K2
17	R x Qch	B x R
18	Kt—K5ch	K—Q1
19	Kt—B7ch	K—K1
20	Kt—Q6ch	K—Q1
21	Q—K8ch!	R x Q
22	Kt—B7 mate	

113. Jackson, Miss., about 1892.

This Galbreath-taking game was played in Jackson, Miss., about 1892.

EVANS GAMBIT

JOHN A. GALBRAITH		H. HARDING
White		Black
1	P—K4	P—K4
2	Kt—KB3	Kt—QB3
3	B—B4	B—B4
4	P—QKt4	B x P
5	P—B3	B—R4
6	O—O	B—Kt3
7	P—Q4	Q—B3
8	B—KKt5	Q—Kt3
9	P x P	Q x P
10	QKt—Q2	Q—Kt3
11	R—K1	P—KR3
12	B—R4	KKt—K2
13	Kt—K4	O—O

Now begins a far-sighted combination.

14	Kt—B6ch	P x Kt
15	B x P	Kt—B4
16	B—Q3	Q—R4
17	P—Kt4	Q x Pch
18	K—R1	B x P
19	R—K4	Q—R6
20	Q—Kt1ch!	Kt—Kt6ch

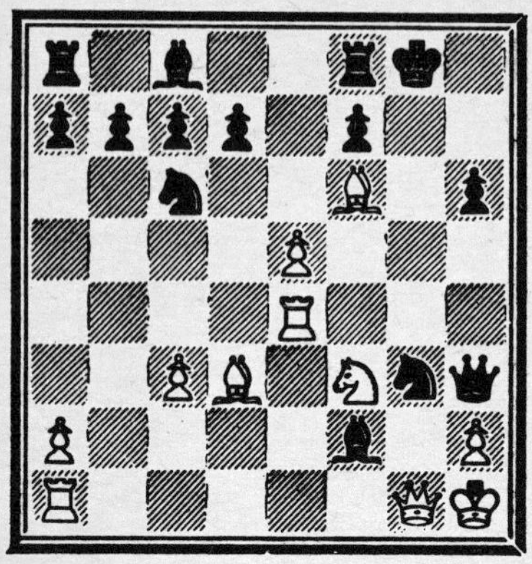

21 Q x Ktch	B x Q
22 R—KKt1	P—Q3
23 R x Bch	Q x R
24 P x Q	B—B4
25 R—KR4	B x B
26 R x P	B—R2
27 Kt—Kt5	Kt x P
28 R x B	Kt—Kt3
29 R—Kt7ch	K—R1
30 R x Kt mate!	

---

114. Vienna, Dec., 1892.

The open KR file triumphs again!

VIENNA GAME

M. POLLAK BARON ALBERT ROTHSCHILD

White	Black
1 P—K4	P—K4
2 Kt—QB3	Kt—QB3
3 P—KKt3	Kt—B3
4 B—Kt2	B—B4
5 KKt—K2	P—Q3
6 P—KR3	B—K3
7 O—O	Q—Q2
8 K—R2	P—KR4
9 P—Q3	O—O—O
10 B—Kt5	Kt—K2
11 P—B4	Kt—Kt5ch!?
12 P x Kt	P x Pch
13 B—R4	Kt—Kt3
14 P—B5	Kt x B
15 P x Kt	Q—K2
16 Q—K1?	R x Pch
17 K—Kt3	Q—Kt4
18 R—R1	. . . .

Black mates in 4 moves: R—R6 ch, etc.

---

115. Vienna, 1893.

Schlechter's Immortal

This sparkling gem ranks as one of the most curious and brilliant on record.

IRREGULAR OPENING

B. FLEISSIG CARL SCHLECHTER

White	Black
1 P—QKt4	P—K3
2 B—Kt2	Kt—KB3
3 P—QR3	P—B4
4 P—Kt5	P—Q4
5 P—Q4	Q—R4ch
6 Kt—B3	Kt—K5
7 Q—Q3	P x P
8 Q x P	B—B4!
9 Q x KtP	B x Pch
10 K—Q1	P—Q5!!

11 Q x Rch	K—K2
12 Q x B	P x Kt

13 B—B1	Kt—Q2
14 Q x R	Q x KtP
15 B—B4	Q—Q4ch
16 K—B1	B—K6ch!
17 B x B	Kt—B7!
18 B x Kt	Q—Q7ch
19 K—Kt1	Q—Q8ch
20 K—R2	Q x P mate

---

116. Played at Kassa in 1893.

A Charousek Gem

DANISH GAMBIT

R. CHAROUSEK	M. WOLLNER
White	Black
1 P—K4	P—K4
2 P—Q4	P x P
3 P—QB3	P x P
4 B—QB4	Kt—KB3
5 Kt—KB3	B—B4
6 Kt x P	P—Q3
7 O—O	O—O
8 Kt—KKt5!	P—KR3
9 Kt x BP	R x Kt
10 P—K5	Kt—Kt5?
11 P—K6!	Q—R5
12 P x Rch	K—B1
13 B—B4	Kt x BP
14 Q—K2!	Kt—Kt5ch
15 K—R1	B—Q2
16 QR—K1	Kt—QB3
17 Q—K8ch	R x Q
18 P x R(Q) ch	B x Q
19 B x QP mate	

---

117. Vienna Chess Club, April 27, 1894.

Inimitable elegance!

FROM'S GAMBIT

L. FRIED	C. SCHLECHTER
White	Black
1 P—KB4	P—K4
2 P x P	Kt—QB3
3 Kt—KB3	P—Q3
4 P x P	B x P
5 P—Q4	Kt—B3
6 B—Kt5	P—KR3
7 B—R4	P—KKt4
8 B—B2	Kt—K5
9 P—K3	P—Kt5
10 B—R4	. . . .

Now follows a very elegant combination.

10	P x Kt!
11 B x Q	P—B7ch
12 K—K2	B—Kt5ch
13 K—Q3	Kt—Kt5ch
14 K x Kt	P—B4 mate!

---

118. Nuremberg, Feb. 9, 1894.

A wonderful combination!

KING'S GAMBIT

DR. S. TARRASCH	HIRSCHLER
White	Black
1 P—K4	P—K4
2 P—KB4	P x P
3 Kt—KB3	P—KKt4
4 P—KR4	P—Kt5
5 Kt—K5	P—Q3
6 Kt x BP	K x Kt
7 B—B4ch	K—Kt3
8 P—Q4	B—K2
9 B x P	Kt—KB3
10 P—R5ch	K—Kt2
11 Kt—B3	Kt—B3
12 P—K5	P x P
13 P—R6ch	K—B1
14 P x P	Q x Qch
15 R x Q	Kt—Q2
16 O—O	K—K1
17 Kt—Q5	B—B4ch
18 K—R1	B—Kt3

19 P—K6	KKt—K4
20 Kt—B6ch	K—K2
21 B—KKt5	Kt x B
22 Kt x KtPch	K—K1
23 Kt—B6ch	K—K2
24 Kt—Kt8ch	K—K1

25 R—Q8ch	Kt x R
26 R—B8ch	K x R
27 P—K7ch	Resigns

---

119. Hastings, 1895.

First Brilliancy Prize

GIUOCO PIANO

W. STEINITZ	C. VON BARDELEBEN
White	Black
1 P—K4	P—K4
2 Kt—KB3	Kt—QB3
3 B—B4	B—B4
4 P—B3	Kt—B3
5 P—Q4	P x P
6 P x P	B—Kt5ch
7 Kt—B3	P—Q4
8 P x P	KKt x P
9 O—O	B—K3
10 B—KKt5	B—K2
11 B x Kt	QB x B
12 Kt x B	Q x Kt
13 B x B	Kt x B
14 R—K1!	P—KB3
15 Q—K2	Q—Q2
16 QR—B1	P—B3?
17 P—Q5!	P x P
18 Kt—Q4	K—B2
19 Kt—K6	KR—QB1
20 Q—Kt4	P—KKt3
21 Kt—Kt5ch	K—K1

22 R x Ktch!!	K—B1
23 R—B7ch	K—Kt1
24 R—Kt7ch	K—R1
25 R x Pch!	Resigns

Steinitz gives this brilliant mate in ten moves.

25	K—Kt1
26 R—Kt7ch	K—R1
27 Q—R4ch	K x R
28 Q—R7ch	K—B1
29 Q—R8ch	K—K2
30 Q—Kt7ch	K—K1
31 Q—Kt8ch	K—K2
32 Q—B7ch	K—Q1
33 Q—B8ch	Q—K1
34 Kt—B7ch	K—Q2
35 Q—Q6 mate!	

---

120. Quadrangular Tourney, St. Petersburg, 1895-96.

One of Pillsbury's memorable games.

PETROFF DEFENSE

DR. E. LASKER White	H. N. PILLSBURY Black
1 P—K4	P—K4
2 Kt—KB3	Kt—KB3
3 Kt x P	P—Q3
4 Kt—KB3	Kt x P
5 P—Q4	P—Q4
6 B—Q3	B—K2
7 O—O	Kt—QB3
8 R—K1	B—KKt5
9 P—B3	P—B4
10 Q—Kt3	O—O
11 B—KB4	B x Kt
12 P x B	Kt—Kt4
13 K—Kt2	Q—Q2
14 Q—B2	Kt—K3!
15 B—QB1	B—Q3
16 Kt—Q2	QR—K1
17 Kt—B1	Kt (K3) x P

18 Q—Q1	R x R
19 Q x R	Kt x P!
20 K x Kt	P—B5
21 Q—Q1	Kt—K4ch
22 K—K2	Q—Kt5ch
23 K—Q2	Q x Qch
24 K x Q	Kt x B
25 K—K2	Kt—K4
26 P—B3	R—K1
27 P—Kt3	Kt—Kt5ch
28 K—Q2	Kt—K6
29 B—Kt2	Kt—Kt7
30 P—KR3	B—B4
31 Kt—R2	B—B7
32 P—B4	P x P
33 P x P	P—KR4!
Resigns	

The manner in which Pillsbury snapped up the Knight with his Bishop at the eleventh move, and his rapid play afterwards, showed clearly that he saw through the game to victory.

---

121. St. Petersburg, 1895-6.

One of Dr. Lasker's finest. A game of many combinations.

QUEEN'S GAMBIT DECLINED

W. STEINITZ White	DR. E. LASKER Black
1 P—Q4	P—Q4
2 P—QB4	P—K3
3 Kt—QB3	Kt—KB3
4 B—B4	B—K2
5 P—K3	O—O
6 R—B1	P—B4
7 P x BP	B x P
8 P x P	P x P
9 Kt—B3	Kt—B3
10 B—Q3	P—Q5!
11 P x P	Kt x P
12 O—O	B—KKt5
13 Kt—QKt5?	B x Kt
14 P x B	Kt—K3!
15 B—K5	Kt—R4
16 K—R1	Q—Kt4
17 B—Kt3	QR—Q1
18 Q—B2	Q—R3

(see diagram next page)

19	QR—Q1	R—B1!
20	Q—Kt3	P—R3
21	Kt—B3	Kt—Q5!
22	Q x P	Kt x Bch
23	P x Kt	R—Kt1
24	Q x P	R—Kt3
25	Q—B4	R x P
26	P—KR4?	B—R2

27	B—K4	Q—Q3
28	P—B4	Q—Q2
29	B—Kt2	Q—Kt5!
30	Q—Q3	Kt—B4
31	Kt—K4	B—K6
32	R—B3	R x B!
33	K x R	Kt x Pch
34	K—R2	Kt x Rch
35	K—Kt2	Kt—R5ch
36	K—R2	Kt—B4
37	R—QKt1	P—R4
38	R—Kt5	R—R1
39	P—R3	R x P!
	Resigns	

---

122. Nuremberg Tournament, July 29, 1896.

One of the deepest combinations ever played.

Awarded Prize for best game.

FRENCH DEFENSE

	H. N. PILLSBURY White	DR. E. LASKER Black
1	P—K4	P—K3
2	P—Q4	P—Q4
3	Kt—QB3	Kt—KB3
4	P—K5	KKt—Q2
5	P—B4	P—QB4
6	P x P	Kt—QB3
7	P—QR3	Kt x BP
8	P—QKt4	Kt—Q2
9	B—Q3	P—QR4
10	P—Kt5	QKt—Kt1
11	Kt—B3	Kt—B4
12	B—K3	QKt—Q2
13	O—O	P—KKt3
14	Kt—K2	B—K2
15	Q—K1	Kt—Kt3
16	KKt—Q4	B—Q2
17	Q—B2	Kt(3)—R5
18	QR—Kt1	P—R4
19	P—Kt6!	Kt x B
20	P x Kt	B x P
21	P—B5!!	. . . .

21	. . . .	KtP x P
22	Kt—B4	P—R5
23	R—R1!	B—K2
24	R x Kt!	B x R
25	Kt(B4) x KP!!	P x Kt
26	Kt x KP	B—Q2

If 26 . . . Q—B1; 27 Q x BP with

a winning attack.

27 Kt x Q	R x Kt
28 B—B5	R—QB1
29 B x B	K x B
30 Q—K3	R—B3
31 Q—Kt5ch	K—B2
32 R—B1	R x Rch
33 Q x R	R—QB1
34 Q—K1	P—R6
35 P x P	R—Kt1ch
36 K—B2	P—R5
37 Q—Kt4	R—Kt3
38 K—B3	P—R6
39 Q x P	R x P
40 Q—B5	R—K3
41 Q—B7	K—K2
42 K—B4	P—Kt3
43 P—R4	R—QB3
44 Q—Kt8	B—K1
45 K x P	R—R3
46 Q—B7ch	K—B1
47 Q—Q8	P—Kt4
48 P—K6	R—R2
49 K—K5	P—Kt5
50 Q—Q6ch	Resigns

123. Nuremberg, 1896.

Bright and witty!

QUEEN'S GAMBIT ACCEPTED

D. JANOWSKI	E. SCHALLOPP
White	Black
1 P—Q4	P—Q4
2 P—QB4	P x P
3 Kt—KB3	P—QB4
4 P—K3	P x P
5 P x P	B—Kt5
6 B x P	P—K3
7 Q—R4ch!	Kt—B3
8 Kt—K5!	Q x P
9 Kt x Kt	Q—K5ch
10 B—K3	P x Kt
11 Kt—B3	Q x P

12 B—Q5!	P x B
13 Q x Pch	K—Q1
14 Q x Rch	K—Q2
15 Q—Kt7ch	K—K3
16 Q—B6ch	B—Q3
17 B—B4!	Resigns

124. Simpson's Divan, London.

"The most summary demolishment of Steinitz on record."

SCOTCH GAME

W. GRIMSHAW (Problem composer)	W. STEINITZ
White	Black
1 P—K4	P—K4
2 Kt—KB3	Kt—QB3
3 P—Q4	P x P
4 Kt x P	Q—R5
5 Kt—Kt5	Q x KPch
6 B—K3	B—Kt5ch
7 Kt—Q2	B x Ktch
8 Q x B	K—Q1
9 O—O—O	Q—K3
10 B—KB4!	P—Q3
11 B x P!!	P x B
12 Kt x QP	Q x P
13 Kt—Kt5ch	K—K1
14 Kt—B7ch!	K—B1

White mates in three.

15 Q—Q6ch	KKt—K2
16 Q—Q8ch	Kt x Q
17 R x Kt mate	

---

125. Eighth game of match. 1897.

Great Match for U. S. Supremacy In this fine game Showalter reveals a grandiose style before which Pillsbury bows in admiration.

RUY LOPEZ

J. SHOWALTER	H. N. PILLSBURY
White	Black
1 P—K4	P—K4
2 Kt—KB3	Kt—QB3
3 B—Kt5	Kt—B3
4 O—O	Kt x P
5 P—Q4	Kt—Q3
6 B—R4	P x P
7 P—B3!	P x P
8 Kt x P	B—K2
9 Kt—Q5	O—O
10 R—K1	B—B3
11 B—B4!	Kt—K1?

12 R x Kt!	Q x R
13 Kt x P	Q—K5
14 B—Q6	R—Kt1
15 B—B2!	Q—KKt5
16 B x R	K x B
17 Q—Q6ch	B—K2
18 R—K1!	P—KKt3
19 Q—Q2	Q—R4
20 Kt—Q5	B—Q1
21 Q—B3	P—B3
22 Kt x P	B—R4

White mates in five.

23 Kt x QPch, etc.

---

126. Correspondence, 1897-98.

QP COUNTER GAMBIT

K. ZAMBELLY	G. MAROCZY
White	Black
1 P—K4	P—K4
2 Kt—KB3	P—Q4
3 P x P	B—Q3?!
4 Kt—B3	Kt—KB3
5 B—Kt5ch	P—B3
6 B—R4	P—K5
7 P x P	O—O
8 Kt—Q4	P x P
9 Kt x BP	Q—Kt3
10 Kt x Kt	R x Kt
11 B—Kt5	R—Q1!!
12 O—O	B x Pch
13 K x B	Kt—Kt5ch
14 K—Kt3	Q—B2ch

15 P—B4	P x P e.p.ch
16 K x P	R—Q5
17 P—Q3	B—Kt2ch
18 Kt—K4	B x Ktch
19 K x Kt	Q—R7
20 P x B	Q x Pch
21 K—R4	R x B!
22 Q x R	R—R4ch!
23 K x R	Q—R6ch
24 K—Kt5	P—R3ch
25 K—B4	P—Kt4ch
26 K—K5	Q—K3 mate

---

127. Cosmopolitan Club Championship, 1898.

A Spark of Genius

MAX LANGE ATTACK

JULIUS FINN	C. NUGENT
White	Black
1 P—K4	P—K4
2 Kt—KB3	Kt—QB3
3 P—Q4	P x P
4 B—QB4	B—B4
5 O—O	Kt—B3
6 P—K5	P—Q4
7 P x Kt	P x B
8 R—K1ch	B—K3
9 Kt—Kt5	Q—Q4
10 Kt—QB3	Q—B4
11 QKt—K4	B—KB1
12 Kt x BP!	K x Kt
13 Kt—Kt5ch	K—Kt1
14 P—KKt4!	Q x P(B3)
15 R x B	Q—Q1
16 Q—B3	Q—Q2
17 R—K7!!	Resigns

---

128. London, 1899.

First Brilliancy Prize; watch for the bombshell on Black's 15th move!

VIENNA GAME

W. STEINITZ	DR. E. LASKER
White	Black
1 P—K4	P—K4
2 Kt—QB3	Kt—KB3
3 P—B4	P—Q4
4 P—Q3	Kt—B3
5 BP x P	QKt x P
6 P—Q4	Kt—Kt3
7 P x P	Kt x P
8 Kt x Kt	Q x Kt
9 Kt—B3	B—Kt5
10 B—K2	O—O—O
11 P—B3	B—Q3
12 O—O	KR—K1!
13 P—KR3	B—Q2
14 Kt—Kt5	Kt—R5!
15 Kt—B3	Kt x P!!
16 K x Kt	B x Pch!
17 K—B2	P—KB3!
18 R—KKt1	P—KKt4
19 B x P	P x B
20 R x P	Q—K3
21 Q—Q3	B—B5
22 R—R1	B x R
23 Kt x B	Q—B3ch
24 B—B3	B—B4
25 Kt x P	Q—KKt3
26 Q—Kt5	P—B3
27 Q—R5	R—K2!
28 R—R5	B—Kt5
29 R—KKt5	Q—B7ch
30 K—Kt3	B x B
Resigns	

---

129. London, 1899.

This sensational victory over Lasker won the second Brilliancy Prize.

RUY LOPEZ

DR. E. LASKER J. H. BLACKBURNE

	White	Black
1	P—K4	P—K4
2	Kt—KB3	Kt—QB3
3	B—Kt5	P—Q3
4	P—Q4	B—Q2
5	P—Q5	Kt—Kt1
6	B—Q3	B—K2
7	Kt—B3	Kt—KB3
8	Kt—K2	P—B3
9	P—B4	Kt—R3
10	Kt—Kt3	Kt—B4
11	B—B2	P—QKt4
12	P—Kt4	Kt—Kt2
13	QP x P	B x P
14	P x P	B x KtP
15	P—QR4	B—Q2
16	O—O	P—Kt3
17	P—R3	P—KR4
18	B—K3	P—R4
19	P—Kt5	R—QB1
20	R—B1	Kt—B4
21	Kt—Q2	P—R5!
22	Kt—K2	P—Kt4!
23	B x P	R—KKt1
24	B x P	B x RP
25	B—KKt3	B—K3
26	R—K1	Kt—Kt5!
27	Kt—B1	B—Kt4!
28	R—Kt1	R—KR1!
29	Kt—B3	B—KB5!
30	Kt—Q5	Q—Kt4!
31	P—B3	....

	White	Black
31	....	R—R8ch!
32	K x R	B x B
33	Kt x B	Kt—B7ch
34	K—Kt1	Kt x Q
35	Kt—B5	B x Kt (B4)
36	P x B	Q—Q7
37	KR x Kt	Q x B
38	QR—B1	Q x BP
39	Kt—Kt6	R—Q1
40	Kt—B4	Kt—Kt2
41	Kt—K3	Q—B5
42	K—B2	Q x P
43	R—B7	Kt—B4
44	R—KR1	R—Q2
45	R—B8ch	K—K2
46	R (1)—R8	Q—Q5
	Resigns	

---

130. Riga, Oct., 1899.

A Russian Gem.

MUZIO GAMBIT

S. NIEMZOVICH (Father of Aron Nimzovich) — N. NEUMANN

	White	Black
1	P—K4	P—K4
2	P—KB4	P x P
3	Kt—KB3	P—KKt4
4	B—B4	P—Kt5
5	O—O	P x Kt
6	Q x P	Q—B3
7	P—Q3	B—Kt2
8	Kt—B3	Kt—B3
9	B x P	Kt—Q5
10	Q—B2	P—Q3
11	Kt—Q5	Q—Q1
12	P—K5	P—QB3
13	B—KKt5!	Q—Q2
14	Kt—B7ch!	Q x Kt
15	B x Pch	K—Q2
16	Q—B5ch!	Kt x Q
17	P—K6 mate!	

---

131. St. Louis, 1899.

Pillsbury's artistry embellishes a hackneyed theme.

QUEEN'S GAMBIT DECLINED

H. N. PILLSBURY	MAX JUDD
White	Black
1 P—Q4	P—Q4
2 P—QB4	P—K3
3 Kt—QB3	P—QKt3
4 Kt—B3	B—Kt2
5 B—B4	B—Q3
6 B x B	Q x B
7 P x P	B x P
8 P—K4	B—Kt2
9 R—B1	P—QR3
10 B—Q3	Kt—K2
11 O—O	O—O?
12 P—K5!	Q—Q1
13 B x Pch	K x B
14 Kt—Kt5ch	K—R3
15 Q—Q2	K—Kt3
16 Kt—K2	Kt—Q4
17 Q—Q3ch!	K x Kt
18 P—B4ch	K—R3
19 Q—R3ch	K—Kt3
20 P—B5ch	P x P
21 KR x P!!	R—R1
22 Q—Kt4ch	K—R2
23 KR x P	Resigns

---

132. Paris, 1900.

Pillsbury finds beautiful sacrifices in a seemingly unpromising position.

FOUR KNIGHTS' GAME

D. JANOWSKI	H. N. PILLSBURY
White	Black
1 P—K4	P—K4
2 Kt—KB3	Kt—KB3
3 Kt—B3	Kt—B3
4 B—Kt5	B—Kt5
5 O—O	O—O
6 P—Q3	B x Kt
7 P x B	P—Q3
8 R—K1	B—Q2
9 R—Kt1	R—K1
10 B—Kt5	P—KR3
11 B—KR4	P—R3
12 B—R4	R—Kt1
13 K—R1	Kt—K2
14 B—QKt3	Kt—Kt3
15 B—Kt3	B—Kt5
16 P—KR3	B—R4
17 R—K3?	Kt—B5
18 B x Kt	P x B
19 R—K1	Q—Q2
20 K—R2	K—R1
21 Q—Q2	B x Kt
22 P x B	R—K4
23 R—KR1	R—KR4
24 K—Kt2	R—R5
25 QR—Kt1	Kt—R2
26 K—B1	Kt—Kt4
27 R—Kt4!	R x P
28 R x R	Kt x R
29 R—R4	P—KKt4!
30 R—R5	P—Kt5
31 R x Pch	K—Kt2
32 R—R5	P x P
33 R—KB5	P—KB3!
34 P—B4	R—K1
35 Q—Kt4	P—B4
36 Q—Kt6	K—B2
37 R—Q5	Q—Kt5
38 K—K1	Kt x P!
39 R x QP	R x Pch!
40 K—Q2	R—K7ch
41 K—B1	R—K3
42 Q x Pch	R—K2
43 Q—Q5ch	K—Kt2
44 R—Q8	Q—K3
45 Q—R5	Q—K8ch

and Black announced mate in five.

---

133. Paris Tournament, 1900.

First Brilliancy Prize.

White's clever sacrifices have been greatly admired.

VIENNA GAME

J. MIESES		D. JANOWSKI
	White	Black
1	P—K4	P—K4
2	Kt—QB3	Kt—QB3
3	B—B4	B—B4
4	P—Q3	P—Q3
5	P—B4	Kt—B3
6	P—B5	Kt—QR4
7	Q—B3	P—B3
8	P—KKt4!	P—KR3
9	P—KR4	P—QKt4
10	B—Kt3	Kt x B
11	RP x Kt	P—KR4
12	P x P	Kt x RP
13	KKt—K2	Q—Kt3
14	Kt—Kt3	Kt—B3
15	B—Kt5	B—Kt2
16	P—R5	Kt—R2
17	B—Q2	O—O—O
18	P—R6!!	P—Kt3
19	O—O—O	KR—Kt1
20	P x P	P x P
21	QR—B1	K—Kt1
22	Q—B7!	R—R1
23	Q x P!	QR—Kt1

24	Q—Kt7!!	B—B1
25	Kt—B5	B x Kt
26	R x B	B—Kt5
27	K—Kt1	B x Kt
28	P x B	Kt—B1
29	KR—KB1	Kt—Kt3
30	Q—Q7	R—Q1
31	Q—K6	Kt—B5
32	B x Kt	P x B
33	R(5) x BP	Q—B4
34	R—B7	Q—Kt4
35	R—B8!!	Q—QB4
36	Q—K7	Resigns

---

134. Paris, 1900.

Marshall's Memorable Game

PETROFF'S DEFENSE

H. N. PILLSBURY		F. J. MARSHALL
	White	Black
1	P—K4	P—K4
2	Kt—KB3	Kt—KB3
3	P—Q4	P—Q4
4	P x QP	P x P
5	B—QB4	B—Kt5ch
6	P—B3	Q—K2ch
7	B—K2	P x P
8	P x P	B—QB4
9	O—O	O—O
10	P—B4	R—K1
11	B—Q3	B—KKt5
12	B—Kt2	Kt—K5
13	QKt—Q2	Kt x P!
14	R x Kt	B x Rch
15	K x B	Q—K6ch
16	K—Kt3	Q x B
17	K x B	R—K7!
18	K—R3	Kt—Q2
19	R—B1	P—KR4
20	Q—B2	Kt—B4
21	P—Kt3	P—KKt4!
22	P—Kt4	R x Kt
23	Q x Q	R x Q
24	R—B3	P—B4
25	K—Kt2	BP x P
26	Kt x P	R—Q7ch
27	K—Kt3	R x B
28	P—KR3	R—KB1

29	P x P	P x P
30	K x P	R(1)—B7
	Resigns	

---

135. Paris, May 25, 1900.

One of the gems of Lasker's "World's Fair" play.

QUEEN'S GAMBIT

DR. E. LASKER		GEZA MAROCZY
White		Black
1	P—Q4	P—Q4
2	P—QB4	P—K3
3	Kt—QB3	Kt—KB3
4	Kt—B3	P x P
5	P—K3	P—B4
6	B x P	P—QR3
7	P—QR4	Kt—B3
8	O—O	P x P
9	P x P	B—K2
10	B—K3	O—O
11	Q—K2!	Q—R4
12	KR—Q1	KR—Q1
13	QR—B1	Kt—QKt5
14	Kt—K5	KKt—Q4
15	B—Kt3	R—B1
16	Kt—K4	Q—Q1
17	P—B4	P—QKt3
18	B—Q2!	B—Kt2
19	Kt—Kt3	R—B1
20	P—B5	R x R
21	R x R	P x P
22	Kt x P(B5)	B—KB3
23	B x Kt(Kt4)	Kt x B
24	Kt x BP!	R x Kt
25	Q—K6	K—R1
26	Q x R	B x Pch
27	K—R1	Kt—Q6
28	R—B1	B x Pch
29	K x B	Q—Kt4ch
30	K—R3	Resigns

---

136. Correspondence Game

Played in Russia, 1900.

Tolstoy plays good Chess.

QUEEN'S GAMBIT

S. F. LEBEDEW		COUNT TOLSTOY
White		Black
1	P—Q4	P—Q4
2	P—QB4	P x P
3	Kt—KB3	Kt—KB3
4	P—K3	B—Kt5
5	B x P	P—K3
6	Q—Kt3	B x Kt
7	P x B	P—QKt3
8	R—Kt1	P—B3
9	Kt—B3	P—QKt4
10	B—K2	P—QR4
11	B—Q2	P—Kt3
12	QR—B1	P—R5
13	Q—B2	Kt—Q4
14	Kt x Kt	KP x Kt
15	P—K4	B—Kt2
16	P—K5	O—O
17	B—Q3	Q—K2
18	P—QR3	B x P
19	P x B	Q x Pch
20	K—B1	Q x RP
21	B x KKtP	Q—R6ch
22	K—K2	Q—K3ch
23	B—K4ch	K—R1
24	Q—B3ch	P—B3
25	B—R6	R—B2
26	R—Kt4	Kt—Q2
27	QR—KKt1	Kt—K4
28	Q—R5	KR—R2
29	R—Kt8ch	R x R
30	Q x R	Kt—Kt3
31	R—Kt4	P x B
32	R x P	Kt—K4
33	Q—Q4	Kt x P!
34	K x Kt	Q—R6ch
35	K—K2	Q x B
36	R—K6	Q—R4ch
37	K—Q2	Q—Kt4ch
38	K—B3	Q—B8ch
39	K—Q3	Q—Q8ch
	Resigns	

White's Rook is lost.

---

137. Augsburg, Aug. 19, 1900.

One of Sixteen Blindfold Games!

PIERCE GAMBIT

H. N. PILLSBURY	HAUSLER
White	Black
1 P—K4	P—K4
2 Kt—QB3	Kt—QB3
3 P—B4	P x P
4 Kt—B3	P—Q3
5 P—Q4	P—KKt4
6 P—KR4	B—Kt5
7 B—Kt5	P—QR3
8 B x Ktch	P x B
9 P x P	Kt—K2
10 B x P	Kt—Kt3
11 Q—Q2	B—Kt2
12 O—O—O	Q—B1
13 P—K5	Q—B4
14 B—R2	P x P
15 P x P	O—O
16 Kt—Q4	Q—Q2
17 Kt—K4!	B x R
18 Kt—B6ch	B x Kt
19 KtP x B	Q—Kt5

If 19 . . . K—R1; 20 Q—R6, R—KKt1; 21 Q x Pch!!

20 Q—R6	Kt—R1
21 Kt—B5	KR—K1
22 R x B	Q—Kt3
23 R—Q7	Q x Qch
24 Kt x Qch	K—B1
25 R x P	QR—B1
26 R—Q7	QR—Q1
27 P—K6!	Resigns

---

138. Franklin Chess Club, Philadelphia, April 28, 1900.

One of twenty simultaneous blindfold games against men, the majority of whom would test the powers of any master single-handed vis-a-vis.

(Score: Pillsbury 14 wins, 5 draws, and 1 loss.)

QUEEN'S GAMBIT DECLINED

H. N. PILLSBURY	C. J. NEWMANN (Club Champion)
White	Black
1 P—Q4	P—Q4
2 P—QB4	P—K3
3 Kt—QB3	Kt—KB3
4 B—Kt5	B—K2
5 P—K3	QKt—Q2
6 Kt—B3	P—QKt3
7 P x P	P x P
8 B—Kt5	B—Kt2
9 Kt—K5	O—O
10 B—B6	R—Kt1
11 B x B	R x B
12 Kt—B6	Q—K1
13 Kt x Bch	Q x Kt
14 Kt x P	Q—K5
15 Kt x Ktch	P x Kt
16 B—R6	Q x KtP
17 K—Q2	. . . .

Q—B3 is even more forcing.

17	Q x Pch
18 K—B1	K—R1
19 R—KKt1	Kt—K4
20 P x Kt	Resigns

---

139. Copenhagen, Oct. 23, 1900.

One of six blindfold games.

VIENNA OPENING

J. MIESES (blindfold)	PRITZEL
White	Black
1 P—K4	P—K4

2	Kt—QB3	Kt—KB3
3	B—B4	Kt—B3
4	P—Q3	B—B4
5	P—B4	P—Q3
6	P—B5	Kt—QR4
7	Q—B3	P—B3
8	P—KKt4	P—KR3
9	P—KR4	Kt—R2
10	P—Kt5	Kt x B
11	P x Kt	P x P
12	P x P	B x Kt
13	P—Kt6	P—B3
14	R x Kt	R—KKt1
15	Q—R3	Q—K2
16	R—R8	Q—B1
17	R x R	Q x R
18	Q—R7	K—B1
19	B—Q2	B—Q2
20	O—O—O	B—Kt3
21	R—R1	B—R4
22	K—Q1	B x Kt
23	B x B	Q x P
24	B—Q2	Q—Kt1
25	B—Kt5!	P x B
26	P—B6	B—Kt5ch
27	K—B1	P x P
28	Q x P	R—Q1
29	R—R8!	B—K3
30	R x Qch	B x R
31	Q—B7	R—K1
32	P—Kt7 mate!	

---

140. Munich, 1900.

Prepared Analysis vs. Genius!

RUY LOPEZ

A. HALPRIN		H. N. PILLSBURY
White		Black
1	P—K4	P—K4
2	Kt—KB3	Kt—QB3
3	B—Kt5	Kt—B3
4	O—O	Kt x P
5	P—Q4	Kt—Q3
6	P x P	Kt x B
7	P—QR4	P—Q3
8	P—K6	P x P
9	P x Kt	Kt—K2
10	Kt—B3	Kt—Kt3
11	Kt—Kt5	B—K2
12	Q—R5	B x Kt
13	B x B	Q—Q2
14	P—Kt6!	BP x P
15	Kt—Q5!	P x Kt
16	KR—K1ch	K—B1!
17	R—R3!	Kt—K4!
18	R x Kt!	P x R
19	R—B3ch	K—Kt1
20	B—R6!!	Q—K2!
21	B x P	K x B
22	R—Kt3ch	K—B1
23	R—B3ch	K—Kt2
24	R—Kt3ch	K—B1

Drawn!!

---

141. Washington, D. C., 1901.

The conclusion is so pretty that it seems as if it were a composition and not an actually played game.

RUY LOPEZ

A. W. FOX		BAUER
White		Black
1	P—K4	P—K4
2	Kt—KB3	Kt—QB3
3	B—Kt5	Kt—B3
4	O—O	Kt x P
5	R—K1	Kt—Q3
6	Kt x P	B—K2
7	B—B1	O—O
8	P—Q4	Kt—B4
9	P—QB3	P—Q4
10	Q—Q3	R—K1
11	P—KB4	Kt—Q3
12	R—K3	Kt—R4?
13	Kt—Q2	Kt—B4
14	R—R3	Kt—R5
15	P—KKt4	Kt—Kt3
16	R—R5	Kt—B3

(see diagram next page)

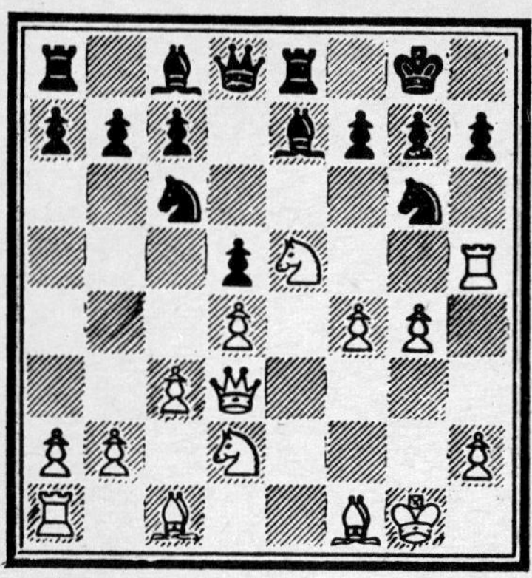

17 QKt—B4!	P x Kt
18 Q x Kt!!	RP x Q
19 Kt x KtP!	P x Kt
20 B x Pch	K—B1
21 R—R8 mate	

---

142. Glasgow, 1902.

Watch White's King walk!

TWO KNIGHTS' DEFENSE

R. TEICHMANN	ALLIES
White	Black
1 P—K4	P—K4
2 Kt—KB3	Kt—QB3
3 B—B4	Kt—B3
4 O—O	Kt x P
5 P—Q4	P x P
6 R—K1	P—Q4
7 B x P	Q x B
8 Kt—B3	Q—KR4
9 Kt x Kt	B—K2
10 B—Kt5	B—K3
11 B x B	Kt x B
12 Kt—Kt3	Q—R3
13 Q x P	O—O
14 QR—Q1	Kt—B3
15 Q—QR4	QR—Q1
16 Kt—Q4!	Kt x Kt
17 R x Kt	R x R
18 Q x R	P—QKt3
19 Q—K5	P—QB4
20 P—KB4	B—B1
21 P—B5	B—Kt2
22 Q—K7	Q—QB3
23 R—K2	P—B3
24 Kt—K4	Q—Q4
25 Kt—Q6	B—B3
26 P—KR3	P—B5
27 P—B3	P—KR3
28 K—R2!	P—QKt4
29 K—Kt3!!	P—QR4
30 K—R4!!	P—Kt3
31 R—K3	Q x KtP
32 R—Kt3	Q—KB7
33 P x P	Q—B5ch
34 R—Kt4	Q—B7ch
35 K—R5	Resigns

---

143. Hanover, 1902.

Second Brilliancy Prize

RUY LOPEZ

DR. A. G. OLLAND	H. WOLF
White	Black
1 P—K4	P—K4
2 Kt—KB3	Kt—QB3
3 B—Kt5	P—QR3
4 B—R4	Kt—B3
5 O—O	P—Q3
6 P—Q4	P x P
7 B x Ktch	P x B
8 Kt x P	B—Q2
9 P—QKt3	B—K2
10 Kt—Q2	O—O
11 B—Kt2	R—K1
12 P—QB4	B—KB1
13 Q—B2	P—Q4
14 P—K5	Kt—Kt5
15 Kt(Q4)—B3	P—B3

16 KP x P	Kt x P(3)
17 KR—K1	B—K2
18 Kt—Kt5	P—Kt3
19 Q—B3	R—KB1
20 QKt—B3	P—KR3
21 Kt—K6	B x Kt
22 R x B	Q—Q2
23 QR—K1	QR—K1
24 Q—Q3	K—R2
25 Kt—K5!!	Q x R
26 Q x Pch	K—R1
27 Q x Pch	K—Kt1
28 R—K3	B—Q1
29 Q—Kt6ch	K—R1
30 R—Kt3	Q—Q2
31 Q—R6ch	Q—R2
32 Kt—Kt6ch	K—Kt1
33 Kt—K7ch	Resigns

---

144. 1902.

Capablanca, at the age of twelve, defeats the champion of Cuba.

ALLGAIER GAMBIT

J. CORZO	J. R. CAPABLANCA
White	Black
1 P—K4	P—K4
2 Kt—QB3	Kt—QB3
3 P—B4	P x P
4 Kt—B3	P—KKt4
5 P—KR4	P—Kt5
6 Kt—KKt5	P—KR3
7 Kt x P	K x Kt
8 P—Q4	P—Q4
9 P x P	Q—K2ch
10 K—B2	P—Kt6ch
11 K—Kt1	Kt x P!
12 Q x Kt	Q—B4!
13 Kt—K2	Q—Kt3
14 Q x Q	RP x Q
15 Kt—Q4	B—QB4
16 P—B3	R—R5
17 B—K2	B x Ktch
18 P x B	R x QP
19 P—Kt3	Kt—B3
20 B—Kt2	R—Q7
21 B—R5ch	Kt x B
22 B x R	P—B6
23 P x P	Kt—B5
24 B—K5	R—Kt7ch
25 K—B1	R—B7ch
26 K—K1	Kt—Q6ch
Resigns	

145.

Superior development tells!

TWO KNIGHTS DEFENSE

A. DAVIS	DEARMAN
White	Black
1 P—K4	P—K4
2 B—B4	Kt—KB3
3 Kt—QB3	Kt—B3
4 Kt—B3	Kt x P
5 Kt x Kt	P—Q4
6 B—Kt5	P x Kt
7 Kt x P	Q—Q4
8 Kt x Kt	Q x B
9 Kt—Q4	Q—Kt4
10 P—KKt3	B—KKt5
11 P—KB3?	P x P
12 Kt x P	Q—R4
13 O—O	O—O—O
14 P—Q3	B—B4ch
15 K—R1	KR—K1
16 P—B3	R—K8!!
17 Q x R	B x Ktch
18 R x B	Q x R mate

---

146. Chicago Championship, Tournament, December, 1902.

A surprising Queen sacrifice

FRENCH DEFENSE

J. R. HOUGHTELING	L. S. CORNELL
White	Black
1 P—K4	P—K3

2	P—Q4	P—Q4
3	Kt—QB3	Kt—KB3
4	P—K5	KKt—Q2
5	Q—Kt4	P—QB4
6	B—K3	P x P
7	B x P	Kt—QB3
8	Kt—B3	P—QR3
9	B—Q3	Q—B2
10	O—O	Kt x B
11	Kt x Kt	B—K2
12	P—B4	B—B4
13	Kt—K2	Q—Kt3
14	P—B3	P—Kt3
15	P—Kt4	B—K2
16	K—R1	Q—B2
17	P—KR4	P—KR4

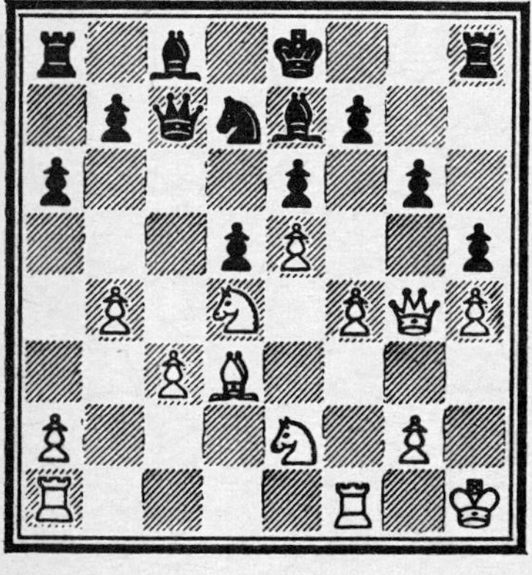

18	Q x KtP!!	Kt—B3
19	Q—Kt7	R—KKt1
20	P x Kt!	R—B1
21	P x B	Q x KP
22	QR—K1	Resigns

---

147. Monte Carlo, 1902.

Pillsbury's fifteen-move combination.

QUEEN'S GAMBIT

H. N. PILLSBURY		I. GUNSBERG
White		Black
1	P—Q4	P—Q4
2	P—QB4	P x P
3	Kt—KB3	P—QB4
4	P—K3	P x P
5	B x P	P—K3
6	P x P	Kt—KB3
7	O—O	B—K2
8	Q—K2	QKt—Q2
9	Kt—B3	Kt—Kt3
10	B—Kt3	QKt—Q4
11	B—Kt5	O—O
12	Kt—K5	Kt x Kt
13	P x Kt	Kt—Q4
14	B—Q2	B—B3
15	P—KB4	P—KKt3
16	R—B3	B—Kt2
17	QR—KB1	P—B3
18	Kt—Q3	P—Kt3
19	P—B5!	KtP x P
20	R—R3	R—B2
21	Q—R5	B—B1
22	R x P!	P x R
23	Kt—B4	B—QKt2
24	R—Kt3ch	B—Kt2
25	R—R3	B—R1
26	Q x P	Q—Q2
27	Kt x Kt	B x Kt
28	Q x B	Q x Q
29	B x Q	R—KB1
30	B—R6	B—Kt2
31	B x B	K x B
32	R—Kt3ch	K—R1
33	B x R	R x B
34	K—B2	R—B2
35	K—K2	R—B5
36	K—Q3	P—Kt4
37	R—K3	R—R5
38	P—Q5!	R x P
39	P—Q6	R—R3
40	R—K6	K—Kt2
41	P—Q7	R x R
42	P—Q8 (Q) and wins	

---

148. Russia, about 1903.

Compare this with Game No. 11!

RUY LOPEZ

A. RABINOVICH	E. SCHIFFERS
White	Black
1 P—K4	P—K4
2 Kt—KB3	Kt—QB3
3 B—Kt5	P—QR3
4 B—R4	KKt—K2
5 P—B3	P—QKt4
6 B—Kt3	Kt—Kt3
7 P—Q4	B—K2
8 P x P	O—O
9 B—Q5	B—Kt2
10 P—KR4	R—Kt1
11 Kt—Kt5	QKt x P
12 Q—R5!	P—R3
13 Kt x P	B x B!!
14 Kt x Q	Kt—Q6ch
15 K—Q2	B x KP
16 R—K1	Kt x R
17 K x Kt	QR x Kt
18 B—K3	Kt x P
19 Kt—Q2	Kt x Pch
20 K—K2	B—QB3
21 B x P	QR—K1
22 B—K3	B—R5
23 K—Q1	R—K3
24 K—B2	B x P
25 B x B	R x B

26 R—R1	Kt—K6ch
27 K—B1	B x R
28 Q x B	R—Q3
29 Q—R5	P—Kt3
30 Q—R3	R—B8ch
Resigns	

---

149. Kiev, 1903.

Tchigorin's Surprise Mate

Played in the Russian Masters' Tournament.

FALKBEER COUNTER GAMBIT

M. TCHIGORIN	ZNOSKO-BOROVSKY
White	Black
1 P—K4	P—K4
2 P—KB4	P—Q4
3 KP x P	P—K5
4 B—Kt5ch	P—B3
5 P x P	Kt x P
6 P—Q4	Q—R4ch
7 Kt—B3	B—QKt5
8 B—Q2	Kt—B3
9 P—QR3	B x Kt
10 B x Ktch	P x B
11 B x B	Q—B2
12 Kt—K2	B—R3
13 Q—Q2	O—O
14 B—R5	Q—Q2
15 O—O—O	P—K6
16 Q—K1	Kt—K5
17 Kt—B3	Kt—B7
18 Q x P	Kt x KR
19 R x Kt	KR—K1
20 Q—B2	Q—B4
21 B—Kt4	R—K3
22 Q—B3	QR—K1
23 P—Kt4	Q—B3
24 Q—B2	R—K6
25 P—Q5	P x P
26 Kt x P	Q—B3
27 R—Q1	R—K7
28 Q—B5	Q—KKt3

(see diagram next page)

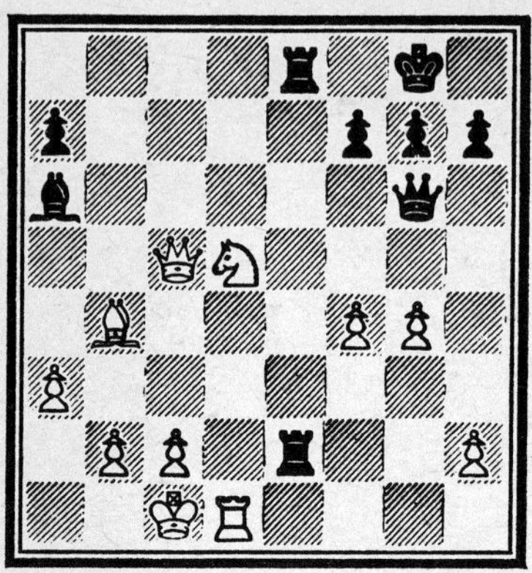

29 Kt—K7ch	R(K1) x Kt
30 R—Q8ch	R—K1
31 Q—B8ch	R x Q
32 R x R mate	

Znosko-Borovsky was only sixteen years of age.

---

150. Cable Match, 1903.
U. S. A. vs. Great Britain

Marshall saves himself with a wonderful combination.

QUEEN'S GAMBIT DECLINED

F. J. MARSHALL White	H. E. ATKINS Black
1 P—Q4	P—Q4
2 P—QB4	P—QB3
3 Kt—QB3	Kt—B3
4 P x P	P x P
5 B—B4	Kt—B3
6 P—K3	P—K3
7 B—Q3	B—K2
8 Kt—B3	O—O
9 Kt—K5	Kt x Kt
10 P x Kt	Kt—Q2
11 Q—B2	P—KKt3
12 P—KR4	Kt—B4
13 P—R5	Kt x Bch
14 Q x Kt	P—KKt4
15 B—Kt3	P—B4
16 P x P e.p.	B x P
17 R—Q1	Q—Kt3
18 R—Q2	B—Q2
19 O—O	QR—B1
20 R—B1	B—Kt4
21 Q—B2	R—B5
22 Q—Kt3	Q—B3
23 R(2)—B2	R—B1
24 Q—R3	B—R3
25 P—Kt3	R—B4

26 Kt x P!!	R x R
27 R x R	Q x R
28 Kt x Bch	K—B2
29 Q—Q6	K x Kt
30 B—K5ch	K—B4
31 P—B3 and wins	

---

151. Vienna Gambit Tournament, 1903.

The great master of the gambit gets a taste of his own medicine.

First Brilliancy Prize

MUZIO GAMBIT

G. MAROCZY White	M. TCHIGORIN Black
1 P—K4	P—K4
2 P—KB4	P x P
3 Kt—KB3	P—KKt4
4 B—B4	P—Kt5
5 Kt—B3	P x Kt
6 Q x P	P—Q3
7 P—Q4	B—K3
8 Kt—Q5!	P—QB3
9 O—O	P x Kt
10 P x P	B—B4
11 B x P	B—Kt3
12 B—Kt5ch	Kt—Q2
13 QR—K1ch	B—K2
14 B x P	K—B1
15 R x B	Kt x R
16 R—K1	K—Kt2
17 QB x Kt	Q—R4
18 Q—K2	Kt—B1
19 B—B6ch	K—Kt1
20 Q—K5	P—KR3
21 B x R	P—B3
22 Q—K7	K x B
23 Q x Pch	K—Kt1
24 R—K7	Resigns

---

152. Berlin, January, 1904.

Caro's Brilliancy.

QUEEN'S PAWN GAME

H. CARO White	W. KUNZE Black
1 P—Q4	P—Q4
2 Kt—KB3	P—K3
3 P—K3	Kt—KB3
4 B—Q3	B—Q3
5 QKt—Q2	O—O
6 P—K4	P x P
7 Kt x P	Kt x Kt
8 B x Kt	P—KB4
9 B—Q3	Kt—Q2
10 O—O	P—K4
11 B—B4ch	K—R1
12 Kt—Kt5	Q—K1
13 R—K1	P—K5
14 Q—B3!	Kt—B3
15 Q—QKt3	Q—R4
16 P—KR3	P—KR3
17 Kt—B7ch	K—R2
18 Kt—K5	B x Kt
19 P x B	Kt—Q2
20 B—B4	P—KKt4
21 B—R2	Kt—B4
22 Q—Kt5	Kt—Q2
23 QR—Q1	P—B3
24 R x Ktch	K—R1
25 P—K6!!	. . . .

25	P x Q
26 B—K5ch	K—Kt1
27 R—Kt7ch	K—R1
28 P—K7	R—K1
29 R—B7ch	K—Kt1
30 R—B8ch	K—R2
31 B—Kt8ch	K—Kt3
32 B—B7ch	Resigns

---

153. Cambridge Springs Tourney, 1904.

"Peerless boy, thou art unique, triumphant, grand."
Morphy himself might envy your style!

QUEEN'S GAMBIT DECLINED

H. N. PILLSBURY	DR. E. LASKER
White	Black
1 P—Q4	P—Q4
2 P—QB4	P—K3
3 Kt—QB3	Kt—KB3
4 Kt—B3	P—B4
5 B—Kt5	P x QP
6 Q x P	Kt—B3
7 B x Kt!	P x B
8 Q—R4	P x P
9 R—Q1	B—Q2
10 P—K3	Kt—K4
11 Kt x Kt	P x Kt
12 Q x BP	Q—Kt3
13 B—K2!	Q x KtP
14 O—O!	R—B1
15 Q—Q3!	R—B2
16 Kt—K4	B—K2
17 Kt—Q6ch	K—B1
18 Kt—B4	Q—Kt4
19 P—B4	P x P
20 Q—Q4!	P—B3
21 Q x P(B4)	Q—QB4
22 Kt—K5	B—K1
23 Kt—Kt4	P—B4
24 Q—R6ch	K—B2
25 B—B4!	R—B3

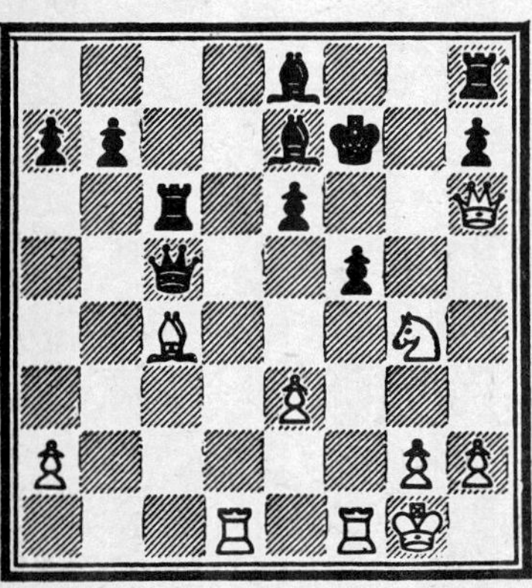

26 R x Pch	Q x R
27 R—KB1	Q x Rch
28 K x Q	B—Q2
29 Q—R5ch	K—Kt1
30 Kt—K5	Resigns

This historic game, played in the grand manner by Pillsbury, created a sensation at the time.

He had waited eight years for the "sweet revenge" that now was his. It proved to be the last flickering of his genius, and the final encounter of these two great masters.

---

154. Cambridge Springs Tournament, 1904.

First Brilliancy Prize: Lasker tries to trap White's Bishop, but runs into a trap himself!

QUEEN'S GAMBIT DECLINED

C. SCHLECHTER	DR. E. LASKER
White	Black
1 P—Q4	P—Q4
2 P—QB4	P—K3
3 Kt—QB3	Kt—KB3
4 B—Kt5	B—K2
5 P—K3	O—O
6 Kt—B3	P—QKt3
7 B—Q3	B—Kt2
8 P x P	P x P
9 Kt—K5	P—B4
10 QR—B1	Kt—B3
11 O—O	Kt x Kt
12 P x Kt	Kt—K1
13 B—KB4	P—B4
14 Q—B2!	P—KKt4
15 B—Kt3	P—KB5?
16 B x Pch	K—R1
17 Q—Kt6	Kt—B3
18 P x Kt	R x P
19 Q—R5	K—Kt2
20 Q x Pch	K x B
21 B x P	R—Kt3
22 Q—R5ch	K—Kt2
23 KR—Q1	P—Q5

24	B—Kt3	R—Kt4
25	B—K5ch	K—Kt1
26	Q—R8ch	K—B2
27	Q—R7ch	K—K3
28	B—Kt3	P x Kt
29	R x Q	P x P
30	R(8)—Q1	P x R(Q)
31	R x Q	R—Q1
32	P—B4	R(4)—Q4
33	P—K4	R—Q8ch
34	R x R	R x Rch
35	K—B2	R—Q5
36	P—B5ch	K—Q2
37	P—K5	Resigns

---

155. Cambridge Springs, 1904.

One of the grandest games ever played.

SICILIAN DEFENSE

DR. E. LASKER		W. E. NAPIER
White		Black
1	P—K4	P—QB4
2	Kt—QB3	Kt—QB3
3	Kt—B3	P—KKt3
4	P—Q4	P x P
5	Kt x P	B—Kt2
6	B—K3	P—Q3
7	P—B3	Kt—B3
8	P—KKt4?!	O—O
9	P—Kt5	Kt—K1
10	P—KR4	Kt—B2
11	P—B4	P—K4!
12	KKt—K2	P—Q4!?
13	KP x P	Kt—Q5!
14	Kt x Kt	Kt x P!
15	Kt—B5!!	. . . .

(see diagram next column)

15	. . . .	Kt x Kt!
16	Q x Q	R x Q
17	Kt—K7ch!	K—R1!
18	P—KR5!!	R—K1!

19	B—B5!	P x RP!
20	B—B4!!	KP x P!!
21	B x BP!	Kt—K5!
22	B x R	B x P
23	R—QKt1	B—B6ch
24	K—B1	B—KKt5!
25	B x KRP!	B x B
26	R x B	Kt—Kt6ch
27	K—Kt2	Kt x R
28	R x P	P—R4
29	R—Kt3!	B—Kt2
30	R—KR3	Kt—Kt6
31	K—B3!	R—R3
32	K x P	Kt—K7ch
33	K—B5	Kt—B6
34	P—R3	Kt—R5
35	B—K3	Resigns

Magnificent!

---

156. At the Last Bivouac, 1904.

This game was contested by two Russian officers in Manchuria on the eve of an assault in which the Captain was killed. Lieutenant Denn was severely wounded in the same engagement and sent the score of the game to M. Alapin, adding that "the furious attack of the Captain during the battle was equal to the present brilliant en-

counter."

RUY LOPEZ

LIEUT. DENN White	CAPT. R. PERWAGO Black
1 P—K4	P—K4
2 Kt—KB3	Kt—QB3
3 B—Kt5	B—Kt5
4 P—B3	B—R4
5 O—O	KKt—K2
6 Kt—R3	O—O
7 Q—R4	P—Q4
8 B x Kt	Kt x B
9 Kt x P	Kt x Kt
10 Q x B	Kt—B6ch!
11 K—R1	Q—Q3!
12 P x Kt	Q—B5
13 K—Kt2	B—R6ch!
14 K x B	Q x BPch
15 K—R4	P—Kt4ch
16 K x P	K—R1
17 K—R4	R—KKt1
18 P—R3	Q—B5ch
19 K—R5	Q—Kt4 mate

---

157. Chicago, about 1905.

The Power of the Vigilantes. A symmetrical mate with Bishops and Knights marks the following curious game.

ALBIN COUNTER GAMBIT

DODGE White	HOUGHTELING Black
1 P—Q4	P—Q4
2 P—QB4	P—K4
3 P—K3	P x QP
4 Q x P	Kt—KB3
5 Kt—QB3	Kt—B3
6 Q—Q1	B—KB4
7 P—B3?	Kt—QKt5
8 Q—R4ch?	Q—Q2
9 Q x Qch	K x Q
10 P—K4?	P x KP
11 P x P	Kt x KP
12 R—Kt1	Kt—B7ch
13 K—Q1	Kt—B7ch
14 K—K2	B—B4
15 Kt—B3	B—Q6ch
16 K—Q2	B—K6 mate

One of the most extraordinary mates ever given in actual play.

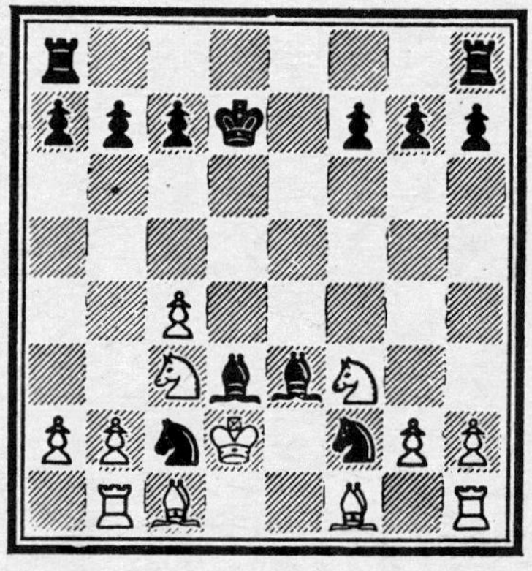

PART VI

Moderns, Hypermoderns and Eclectics

Shortly after the turn of the century there appeared a new group of masters, the outstanding members of this group being Rubinstein, Nimzovich, Bernstein, Capablanca, Duras, Tartakower, Spielmann and Vidmar. They not only applied in their games what they had learned from the reigning gods of the chessboard, but they also rebelled, as is the way of youth, and made their own additions and corrections. By the time the fateful year of 1914 arrived, it had become pretty clear that Nimzovich and his young countryman Alekhine were evolving a new school of chess thought, whose effect, if not always its objective, was to turn the current chess theories upside down.

During and after the World War, these players were joined by such masters as Reti, Bogolyubov and Breyer, and as they garnered one first prize after another, the hypermodern theories began to get a respectful hearing in some quarters. Once the new theories had become respectable and acceptable, still younger players, such as Euwe, applied them as a matter of course. About 1927 we see a new tendency toward a reconciliation of the old and the new, and our contemporary crop of masters, among them Flohr, Kashdan, Fine, Reshevsky, Botvinnik and Keres, have the reputation, despite their disparate styles, of being at home in all kinds of play, and having few preconceptions and strongly marked individual styles. It is an age where "anything goes." Each game is played on its own merits, and every occasion is treated in whatever way the situation seems to demand; the older masters were rarely capable of such elasticity and objectivity.

158. Nuremberg, 1906.

One of Marshall's immortal combinations.

QUEEN'S GAMBIT

F. J. MARSHALL White	H. WOLF Black
1 P—Q4	P—Q4
2 P—QB4	P x P
3 Kt—KB3	Kt—KB3
4 Kt—B3	P—QR3
5 P—K3	P—K3
6 B x P	P—B4
7 O—O	Kt—B3
8 P—QR3	Q—B2
9 Q—K2	P—QKt4
10 B—R2	B—Kt2
11 P x P	B x P
12 P—QKt4	B—Q3
13 B—Kt2	O—O
14 QR—B1	QR—Q1
15 B—Kt1	B—R1
16 Kt—K4	Kt—Q4
17 QKt—Kt5	P—Kt3

18 Kt x RP!	K x Kt
19 Kt—Kt5ch	K—Kt1
20 Q—R5!	P—B3
21 B x KtP	R—Q2
22 Kt x P	R—R2
23 B x Rch	Q x B
24 Q x Qch	K x Q
25 Kt x Rch	B x Kt
26 KR—Q1	Kt(3)—K2
27 P—K4	Kt—QKt3
28 R—B7	K—Kt1
29 B x P	Kt—Kt3
30 R—Q8	Resigns

---

159. Vienna, 1906.

Tartakower as a youngster.

SICILIAN DEFENSE

DR. S. TARTAKOWER White	DR. M. VIDMAR Black
1 P—K4	P—QB4
2 Kt—KB3	Kt—QB3
3 P—Q4	P x P
4 Kt x P	P—KKt3
5 B—K3	B—Kt2
6 Kt—QB3	Kt—B3
7 B—K2	P—Q3
8 P—KR3	O—O
9 Q—Q2	B—Q2
10 P—KKt4	P—QR3
11 P—Kt5	Kt—K1
12 P—KR4	R—B1
13 P—R5	Kt—R4
14 P x P	RP x P
15 O—O—O	P—Kt4
16 P—B3	Kt—B2
17 B—Q3!	Kt—K3
18 Q—R2	R—K1
19 Q—R7ch	K—B1
20 Kt x Ktch	B x Kt
21 R—R6!	B—B5
22 P—K5!!	B x B
23 P—K6!!	R x Kt
24 P x R	Q—B1
25 B—Q4	P—B3
26 P x P	P x P
27 B x P	Q—Kt2
28 Q—R8ch!	B x Q
29 R x B mate	

---

160. Lodz, 1907.

Rubinstein's Immortal Game

QUEEN'S GAMBIT DECLINED

G. ROTLEWI	A. RUBINSTEIN
White	Black
1 P—Q4	P—Q4
2 Kt—KB3	P—K3
3 P—K3	P—QB4
4 P—B4	Kt—QB3
5 Kt—B3	Kt—B3
6 P x BP	B x P
7 P—QR3	P—QR3
8 P—QKt4	B—Q3
9 B—Kt2	O—O
10 Q—Q2	Q—K2!
11 B—Q3	P x P
12 B x P	P—QKt4
13 B—Q3	R—Q1
14 Q—K2	B—Kt2
15 O—O	Kt—K4
16 Kt x Kt	B x Kt
17 P—B4	B—B2
18 P—K4?	QR—B1
19 P—K5?	B—Kt3ch
20 K—R1	Kt—Kt5!!

Beginning a series of brilliant sacrifices.

21 B—K4	Q—R5
22 P—Kt3	. . . .

22	R x Kt!!
23 P x Q	R—Q7!!!
24 Q x R	. . . .

Black mates in five.

24	B x Bch
25 Q—Kt2	R—R6!
26 B—Q4	B x B
27 R—B2	B x R
28 Any move	R x P mate

---

161. Vienna, 1907.

Sparkling middle-game play.

CENTER COUNTER GAME

O. DURAS	R. SPIELMANN
White	Black
1 P—K4	P—Q4
2 P x P	Q x P
3 Kt—QB3	Q—QR4
4 P—Q4	Kt—KB3
5 Kt—B3	B—Kt5
6 B—K2	Kt—B3
7 B—K3	O—O—O
8 Kt—Q2!	B x B
9 Q x B	Q—KB4
10 Kt—Kt3	P—K3
11 P—QR3	B—Q3
12 O—O—O	Kt—Q4!
13 Kt—R4	P—K4!

14 P x P	B x KP?
15 Kt(4)—B5	Kt—Kt3
16 P—QR4!	P—QR4
17 P—Kt4	Q—B3
18 P—QB3	KR—K1
19 Kt x KtP!	R x Rch
20 R x R	B x BP!
21 Kt(7)—B5	Kt—Kt5
22 P—Kt5!	Q—K4
23 Kt x P!!	P—R4
24 P x B	Q x Pch
25 K—Kt1	Q x Kt
26 R—Q8ch!	Resigns

---

162. Ostend, 1907.

A Lesson in Dynamics

FOUR KNIGHTS' GAME

E. A. ZNOSKO-BOROVSKY — A. RUBINSTEIN

White	Black
1 P—K4	P—K4
2 Kt—KB3	Kt—QB3
3 Kt—B3	Kt—B3
4 B—Kt5	P—QR3
5 B x Kt	QP x B
6 Kt x P	Kt x P
7 Kt x Kt	Q—Q5
8 O—O	Q x KKt
9 R—K1	B—K3
10 P—Q4	Q—KB4
11 B—Kt5	B—Q3
12 P—KKt4!	Q—Kt3
13 P—KB4	P—KB4
14 Kt x Bch	P x Kt
15 P—Q5!	O—O
16 R x B	Q—B2
17 Q—K2	P x KtP
18 Q x KtP	P x P
19 QR—K1	QR—B1
20 Q—Kt2	Q—B4
21 B—R6	R—QB2
22 R—K7	R—B2
23 R—K8ch	R—B1
24 QR—K7	Q—B3
25 Q x QPch	K—R1
26 R x Rch	Q x R
27 R x R	Resigns

---

163. Ostend, 1907.

An Indian war-dance

INDIAN DEFENSE

F. J. MARSHALL — A. BURN

White	Black
1 P—Q4	Kt—KB3
2 Kt—KB3	P—Q3
3 B—B4	QKt—Q2
4 P—K3	P—KKt3
5 B—Q3	B—Kt2
6 QKt—Q2	O—O
7 P—KR4	R—K1
8 P—R5	Kt x P
9 R x Kt?!	P x R
10 B x Pch	K x B?
11 Kt—Kt5ch	K—Kt3
12 QKt—B3	P—K4
13 Kt—R4ch	K—B3
14 Kt—R7ch	K—K2
15 Kt—B5ch	K—K3
16 Kt x Bch	K—K2
17 Kt—B5ch	K—K3
18 P—Q5ch	K x Kt
19 Q x Pch	K—K5
20 O—O—O	Resigns

---

164. Ostend, 1907.

CENTER GAMBIT

DR. J. PERLIS — J. H. BLACKBURNE

White	Black
1 P—K4	P—K4
2 P—Q4	P x P
3 P—QB3	P—Q4
4 KP x P	Q x P
5 P x P	Kt—QB3
6 Kt—KB3	B—Kt5

7	B—K2	Kt—B3
8	O—O	B—Q3
9	Kt—B3	Q—KR4
10	R—K1	O—O
11	P—KR3	QR—Q1!

12	P x B	Kt x KtP
13	B—KKt5	B—R7ch
14	K—B1	B—K4!
15	B—Q3	R x P!
16	Kt x B	R—K1!
17	R—K4	R x R
18	B x R	QKt x Kt
19	B—B4	Kt—Kt3
20	B—Kt3	Q—R8ch
21	K—K2	Q x P
22	Q—R1	Q x Q
23	R x Q	P—KB4
24	K—B3	Kt (5)—K4ch
25	K—Kt2	P x B
26	Kt x P	Kt—B2
27	R—K1	R—K2
28	P—B3	Kt—Q3
29	B x Kt	P x B
30	R—Q1	P—Q4
31	Kt—B3	R—Q2
32	K—B2	Kt—K2
33	K—K3	P—Q5ch
34	K—K4	P x Kt!
35	Resigns	

165. Correspondence Game, Russia, 1908.

Alekhine at the age of sixteen.

VIENNA GAME

	A. WJAKHIREFF White	A. ALEKHINE Black
1	P—K4	P—K4
2	Kt—QB3	Kt—KB3
3	B—B4	Kt—B3
4	P—Q3	B—Kt5
5	Kt—K2	P—Q4
6	P x P	Kt x P
7	B x Kt	Q x B
8	O—O	Q—Q1
9	Kt—Kt3	O—O
10	P—B4	P—B4
11	QKt—K2	Q—R5
12	K—R1	B—Q3
13	P—Q4	P—K5
14	P—B4	R—B3
15	P—B5	R—R3
16	P—KR3	B—B1
17	Q—Kt3ch	K—R1
18	Q—B3?	Kt—K2!
19	B—K3	B—K3
20	B—B2	Q—B3
21	P—R3	B—Q4
22	B—K3	Kt—Kt3
23	P—Kt4	Kt—R5
24	K—Kt1	Kt—B6ch
25	K—B2	Q—R5!

26 P—Kt5	R—KKt3
27 KR—B1	B—K2!
28 K—B1	R x Kt
29 Kt x R	Q x Kt
30 B—B2	Q—R7
31 P x Kt	P x P
32 R—B2	R—K1!
33 B—K3	Q—R8ch
34 B—Kt1	B—R5!
35 R—KR2	. . . .
35	Q—Kt7ch
36 R x Q	P x R mate

---

166. St. Petersburg Congress, 1909.

First Brilliancy Prize: beautifully sustained attack.

RUY LOPEZ

C. SCHLECHTER	G. SALWE
White	Black
1 P—K4	P—K4
2 Kt—KB3	Kt—QB3
3 B—Kt5	P—QR3
4 B—R4	Kt—B3
5 O—O	B—K2
6 R—K1	P—QKt4
7 B—Kt3	P—Q3
8 P—B3	Kt—QR4
9 B—B2	P—B4
10 P—Q3	Kt—B3
11 QKt—Q2	O—O
12 Kt—B1	Q—B2
13 B—Kt5	Kt—K1
14 Kt—K3	B x B
15 Kt x B	Kt—K2
16 P—QR4	R—Kt1
17 P x P	P x P
18 Q—Q2	P—R3
19 Kt—B3	B—K3
20 P—Q4	Kt—KB3
21 R—R6	R—R1

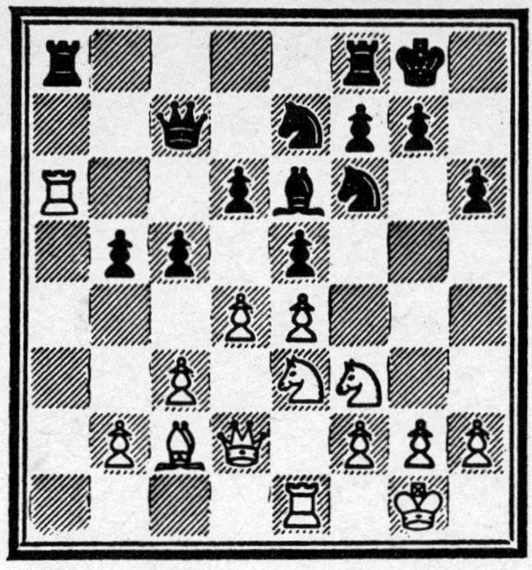

22 P x P!?	R x R?

(. . . *Kt x P!*)

23 P x Kt	P x P
24 Kt—Q5!	B x Kt
25 P x B	K—Kt2
26 Kt—R4	R—K1
27 P—R3	Q—Q1
28 R—K3	Kt—Kt3
29 Kt—B5ch	K—B1
30 R—K6!	R x R
31 P x R	P—Q4
32 Q x Pch	K—K1
33 P x Pch	K x P
34 Q—R7ch	K—K3
35 Q x Kt	R—R7
36 P—QKt4!	P x P
37 Kt—Q4ch	K—Q2
38 B—B5ch	Resigns

---

167. St. Petersburg Congress, 1909.

Black's position is smashed in elegant style.

FRENCH DEFENSE

DR. O. S. BERNSTEIN
E. A. ZNOSKO-BOROVSKY

	White	Black
1	P—K4	P—K3
2	P—Q4	P—Q4
3	Kt—QB3	Kt—KB3
4	B—Kt5	B—Kt5
5	P x P	Q x P
6	B x Kt	B x Ktch
7	P x B	P x B
8	Kt—B3	P—Kt3
9	P—Kt3	B—Kt2
10	B—Kt2	Q—KR4
11	O—O	Kt—Q2
12	Q—K2	R—QB1
13	Q—K3	P—QB4
14	Kt—R4	B x B
15	Kt x B	P x P
16	P x P	O—O
17	Q—K4	R—B2
18	Kt—B4	Q—Kt5
19	P—KB3	Q—Kt4
20	R—B2	R—Q1
21	P—KR4	Q—R3
22	P—Kt4!	Q x P
23	R—R2	Q—Kt4
24	Kt x P!	P x Kt
25	Q x KPch	K—R1
26	Q—K7	Q—Kt1
27	R x Pch	Q x R
28	Q x Rch	Kt—B1
29	Q x Ktch	Q—Kt1
30	Q x Pch	Resigns

---

168. St. Petersburg Congress, 1909.

Dynamic Tactics.

KING'S GAMBIT DECLINED

DR. S. TARTAKOWER

C. SCHLECHTER

	White	Black
1	P—K4	P—K4
2	P—KB4	B—B4
3	Kt—KB3	P—Q3
4	P x P	P x P
5	P—B3	Kt—KB3
6	Kt x P	O—O
7	P—Q4	B—Q3
8	Kt—B3	Kt x P
9	B—Q3	R—K1
10	O—O	P—KR3
11	QKt—Q2	Kt—KB3
12	Kt—B4	P—B4
13	Kt (B3)—K5	P x P

14	Kt x P!	K x Kt
15	Q—R5ch	K—Kt1
16	R x Kt!	R—K8ch
17	R—B1	R x Rch
18	B x R	B—B1
19	B x P!!	Q—B3
20	B—Kt5	Q—B4
21	Kt—Q6!!	B x Kt
22	B—B4ch	B—K3
23	R—KB1	Q x Rch
24	B x Q	Kt—Q2
25	B—Q3	Kt—B1
26	P x P	B—KB2
27	Q—B3	Kt—K3
28	B—K3	R—Kt1
29	P—KKt4	P—KKt4
30	Q—KB6	B—B1
31	B—R7ch	K x B
32	Q x Bch	Resigns

---

169. St. Petersburg Congress, 1909.

Brilliancy Prize
An electric storm in the offing.

FRENCH DEFENSE

FORGACS White	DR. S. TARTAKOWER Black
1 P—K4	P—K3
2 P—Q4	P—Q4
3 Kt—QB3	Kt—KB3
4 B—Kt5	B—K2
5 P—K5	Kt—K5
6 Kt x Kt	B x B
7 Kt x B	Q x Kt
8 P—KKt3	P—QB4
9 P—QB3	Kt—B3
10 P—KB4	Q—K2
11 Kt—B3	B—Q2
12 Q—Q2	O—O
13 B—Q3	P—B5
14 B—B2	P—QKt4
15 O—O	P—QR4
16 QR—K1	P—Kt5

17 P—B5!	P x KBP
18 P—Kt4!!	P x KtP
19 Kt—Kt5	P—Kt3
20 R—B6!	K—Kt2
21 R(1)—KB1	B—K1
22 Q—B4	Kt—Q1
23 P—K6	R—R3
24 Q—K5	K—R3
25 R(1)—B5!!	P x KP
26 Kt—B7ch	Q x Kt
27 R—R5ch	K—Kt2
28 R x P mate	

---

170. St. Petersburg Congress, 1909.

A great battle for supremacy.

QUEEN'S GAMBIT DECLINED

A. RUBINSTEIN White	DR. E. LASKER Black
1 P—Q4	P—Q4
2 Kt—KB3	Kt—KB3
3 P—B4	P—K3
4 B—Kt5	P—B4
5 BP x P	KP x P
6 Kt—B3	P x P
7 KKt x P	Kt—B3
8 P—K3	B—K2
9 B—Kt5	B—Q2
10 B x KKt	B x B
11 Kt x P	B x Kt
12 P x B	Q—Kt4!
13 B x Kt	B x B
14 Kt—K3	O—O—O
15 O—O	KR—K1
16 R—B1!!	. . . .
16	R x Kt?
17 R x Bch	P x R
18 Q—B1!!	R x P!
19 P x R	R—Q2

20 Q x Pch	K—Q1
21 R—B4!	P—B4
22 Q—B5!	Q—K2
23 Q x Qch	K x Q
24 R x P	R—Q8ch
25 K—B2	R—Q7ch
26 K—B3	R x QKtP
27 R—QR5!	R—Kt2
28 R—R6!	K—B1
29 P—K4	R—B2
30 P—KR4	K—B2
31 P—Kt4	K—B1
32 K—B4	K—K2
33 P—R5	P—R3
34 K—B5	K—B2
35 P—K5	R—Kt2
36 R—Q6	K—K2
37 R—R6	K—B2
38 R—Q6	K—B1
39 R—B6	K—B2
40 P—R3!	Resigns

---

171. Paris, 1909

Magnificent!

DANISH GAMBIT

White	Black
D. JANOWSKI	DR. E. LASKER
B. SOLDATENKOFF	J. TAUBENHAUS
1 P—K4	P—K4
2 P—Q4	P x P
3 P—QB3	P x P
4 B—QB4	P x P
5 B x P	Kt—KB3
6 P—K5	B—Kt5ch
7 Kt—B3	Q—K2
8 Kt—K2	Kt—K5
9 O—O	Kt x Kt
10 B x Kt	B x B
11 Kt x B	O—O
12 Kt—Q5!	Q x P
13 R—K1	Q—Q3
14 Q—R5	P—QB3
15 Kt—B7!	P—KKt3
16 Q—R6	Q x Kt
17 B x Pch!	K x B
18 Q x RPch	K—B3
19 Q—R4ch	K—Kt2
20 R—K7ch	R—B2
21 Q—Q4ch	K—B1
22 Q—R8ch	K x R
23 R—K1ch!	K—Q3
24 Q—K5 mate	

---

172. Vienna, 1910.

A Grandmaster who has written many books on chess was once checkmated in eleven moves. Here is the game:

CARO-KANN DEFENSE

R. RETI	DR. S. TARTAKOWER
White	Black
1 P—K4	P—QB3
2 P—Q4	P—Q4
3 Kt—QB3	P x P
4 Kt x P	Kt—KB3
5 Q—Q3	P—K4?
6 P x P	Q—R4ch
7 B—Q2	Q x KP
8 O—O—O	Kt x Kt?
9 Q—Q8ch!!	K x Q
10 B—Kt5ch	K—B2
11 B—Q8 mate	

---

173. Match, 1910.

White's 32nd and 38th moves have been greatly admired.

QUEEN'S GAMBIT DECLINED

R. SPIELMANN White	J. MIESES Black
1 P—Q4	P—Q4
2 P—QB4	P—K3
3 Kt—QB3	Kt—KB3
4 B—Kt5	QKt—Q2
5 Kt—B3	P—B3
6 P—K3	Q—R4
7 Kt—Q2	B—Kt5
8 Q—B2	P x P
9 B x Kt	Kt x B
10 Kt x P	Q—B2
11 B—Q3	B—Q2
12 P—QR3	B—Q3?
13 P—K4	P—K4
14 P—B4!	P x QP
15 P—K5	B—KB1
16 P x Kt	P x Kt
17 Q—K2ch!	K—Q1
18 O—O—O!	Q x Pch
19 K—Kt1	K—B2
20 KR—B1	Q—Kt4
21 P—KR4!	Q—QB4
22 P x P	B x P
23 R x P	B—Q5
24 R x Bch!	K x R
25 Q—Kt4ch	K—B2

26 Q—B4ch	B—K4
27 Kt x B	QR—KB1
28 Q—R2!	Q—B7!
29 B—B2	KR—Kt1
30 R—Q7ch	K—Kt3
31 Kt—B4ch	K—R3
32 Q—B7!!	Q—B8ch
33 K—R2	Q x Ktch
34 P—Kt3	Q—Kt4
35 P—R4!	Q—Kt3
36 B—Q3ch	K—R4
37 Q—K5ch!	P—B4
38 R x KtP!!	R x Pch
39 K—R3	R—Kt5
40 R x Q	P x R
41 Q—B7	Resigns

---

174. San Sebastian, 1911.

Brilliancy Prize

RUY LOPEZ

J. R. CAPABLANCA White	DR. BERNSTEIN Black
1 P—K4	P—K4
2 Kt—KB3	Kt—QB3
3 B—Kt5	Kt—B3
4 O—O	B—K2
5 Kt—B3	P—Q3
6 B x Ktch	P x B
7 P—Q4	P x P
8 Kt x P	B—Q2
9 B—Kt5	O—O
10 R—K1	P—KR3
11 B—R4	Kt—R2
12 B x B	Q x B
13 Q—Q3	QR—Kt1
14 P—QKt3	Kt—Kt4
15 QR—Q1	Q—K4
16 Q—K3	Kt—K3
17 QKt—K2	Q—QR4
18 Kt—B5!	Kt—B4
19 Kt(2)—Q4	K—R2
20 P—KKt4	QR—K1
21 P—KB3	Kt—K3
22 Kt—K2!	Q x P

23 Kt(2)—Kt3!	Q x BP
24 R—QB1	Q—Kt7
25 Kt—R5	R—KR1
26 R—K2	Q—K4
27 P—B4	Q—Kt4
28 Kt(B5) x KtP!	Kt—B4?
29 Kt x R	B x Kt
30 Q—QB3	P—B3
31 Kt x Pch	K—Kt3
32 Kt—R5	R—Kt1
33 P—B5ch	K—Kt4
34 Q—K3ch	K—R5
35 Q—Kt3ch	K—Kt4
36 P—R4 mate	

The march of the Knight initiated at move 22 and which decides the game is one of the longest combinations on record.

---

175. Carlsbad, 1911.

Black is forced into a tragicomic zugzwang!

FOUR KNIGHTS' GAME

R. SPIELMANN	A. RUBINSTEIN
White	Black
1 P—K4	P—K4
2 Kt—KB3	Kt—QB3
3 Kt—B3	Kt—B3
4 B—Kt5	B—Kt5
5 O—O	O—O
6 P—Q3	P—Q3
7 B—Kt5	B x Kt
8 P x B	Q—K2
9 R—K1	Kt—Q1
10 P—Q4	Kt—K3
11 B—QB1	P—B3
12 B—B1	R—Q1
13 P—Kt3	Q—B2
14 Kt—R4	P—Q4
15 P—KB4!	P x BP
16 P—K5	Kt—K5
17 P x P	P—KB4
18 P x P e. p.	Kt x P(B3)
19 P—B5	Kt—B1
20 Q—B3	Q—B2
21 B—Q3	B—Q2
22 B—KB4	R—K1
23 B—K5	P—B4
24 K—R1	P—B5
25 B—K2	B—B3
26 Q—B4	Kt(1)—Q2
27 B—B3	R—K2
28 R—K2	R—KB1
29 R—KKt1	Q—K1
30 R(2)—Kt2	R(B)—B2
31 Q—R6!	K—B1

32 Kt—Kt6ch!	P x Kt
33 Q—R8ch	Kt—Kt1
34 B—Q6!	Q—Q1
35 R x P	Kt—B3
36 R x Kt!	R x R

Four death dealing blows now terminate the game.

37 R x P	K—K1
38 R x Ktch	R—B1
39 R x Rch	K—Q2
40 R x Q mate	

---

176. Carlsbad, 1911.

A superb game.

RUY LOPEZ

O. DURAS	E. COHN
White	Black
1 P—K4	P—K4
2 Kt—KB3	Kt—QB3
3 B—Kt5	P—QR3
4 B—R4	Kt—B3
5 P—Q3	P—Q3
6 P—B4	P—KKt3
7 P—Q4	P x P
8 Kt x P	B—Q2
9 Kt x Kt	P x Kt
10 O—O	B—Kt2
11 P—B5	O—O
12 Kt—B3	Q—K2
13 P x P	P x P
14 P—B3	P—Q4!
15 R—K1	P—Q5!
16 Kt—K2	P—B4
17 Kt—B4	B—K3
18 P—QKt3	KR—Q1
19 Kt—Q3	B—Q2
20 B x B	Kt x B
21 B—R3	QR—B1
22 R—QB1	B—B1
23 Q—Q2	Q—R5
24 P—Kt3	Q—R4
25 K—Kt2	P—B5
26 Kt—B4	Q—K4
27 B x B	P—B6
28 Q—Q3	Kt x B
29 Kt—Q5!	R x Kt!
30 P x R	Q x P
31 R(K1)—Q1	Kt—K3

32 Q x RP!	R—R1
33 Q—K2	P—Q6!
34 R x QP	Q—KKt4
35 Q—K3!	R x Pch
36 K—Kt1	Q—KR4
37 P—R4	Q—KB4
38 R(3) x P	Q—R6
39 R—B8ch	K—Kt2
40 Q—K5ch	P—B3
41 R(1)—B7ch!	K—R3
42 Q—K3ch!	P—Kt4
43 P x Pch	Kt x P
44 R x Pch!	K x R
45 Q—K7ch	K—Kt3
46 R—Kt8ch	K—B4
47 R x Ktch!	Resigns

---

177. Carlsbad, 1911.

A surprise sacrifice decides

RUY LOPEZ

R. TEICHMANN	C. SCHLECHTER
White	Black
1 P—K4	P—K4
2 Kt—KB3	Kt—QB3
3 B—Kt5	P—QR3
4 B—R4	Kt—B3
5 O—O	B—K2
6 R—K1	P—QKt4
7 B—Kt3	P—Q3
8 P—B3	O—O
9 P—Q3	Kt—QR4
10 B—B2	P—B4
11 QKt—Q2	Q—B2
12 Kt—B1	Kt—B3
13 Kt—K3	B—Kt2
14 Kt—B5	KR—K1
15 B—Kt5	Kt—Q2
16 B—Kt3	Kt—B1
17 B—Q5	Kt—Kt3
18 B x B	Kt(Kt3) x B
19 B x Pch!	K x B
20 Kt—Kt5ch	K—Kt1
21 Q—R5	Kt x Kt
22 Q x Pch	K—B1
23 Q x Ktch	K—Kt1

24 Q—Kt6!	Q—Q2
25 R—K3	Resigns

---

178. St. Petersburg, March, 1912.

Black refutes his opponent's weak play in artistic style.

SICILIAN DEFENSE

POTEMKIN	DR. A. ALEKHINE
White	Black
1 P—K4	P—QB4
2 P—KKt3	P—KKt3
3 B—Kt2	B—Kt2
4 Kt—K2	Kt—QB3
5 P—QB3	Kt—B3
6 Kt—R3	P—Q4
7 P x P	Kt x P
8 Kt—B2	O—O
9 P—Q4	P x P
10 P x P	B—Kt5
11 P—B3	B—B4
12 Kt—K3	Q—R4ch
13 K—B2	Kt(4)—Kt5
14 Kt x B	Q x Kt
15 P—Kt4	Kt—Q6ch
16 K—Kt3	Kt x QP!
17 P x Q	Kt x Pch

Mate in two

---

179. City of London Chess Club Skittle game played in 1912.

Catiline abandoned by the Senators.

EDWARD LASKER	G. A. THOMAS
White	Black
1 P—Q4	P—KB4
2 Kt—QB3	Kt—KB3
3 Kt—B3	P—K3
4 B—Kt5	B—K2?
5 B x Kt	B x B
6 P—K4	P x P
7 Kt x P	P—QKt3
8 Kt—K5	O—O
9 B—Q3	B—Kt2?
10 Q—R5!	Q—K2

White announces *mate* in 8 moves.

11 Q x Pch!!	K x Q
12 Kt x Bch	K—R3
13 Kt(5)—Kt4ch	K—Kt4
14 P—R4ch	K—B5
15 P—Kt3ch	K—B6
16 B—K2ch	K—Kt7
17 R—R2ch	K—Kt8
18 K—Q2 mate	

---

180. Match Game, Biarritz, September, 1912.

A Dare-devil's Challenge.

PETROFF DEFENSE

D. JANOWSKI	F. J. MARSHALL
White	Black
1 P—K4	P—K4
2 Kt—KB3	Kt—KB3
3 Kt x P	P—Q3
4 Kt—KB3	Kt x P
5 P—Q4	P—Q4
6 B—Q3	B—Q3
7 P—B4	B—Kt5ch
8 K—B1	O—O
9 P x P	Q x P

10 Q—B2	R—K1
11 Kt—B3	Kt x Kt
12 P x Kt	Q x Kt!!
13 P x B	Kt—B3
14 B—Kt2	Kt x KtP
15 B x Pch	K—R1
16 P x Q	B—R6ch
17 K—Kt1	Kt x Q
18 B x Kt	R—K7
19 R—QB1	QR—K1
20 B—B3	R(1)—K6!
21 B—Kt4	R(6) x P!
22 B—Q1	R—B3
Resigns	

---

181. Masters' Tournament, Stockholm, 1912.

Brilliancy Prize

RUY LOPEZ

FRIDLIZIUS White	DR. A. ALEKHINE Black
1 P—K4	P—K4
2 Kt—KB3	Kt—QB3
3 B—Kt5	P—QR3
4 B—R4	Kt—B3
5 Kt—B3	B—B4
6 O—O	P—QKt4
7 B—Kt3	P—Q3
8 P—Q3	B—KKt5
9 B—K3	Kt—Q5
10 B x Kt	B x B
11 P—KR3	P—KR4
12 Q—K2	Kt—Q2!?
13 Kt—Q1	Kt—B1
14 P—B3	B—R2
15 Kt—K3	B—Q2
16 P—Q4	Kt—Kt3
17 Q—Q2	B—B3
18 Kt—Q5	R—QB1
19 QR—Q1	O—O
20 K—R2	B—Kt2
21 R—KKt1	P—QB3
22 Kt—K3	Q—B3
23 Kt—B5	P—Q4
24 Kt—Kt3!	P—R5
25 Kt—R5	Q—Q3
26 Q—Kt5!	P x Pch
27 P—K5	Q—K3
28 P x P	P—QB4
29 Kt x RP	P x P
30 KR—K1	B—Kt1
31 P—B4	Q—K2

32 Kt—B6ch!!	P x Kt
33 P x P	B x Pch
34 Q x B	Q xR
35 Kt x Kt	Q—K5
36 Kt—K7ch	K—R1
37 R x P!!	Q—R2
38 Q—R4	R—B5
39 B x R	QP x B
40 Q x Qch	K x Q
41 R—R4 mate	

---

182. International Tourney, Breslau, 1912.

This contains the most beautiful move ever played!

FRENCH DEFENSE

S. LEWITZKY White	F. J. MARSHALL Black
1 P—Q4	P—K3
2 P—K4	P—Q4
3 Kt—QB3	P—QB4

4	Kt—B3	Kt—QB3
5	KP x P	KP x P
6	B—K2	Kt—B3
7	O—O	B—K2
8	B—KKt5	O—O
9	P x P	B—K3
10	Kt—Q4	B x P
11	Kt x B	P x Kt
12	B—Kt4	Q—Q3
13	B—R3	QR—K1
14	Q—Q2	B—Kt5!
15	B x Kt	R x B
16	QR—Q1	Q—B4
17	Q—K2	B x Kt
18	P x B	Q x P
19	R x P	Kt—Q5
20	Q—R5	QR—KB1
21	R—K5	R—R3
22	Q—Kt5	R x B
23	R—QB5	Q—KKt6!!
	Resigns	

183. Havana, 1913.

First Brilliancy Prize

INDIAN DEFENSE

J. Corzo — J. R. Capablanca

	White	Black
1	P—Q4	Kt—KB3
2	P—QB4	P—Q3
3	Kt—QB3	QKt—Q2
4	P—K4	P—K4
5	P—B4	P x QP
6	Q x P	Kt—B4
7	B—K3	Q—K2
8	Kt—Q5	Kt x Kt
9	KP x Kt	B—B4
10	Kt—B3	P—KKt3!
11	K—B2	R—KKt1
12	R—K1	B—Kt2
13	Q—Q1	Kt—K5ch
14	K—Kt1	K—B1
15	B—Q4	P—KKt4*
16	B x Bch	R x B
17	Kt—Q4	B—Q2
18	P—KB5	Q—K4
19	Q—Q3	R—K1
20	Kt—K6ch	P x Kt
21	BP x P	R x P!
22	P x R	B—B3
23	Q—B3ch	Q—B5!
24	Q—K3	K—K2
25	P—QKt4	P—Kt3
26	P—Kt5	B—Kt2
27	P—Kt3	Kt—Q7!
28	Q—QB3	Kt—B6ch
29	K—B2	Q—B1
30	P—B5	Kt—K4ch
31	K—Kt1	Kt—B6ch
32	K—B2	KtP x P
33	Q—R5	Kt—K4ch
34	K—Kt1	Q—B6
35	Q x Pch	K—B3
36	Q x QP	Q x Rch
	Resigns	

**If now 16 P x P, Kt x P!! 17 B x Bch, R x B; 18 R x Q, Kt—R6 mate!*

184. Abbazia, January, 1913.

This fine game was awarded two brilliancy prizes, the Rothschild prize, and the Hallgarten Muzio-prize.

MUZIO GAMBIT

R. RETI White	A. FLAMBERG Black
1 P—K4	P—K4
2 P—KB4	P x P
3 Kt—KB3	P—KKt4
4 B—B4	P—Kt5
5 O—O	P—Q4
6 P x P	P x Kt
7 Q x P	B—Q3
8 P—Q4	Q—B3
9 Q—K4ch	Q—K2
10 Kt—B3	Kt—Q2
11 B x P	Q x Q
12 Kt x Q	B x B
13 R x B	P—KB4
14 R x P	Kt—K2
15 R—K1	Kt—QKt3
16 B—Kt5ch	K—Q1
17 R—K5	Kt—Kt3
18 Kt—Kt5!	Kt x R
19 R x Kt	B—Q2
20 Kt—B7ch	K—B1

21 Kt x R	B x B
22 R—R5	B—B5
23 R x P	B x QP
24 P—KR4	B—K5
25 R—Kt7	B x BP
26 P—R5	P—R4
27 P—R6	P—R5
28 P—R7	B x P
29 R x B	Kt—B5
30 Kt—B7	R—R3
31 P—KKt4	Kt x P
32 R—R8ch	K—Q2
33 Kt—K5ch	K—K3
34 P—Kt5	Kt—Q8
35 R—KB8	Kt—K6
36 K—B2	Kt—Q4
37 P—Kt6	Resigns

---

185. Debreczin, 1913.

Breyer's dynamic style and championship calibre, even at this early stage, are here admirably exemplified. The game terminates with an extraordinarily beautiful mate.

QUEEN'S GAMBIT DECLINED

DR. L. ASZTALOS White	J. BREYER Black
1 P—Q4	P—Q4
2 P—QB4	P—QB3
3 P—K3	Kt—B3
4 Kt—KB3	P—K3
5 Kt—B3	Kt—K5
6 Kt x Kt	P x Kt
7 Kt—Q2	P—KB4
8 P—B3	B—Q3
9 P—B4?	P—B4!
10 Kt—Kt3	Kt—Q2
11 B—K2	Q—R5ch
12 P—Kt3	Q—K2
13 O—O	P—KKt4!
14 B—R5ch	K—B1
15 P x KtP	Q x P
16 R—B2	R—KKt1
17 R—Kt2	K—K2
18 B—K2	P—Kt3
19 P—QR4	P—QR4
20 P x P	P x P
21 Q—K1	Kt—K4!
22 Kt x RP	R x Kt!
23 Q x R	Kt—B6ch

24 K—R1	Q—R4!
25 Q—K1	B x P!!
26 B x Kt	P x B
27 R x B	. . . .

27	P—B7!!
28 Q x P	Q—Q8ch
29 Q—Kt1	B—Kt2ch
30 R—Kt2	B x R mate

186. St. Petersburg, December, 1913.

Two future World Champions

QUEEN'S GAMBIT DECLINED

J. R. CAPABLANCA	A. ALEKHINE
White	Black
1 P—Q4	P—Q4
2 P—QB4	P—QB3
3 P—K3	Kt—B3
4 Kt—KB3	P—K3
5 QKt—Q2	QKt—Q2
6 B—Q3	B—K2
7 O—O	O—O
8 Q—B2	P x P?
9 Kt x P	P—B4
10 QKt—K5	P x P
11 P x P	Kt—Kt3
12 Kt—Kt5!	P—Kt3
13 Kt(Kt5)—B3!	K—Kt2
14 B—KKt5	QKt—Q4
15 QR—B1	B—Q2
16 Q—Q2	Kt—Kt1
17 B x B	Q x B
18 B—K4!	B—Kt4
19 KR—K1	Q—Q3?
20 B x Kt!	P x B
21 Q—R5	P—QR3
22 Q—B7!	Q x Q
23 R x Q	P—R3
24 R x P	QR—B1
25 P—QKt3	R—B7
26 P—QR4	B—K7
27 Kt—R4	P—KR4
28 Kt(4) x P	R—K1
29 R x Pch	K—R3
30 P—B4	P—R4
31 Kt—R4	R x Kt
32 BP x R	K—Kt4
33 P—Kt3	K—Kt5
34 R—Kt7ch	K—R6
35 Kt—Kt2	Resigns

187. Riga, 1913.

Emulating Morphy in a coruscating brilliant.

FRENCH DEFENSE

A. NIMZOVICH	S. ALAPIN
White	Black
1 P—K4	P—K3
2 P—Q4	P—Q4
3 Kt—QB3	Kt—KB3
4 P x P	Kt x P
5 Kt—B3	P—QB4
6 Kt x Kt	Q x Kt
7 B—K3	P x P
8 Kt x P	P—QR3
9 B—K2	Q x KtP
10 B—B3	Q—Kt3
11 Q—Q2	P—K4
12 O—O—O!?	P x Kt
13 B x QP	Kt—B3

14 B—B6!!	Q x B
15 KR—K1ch	B—K2
16 B x Ktch	K—B1
17 Q—Q8ch	B x Q
18 R—K8 mate	

---

188. Moscow, Feb. 4, 1914.

This ends with one of the most surprising moves ever made!

QUEEN'S GAMBIT DECLINED

DR. O. BERNSTEIN

J. R. CAPABLANCA

White	Black
1 P—Q4	P—Q4
2 P—QB4	P—K3
3 Kt—QB3	Kt—KB3
4 Kt—B3	B—K2
5 B—Kt5	O—O
6 P—K3	QKt—Q2
7 R—B1	P—QKt3
8 P x P	P x P
9 Q—R4	B—Kt2
10 B—R6	B x B
11 Q x B	P—B4
12 B x Kt	Kt x B
13 P x P	P x P
14 O—O	Q—Kt3
15 Q—K2	P—B5
16 KR—Q1	KR—Q1
17 Kt—Q4	B—Kt5

18 P—QKt3	QR—B1
19 P x P	P x P
20 R—B2	B x Kt
21 R x B	Kt—Q4
22 R—B2	P—B6
23 KR—QB1	R—B4
24 Kt—Kt3	R—B3
25 Kt—Q4	R—B2
26 Kt—Kt5	R—B4
27 Kt x BP?	Kt x Kt
28 R x Kt	R x R
29 R x R	Q—Kt7!!
Resigns	

---

189. St. Petersburg, 1914.

A Great Historic Classic.

RUY LOPEZ

DR. E. LASKER J. R. CAPABLANCA

White	Black
1 P—K4	P—K4
2 Kt—KB3	Kt—QB3
3 B—Kt5	P—QR3
4 B x Kt	QP x B
5 P—Q4	P x P
6 Q x P	Q x Q
7 Kt x Q	B—Q3
8 Kt—QB3	Kt—K2
9 O—O	O—O
10 P—B4	R—K1
11 Kt—Kt3	P—B3
12 P—B5!	P—QKt3
13 B—B4	B—Kt2
14 B x B	P x B
15 Kt—Q4	QR—Q1?
16 Kt—K6	R—Q2
17 QR—Q1	Kt—B1
18 R—B2	P—QKt4
19 R(2)—Q2	R(2)—K2
20 P—QKt4	K—B2
21 P—QR3	B—R1
22 K—B2	R—R2
23 P—Kt4	P—R3
24 R—Q3	P—QR4
25 P—KR4	P x P

26	P x P	R(2)—K2
27	K—B3	R—Kt1
28	K—B4	P—Kt3
29	R—Kt3	P—Kt4ch
30	K—B3!	Kt—Kt3
31	P x P	RP x P
32	R—R3!	R—Q2
33	K—Kt3!	K—K1
34	R(1)—KR1	B—Kt2
35	P—K5!	QP x P
36	Kt—K4?	Kt—Q4
37	Kt(6)—B5	B—B1
38	Kt x R	B x Kt
39	R—R7	R—B1
40	R—R1	K—Q1
41	R—R8ch	B—B1
42	Kt—B5	Resigns

---

190. St. Petersburg, 1914.

Youth vs. Old Age!

ALBIN COUNTER GAMBIT

DR. E. LASKER DR. A. ALEKHINE

	White	Black
1	P—Q4	P—Q4
2	P—QB4	P—K4
3	QP x P	P—Q5
4	Kt—KB3	Kt—QB3
5	P—QR3	B—Kt5
6	QKt—Q2	Q—K2
7	P—R3	B x Kt
8	Kt x B	O—O—O
9	Q—Q3	P—KR3
10	P—KKt3	P—KKt3
11	B—Kt2	B—Kt2
12	O—O	Kt x P
13	Kt x Kt	B x Kt
14	P—QKt4	P—KB4
15	P—B5	Q—K3
16	P—B6!	Kt—K2
17	P x Pch	K—Kt1
18	B—Kt2	R—Q3
19	QR—B1	KR—Q1
20	R—B2	P—B5
21	P x P	B x P
22	R—Q1	Kt—B4
23	QB—B1?	Kt—K6!!
24	R—B5!	Q—B3
25	Q—K4	Kt x R!
26	B x B	Kt—B6?
27	B x R!!	Q x B
28	Q—K5	Q—Kt3
29	Q—K7	Q—Q3
30	R—K5	P—Q6
31	P x P	Q x QP
32	R—K3	Q—Q8ch
33	K—R2	Kt—Kt4
34	R—K6	Kt x P
35	R—KB6	Resigns

---

191. St. Petersburg, 1914.

First Brilliancy Prize

QUEEN'S GAMBIT DECLINED

J. R. CAPABLANCA DR. O. S. BERNSTEIN

	White	Black
1	P—Q4	P—Q4
2	Kt—KB3	Kt—KB3
3	P—B4	P—K3
4	Kt—B3	QKt—Q2
5	B—Kt5	B—K2
6	P—K3	P—B3
7	B—Q3	P x P
8	B x BP	P—Kt4
9	B—Q3	P—QR3
10	P—K4	P—K4
11	P x P	Kt—Kt5
12	B—KB4	B—B4
13	O—O	Q—B2
14	R—B1	P—B3
15	B—Kt3	P x P
16	P—Kt4!	B—R2
17	KB x P!	RP x B
18	Kt x KtP	Q—Q1
19	Kt—Q6ch	K—B1
20	R x P	Kt—Kt3

(see diagram next page)

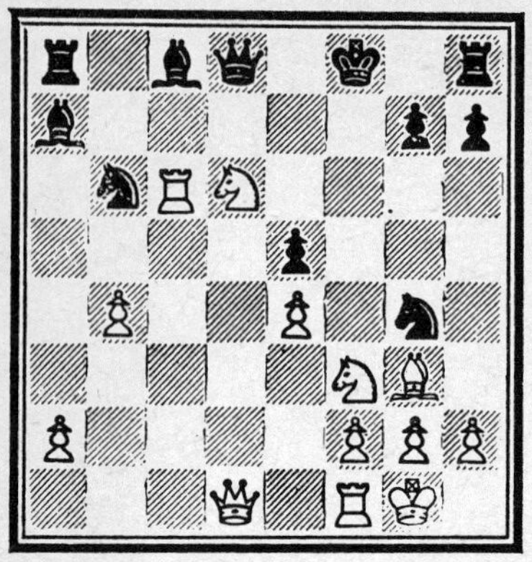

21 B—R4!	Q—Q2
22 Kt x B!	Q x R
23 Q—Q8ch?	Q—K1
24 B—K7ch	K—B2
25 Kt—Q6ch	K—Kt3
26 Kt—R4ch	K—R4
27 Kt x Q	R x Q
28 Kt x Pch	K—R3
29 Kt(7)—B5ch	K—R4
30 P—KR3!	Kt—B1
31 P x Ktch	K x P
32 B x R	R x B
33 P—Kt3	R—Q7
34 K—Kt2	R—K7
35 P—R4	Kt—Kt3
36 Kt—K3ch	K—R4
37 P—R5	Kt—Q2
38 Kt(4)—B5	Kt—B3
39 P—Kt5	B—Q5
40 K—B3	R—R7
41 P—R6	B—R2
42 R—B1	R—Kt7
43 P—Kt4ch	K—Kt4
44 R—B7	R x Pch
45 K x R	Kt x KtPch
46 K—B3	Resigns

---

192. St. Petersburg, 1914.

Brilliancy Prize

QUEEN'S GAMBIT DECLINED

A. NIMZOVICH White	DR. S. TARRASCH Black
1 P—Q4	P—Q4
2 Kt—KB3	P—QB4
3 P—B4	P—K3
4 P—K3	Kt—KB3
5 B—Q3	Kt—B3
6 O—O	B—Q3
7 P—QKt3	O—O
8 B—Kt2	P—QKt3
9 QKt—Q2	B—Kt2
10 R—B1	Q—K2
11 BP x P	KP x P
12 Kt—R4	P—Kt3
13 Kt(4)—B3	QR—Q1
14 P x P	P x P
15 B—Kt5	Kt—K5
16 B x Kt	B x B
17 Q—B2	Kt x Kt
18 Kt x Kt	P—Q5
19 P x P	B x Pch!!
20 K x B	Q—R5ch
21 K—Kt1	B x P!
22 P—B3	KR—K1
23 Kt—K4	Q—R8ch
24 K—B2	B x R
25 P—Q5	P—B4
26 Q—B3	Q—Kt7ch
27 K—K3	R x Ktch
28 P x R	P—B5ch!
29 K x P	R—B1ch
30 K—K5	Q—R7ch
31 K—K6	R—K1ch
32 K—Q7	B—Kt4 mate

The King hunt is an attractive feature of the game.

---

193. 1914.

Blindfold Chess in Prison. After the disruption of the Mannheim Congress, 1914

SICILIAN DEFENSE

E. BOGOLYUBOV DR. A. ALEKHINE

	White	Black
1	P—K4	P—QB4
2	P—KKt3	P—KKt3
3	B—Kt2	B—Kt2
4	Kt—K2	Kt—QB3
5	P—QB3	P—K3
6	Kt—R3	KKt—K2
7	P—Q4	P x P
8	P x P	P—Q4
9	P—K5	O—O
10	Kt—B2	B—Q2
11	O—O	R—B1
12	B—Kt5	P—KR3
13	B—Q2	Q—Kt3
14	B—B3	Kt—R4
15	B x Kt	Q x B
16	Kt—K3	B—R5
17	P—Kt3	B—Kt4
18	R—K1	Q—R6
19	Q—Q2	P—KR4
20	Kt—B3	Q—R4
21	KR—QB1	B—QR3
22	B—B1	B x B
23	K x B	B—R3
24	P—B4	Kt—B3
25	R—Q1	KR—Q1
26	Kt—K2	Q—Kt3
27	K—B2	B—B1
28	P—KR3	B—Kt5
29	Q—Kt2	R—B2
30	P—R3	B—K2
31	P—QKt4	KR—QB1
32	P—Kt4	P x P
33	P x P	K—Kt2
34	P—B5	B—R5ch
35	K—B3	B—Kt4
36	Kt—KB4	Kt x KPch
37	P x Kt	R—B6
38	Q—Q2	KR—B5
39	Kt—Kt2	P—Q5
40	R—R1	K—Kt1
41	R—R3	P x Kt
	Resigns	

---

194. New York, May 23, 1915.

A most extraordinary game in that the final moves were wholly unexpected.—A preachment on foraging.

DUTCH DEFENSE

	SMYTH White	H. HELMS Black
1	P—Q4	P—KB4
2	Kt—KB3	Kt—KB3
3	P—B4	P—K3
4	Kt—B3	P—QKt3
5	P—K3	B—Kt2
6	B—Q3	B—Q3
7	P—QR3	P—QR4
8	O—O	O—O
9	Q—B2	Kt—B3
10	P—K4?	P x P
11	Kt x P	Kt x Kt
12	B x Kt	Kt x P!
13	B x Pch	K—R1
14	Kt x Kt	Q—R5
15	P—KKt3	Q x Kt
16	B—Q3	R—B6
17	B—K3	Q—K4
18	QR—K1	QR—KB1
19	B x P	Q—R4
20	B—K3	Q—R6
21	B—K4	QR—B4!

22 B x QR	Q—Kt7ch!!
23 K x Q	R x KtP mate

---

195. Moscow Championship Tourney, 1916.

Brilliancy Prize.

INDIAN DEFENSE

DR. A. ALEKHINE	N. ZUBAREFF
White	Black
1 P—Q4	Kt—KB3
2 P—QB4	P—K3
3 Kt—QB3	B—Kt5
4 Q—B2	P—QKt3?
5 P—K4	B—Kt2
6 B—Q3	B x Ktch
7 P x B	P—Q3
8 Kt—K2	QKt—Q2
9 O—O	O—O
10 P—B4	P—KR3
11 Kt—Kt3	Q—K2
12 Q—K2!	QR—K1
13 B—R3	P—B4
14 QR—K1	K—R1
15 P—Q5!	Kt—KKt1
16 P—K5	P—Kt3
17 Q—Q2	KP x P
18 BP x P	P x P
19 P—B4!	K—R2
20 B—Kt2	Kt(1)—B3
21 P x P	Kt—Kt5
22 P—K6	Q—R5

(see diagram next column)

White now mates in at most fifteen moves.

23 R x Pch	R x R
24 B x Pch!	K x B
25 Q—Q3ch	K—Kt4
26 B—B1ch	K—B3
27 Q—B5ch	K—Kt2
28 Q x Rch	K—R1
29 Q x Rch	K—R2

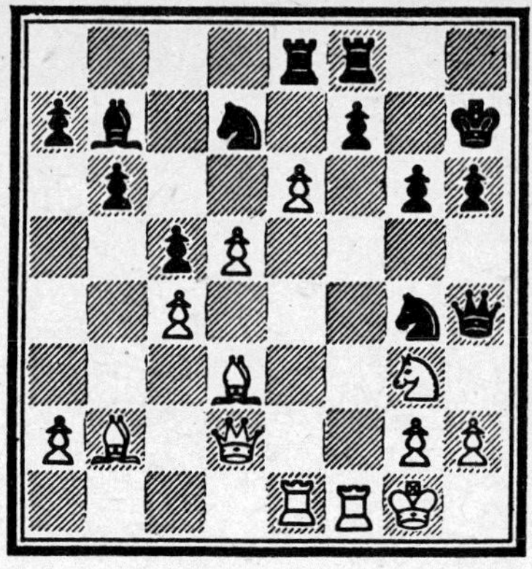

30 Q x Ktch	K—R1
31 Q—K8ch	K—R2
32 Q—B7ch	K—R1
33 B—Kt2ch	Kt—B3
34 B x Ktch	Q x B
35 Q x Qch	K—R2
36 Kt—R5	Any move
37 Q—Kt7 mate	

However, Black resigned at the 26th move.

---

196. September, 1916.

Played in a blindfold seance at the Military Hospital in Tarnopol, Austria.

FRENCH DEFENSE

DR. A. ALEKHINE	M. VON FELDT
White	Black
1 P—K4	P—K3
2 P—Q4	P—Q4
3 Kt—QB3	Kt—KB3
4 P x P	Kt x P
5 Kt—K4	P—KB4
6 Kt—Kt5!	B—K2
7 Kt(5)—B3	P—B3
8 Kt—K5	O—O
9 KKt—B3	P—QKt3
10 B—Q3	B—Kt2

11	O—O	R—K1
12	P—B4	Kt—B3
13	B—B4	QKt—Q2
14	Q—K2	P—B4

15	Kt—B7!!	K x Kt
16	Q x Pch!	K—Kt3
17	P—KKt4!	B—K5
18	Kt—R4 mate	

Certainly an amazing combination.

---

197. January, 1917.

When Checker Champions play Chess.

KING'S KNIGHT'S OPENING

ALFRED JORDAN		NEWELL BANKS
White		Black
1	P—K4	P—K4
2	Kt—KB3	Kt—QB3
3	B—B4	Kt—Q5
4	Kt x P?	Q—Kt4
5	Kt x BP	Q x P
6	R—B1	Q x KPch
7	B—K2	Kt—B6 mate

---

198. Los Angeles Chess Club, October, 1917.

An Example of Testa's Trenchant Style.

"Mr. Testa, director, actor and scenario-writer with Universal, got a strangle-hold on me in the early stages, which I was never able to shake off."—S. MLOTKOWSKI.

KING'S GAMBIT

M. W. TESTA		S. MLOTKOWSKI
White		Black
1	P—K4	P—K4
2	P—KB4	P x P
3	Kt—KB3	P—KKt4
4	P—Q4	P—Kt5
5	B x P	P x Kt
6	Q x P	P—Q4
7	P x P	B—Q3
8	B—Kt5ch	B—Q2
9	QB x B	P x B
10	O—O	P—B3
11	Kt—B3	K—B1
12	Q—B4	P—QR3
13	B—Q3	Q—Kt3
14	QR—K1	P—KR4
15	Q—K3	R—R3
16	Kt—K4	Q—Q1
17	Kt x QP	B—Kt4
18	Kt x P	Q—K2
19	Q x Qch	Kt x Q
20	P—B4	B—K1
21	P—Q6	Kt—Kt1
22	P—Q5	B—B2
23	Kt—B5	R—QR2
24	B—B5	B—K1
25	Kt—K6ch	K—B2
26	Kt—B7	B—Q2
27	B—K6ch	K—Kt2
28	B x Kt	K x B
29	R—K7	R—Kt3
30	KR—K1	QR—Kt2
31	P—QKt3	QR—Kt5
32	Kt x P	Kt x Kt
33	R x B	R—Kt1
34	R—QR7	Kt—B4
35	P—Q7	K—B1
36	R—B7	R—Q1

37 R—K8ch	R x R
38 P x R(Q)ch	K x Q
39 R x Kt	R—Kt5
40 P—QR4	Resigns

---

199. New York, 1918.

The trapper trapped

RUY LOPEZ

J. R. CAPABLANCA White	FONAROFF Black
1 P—K4	P—K4
2 Kt—KB3	Kt—QB3
3 B—Kt5	Kt—B3
4 O—O	P—Q3
5 P—Q4	B—Q2
6 Kt—B3	B—K2
7 R—K1	P x P
8 Kt x P	Kt x Kt
9 Q x Kt	B x B
10 Kt x B	O—O
11 Q—B3	P—B3
12 Kt—Q4	Kt—Q2
13 Kt—B5	B—B3
14 Q—KKt3	Kt—K4
15 B—B4	Q—B2
16 QR—Q1	QR—Q1

17 R x P!	R x R
18 B x Kt	R—Q8?

18 . . . Q—R4 relatively best.

19 R x R	B x B
20 Kt—R6ch	K—R1
21 Q x B	Q x Q
22 Kt x Pch	Resigns

---

200. Odessa, December, 1918.

One of six blindfold games.

BISHOP'S OPENING

W. GONSSIOROVSKI White	A. ALEKHINE Black
1 P—K4	P—K4
2 B—B4	Kt—KB3
3 P—Q3	P—B3
4 Q—K2	B—K2
5 P—B4	P—Q4!
6 KP x P	KP x P
7 B x P	O—O
8 Kt—Q2	P x P
9 B—Kt3	P—QR4!
10 P—B3	P—R5
11 B—B2	P—R6
12 P—QKt3	R—K1
13 O—O—O	B—QKt5
14 Q—B2	B x P
15 B—Kt5	Kt—B3
16 KKt—B3	P—Q5!
17 KR—K1	B—Kt7ch
18 K—Kt1	Kt—Q4!
19 R x Rch	Q x R
20 Kt—K4	Q x Kt!
21 B—Q2	Q—K6!!

22 R—K1	B—B4
23 R x Q	P x R
24 Q—B1	. . . .

Black here called mate in three, thus:

24	P x B
25 B—Q1	Kt(3)—Kt5!
26 Any	Kt—B6 mate

Shade of Paul Morphy, check!!

---

201. Moscow, May, 1918.

When a Mite of a Pawn becomes Mighty.

PETROFF DEFENSE

DR. A. ALEKHINE	A. RABINOVICH
White	Black
1 P—K4	P—K4
2 Kt—KB3	Kt—KB3
3 Kt x P	P—Q3
4 Kt—KB3	Kt x P
5 Kt—B3	P—Q4
6 Q—K2	B—K2
7 Kt x Kt	P x Kt
8 Q x P	O—O
9 B—B4	B—Q3
10 O—O	R—K1
11 Q—Q3	Kt—B3
12 P—QKt3!	Q—B3
13 B—Kt2!	Q x B
14 Kt—Kt5	B—K3
15 B x B	P x B
16 Q x Pch	K—B1
17 QR—K1	Q—B3
18 Q—R5	K—Kt1
19 R—K3!	B—B5
20 Q—R7ch	K—B1
21 Q—R8ch	K—K2
22 R x Pch	Q x R
23 Q x Pch	K—Q3
24 Kt x Q	R x Kt
25 P—Q4	QR—K1
26 P—B4	R(1)—K2
27 Q—B8	R—K5

28 Q—B5!	R x P
29 P—B5 mate	

---

202. New York, October, 1918.

War for Survival.

RUY LOPEZ

J. R. CAPABLANCA	F. J. MARSHALL
White	Black
1 P—K4	P—K4
2 Kt—KB3	Kt—QB3
3 B—Kt5	P—QR3
4 B—R4	Kt—B3
5 O—O	B—K2
6 R—K1	P—QKt4
7 B—Kt3	O—O
8 P—B3	P—Q4
9 P x P	Kt x P
10 Kt x P	Kt x Kt
11 R x Kt	Kt—B3
12 R—K1	B—Q3
13 P—KR3	Kt—Kt5!
14 Q—B3	Q—R5
15 P—Q4	Kt x P!

(see diagram next page)

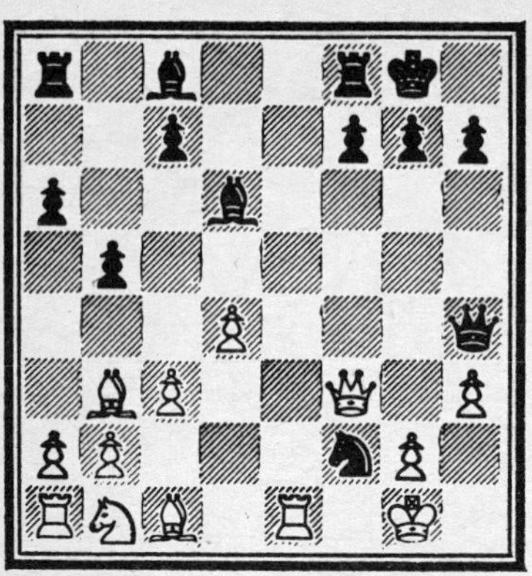

16 R—K2	B—KKt5!?
17 P x B	B—R7ch
18 K—B1	B—Kt6
19 R x Kt	Q—R8ch
20 K—K2	B x R
21 B—Q2	B—R5
22 Q—R3	QR—K1ch
23 K—Q3	Q—B8ch
24 K—B2	B—B7
25 Q—B3	Q—Kt8
26 B—Q5	P—B4
27 P x P	B x P
28 P—Kt4	B—Q3
29 P—R4	P—QR4
30 P x KtP	P x P
31 R—R6	P x P
32 Kt x P	B—Kt5
33 P—Kt6	B x Kt
34 B x B	P—R3
35 P—Kt7	R—K6
36 B x Pch	R x B

White mates in five.

37 P—Kt8 (Q) ch	R—K1
38 Q x R (K8) ch etc.	

---

203. Stockholm, 1919.

A modern classic of attacking play.

FRENCH DEFENSE

E. BOGOLYUBOV	AMATEUR
White	Black
1 P—K4	P—K3
2 P—Q4	P—Q4
3 Kt—QB3	Kt—KB3
4 B—Kt5	B—K2
5 P—K5	KKt—Q2
6 P—KR4	B x B
7 P x B	Q x P
8 Kt—R3	Q—K2
9 Q—Kt4	P—KKt3
10 Kt—B4	P—QR3
11 O—O—O	P—QB4
12 Q—Kt3	Kt—Kt3
13 P x P	Q x P
14 B—Q3	Q—B1
15 B—K4!!	P x B
16 QKt x P	QKt—Q2
17 Q—QB3!	Q—K2
18 Kt—B6ch	Kt x Kt
19 P x Kt	Q—B1
20 Q—B7	Kt—Q2
21 Kt—Q5!	P x Kt
22 KR—K1ch	Kt—K4
23 R x Ktch	B—K3
24 K—Kt1!	R—Q1
25 QR x P!	R x R
26 R x R	B x R
27 Q—B8 mate	

---

204. Gothenberg, 1920.

A magnificent specimen of Tarrasch's methodical style.

QUEEN'S GAMBIT DECLINED

J. BREYER	DR. S. TARRASCH
White	Black
1 P—Q4	P—Q4
2 P—K3	Kt—KB3
3 Kt—KB3	P—K3
4 QKt—Q2	B—Q3
5 P—B4	P—QKt3
6 Q—B2	B—Kt2
7 P—B5	P x P

8 P x P	B—K2
9 P—QKt4	O—O
10 B—Kt2	P—QR4
11 P—Kt5	P—B3
12 P—QR4	QKt—Q2
13 B—Q4	R—K1!
14 R—B1	B—KB1
15 Q—Kt2	Kt—Kt5!
16 P—R3	Kt—R3
17 Kt—Kt3	P—B3
18 Q—R3	P—K4
19 B—B3	Q—B2
20 B—Kt2	KR—B1!
21 Q—R2!	Q—Q1!
22 P—Kt6	B—K2
23 Q—Kt1	Q—B1
24 Q—B2	Kt—B2
25 P—R4	Kt—Q1
26 P—Kt3	Kt—K3
27 B—KR3	Kt(3) x P!
28 Kt x Kt	Kt x Kt
29 B—R3	Kt—Q6ch
30 Q x Kt	B x B
31 B x R	R x B
32 R—R1	B—Kt5ch
33 Kt—Q2	P—K5
34 Q—Kt3	P—QB4
35 K—Q1	P—B5
36 Q—R2	Q—Q3
37 K—K2	B—R3
38 P—Kt7	R—Kt1
39 K—Q1	R x P
40 P—B3	K—R1
41 P x P	P x P
42 K—B1	Q x P
43 Kt—B1	Q—K8ch
44 K—B2	Q—B6ch
45 K—Q1	Q—Q6ch
46 K—B1	R—Q2
Resigns	

---

205. Match, 1921

Just the kind of swashbuckling gambit play that Blackburne would have relished!

KING'S GAMBIT DECLINED

DR. M. EUWE	G. MAROCZY
White	Black
1 P—K4	P—K4
2 P—KB4	B—B4
3 Kt—KB3	P—Q3
4 P—B3	B—KKt5
5 P x P	P x P
6 Q—R4ch	B—Q2
7 Q—B2	Q—K2
8 P—Q4	P x P
9 P x P	B—Kt5ch
10 Kt—B3	B—B3
11 B—Q3	B x Ktch
12 P x B	B x P
13 B x B	P—KB4
14 O—O	P x B
15 Q—Kt3!	P—B4
16 B—R3	Kt—KB3
17 B x P	Q—KB2
18 P—B4!	P—QKt3
19 Kt—Kt5	Q—Q2
20 R x Kt!	P x R
21 Kt x KP	Q—K3
22 R—K1!	P x B
23 Kt x Pch	K—B2
24 Q—Kt7ch	Resigns

---

206. Budapest, September, 1921.

Brilliancy Prize: White extricates himself from a difficult position by highly original moves.

QUEEN'S GAMBIT DECLINED

DR. A. ALEKHINE	K. STERK
White	Black
1 P—Q4	P—Q4
2 Kt—KB3	Kt—KB3
3 P—B4	P—K3
4 Kt—B3	QKt—Q2
5 P—K3	B—Q3
6 Kt—QKt5	B—K2
7 Q—B2	P—B3

8	Kt—B3	O—O
9	B—Q3	P x P
10	B x P	P—B4
11	P x P	B x P
12	O—O	P—QKt3
13	P—K4	B—Kt2
14	B—KKt5	Q—B1
15	Q—K2	B—Kt5
16	B—Q3	B x Kt
17	KR—B1!!	Kt x P
18	B x Kt	B x B
19	Q x B	Kt—B4
20	Q—K2	B—R4
21	QR—Kt1	Q—R3
22	R—B4!	Kt—R5
23	B—B6!	KR—B1
24	Q—K5!	R—B4
25	Q—Kt3	P—Kt3
26	R x Kt	Q—Q6
27	R—KB1	Q—B4
28	Q—B4	Q—B7
29	Q—R6	Resigns

207. Vienna, 1922.

Charming reminiscence of a famous endgame compostion.

CARO-KANN DEFENSE

DR. S. TARRASCH		R. RETI
White		Black
1	P—K4	P—QB3
2	Kt—QB3	P—Q4
3	Kt—B3	Kt—B3
4	P x P	P x P
5	P—Q4	B—Kt5
6	P—KR3!	B x Kt
7	Q x B	P—K3
8	B—Q3	Kt—B3
9	B—K3	B—K2
10	O—O	O—O
11	P—R3	P—QR3
12	Kt—K2	P—QKt4
13	B—KB4	Q—Kt3
14	P—B3	Kt—QR4
15	QR—Q1	Kt—B5
16	B—B1	Q—B3
17	Kt—Kt3	P—QR4
18	KR—K1!	P—Kt5
19	RP x P	P x P
20	Kt—B5!	P x Kt
21	R x B	P x P
22	P x P	P—Kt3
23	B—R6!	Kt—Kt7
24	R—Kt1	Kt x B
25	Q x Kt	KR—Kt1
26	R x Rch	R x R
27	Q—Kt3	R—Q1
28	Q—K5	R—R1
29	R—B7!	Q—K3
30	Q x Q	P x Q
31	R—Kt7ch	K—R1
32	R—K7	K—Kt1
33	P—B3!	Kt—K1
34	K—R2!	Kt—Q3
35	R—Kt7ch	K—R1
36	R—Q7	Kt—Kt4
37	K—Kt3	Kt x BP
38	K—B4	Kt—Kt4
39	K—K5	R—K1
40	K—B6	Resigns

(*No defense against K—B7!*)

208. Vienna, 1922.

First Brilliancy Prize

INDIAN DEFENSE

A. RUBINSTEIN		E. BOGOLYUBOV
White		Black
1	P—Q4	Kt—KB3
2	P—QB4	P—KKt3
3	Kt—QB3	P—Q4
4	P—K3	B—Kt2
5	Kt—B3	O—O
6	B—K2	P—B3
7	O—O	QKt—Q2?
8	P x P!	Kt x P
9	Kt x Kt	P x Kt
10	Q—Kt3	Kt—B3
11	B—Q2	Kt—K5
12	KR—Q1	Kt x B

13 R x Kt	Q—Q3
14 R—QB1	P—Kt3
15 KR—B2	B—Kt2
16 Q—R4!	P—QR3
17 R—B7	P—QKt4
18 Q—R5!	QR—Kt1
19 R(1)—B5!	KR—Q1
20 Kt—K5!	B—KB3
21 Kt—B6!	P—K3
22 P—KKt3!!	KR—QB1
23 Kt x R	R x Kt

24 B x P!!	B—Q1
25 B—K8!	Q—B1
26 R x B!!	B x Q
27 R x R	Q—Q3
28 R—Kt7	B—Kt3
29 R—B6	Q—Kt5
30 B x Pch	Resigns

---

209. Pistyan, 1922.

Brilliancy Prize

QUEEN'S PAWN GAME

A. ALEKHINE	H. WOLF
White	Black
1 P—Q4	P—Q4
2 Kt—KB3	P—QB4
3 P—B4	BP x P
4 P x P	Kt—KB3
5 Kt x P	P—QR3
6 P—K4!	Kt x KP
7 Q—R4ch!	B—Q2
8 Q—Kt3	Kt—B4
9 Q—K3!	P—KKt3
10 Kt—KB3	Q—B2
11 Q—B3	R—Kt1
12 B—K3	P—Kt3
13 QKt—Q2	B—Kt2
14 B—Q4	B x B
15 Q x B	B—Kt4
16 B x Bch	P x B
17 O—O	R—R5
18 P—QKt4	Q—Q1
19 P—QR3!	QKt—Q2
20 KR—K1	K—B1
21 P—Q6!	Kt—K3
22 R x Kt!	P x R
23 Kt—Kt5	Q—Kt1
24 Kt x KPch	K—B2
25 Kt—Kt5ch	K—B1
26 Q—Q5!	R—Kt2
27 Kt—K6ch	K—Kt1
28 Kt x Rch	K x Kt
29 P x P	Kt—B3
30 Q x P	R—R2
31 R—K1	Q—Q3
32 P—K8(Q)	Kt x Q
33 Q x Kt	Q x Kt
34 Q—K5ch	K—B2
35 P—KR4	R x P
36 Q—K8ch	K—Kt2
37 R—K7ch	K—R3
38 Q—B8ch	K—R4
39 R—K5ch	K—Kt5
40 R—Kt5ch	Resigns

---

210. Pistyan, April, 1922.

Brilliancy Prize

BLUMENFELD COUNTER GAMBIT

DR. S. TARRASCH	A. ALEKHINE

	White	Black
1	P—Q4	Kt—KB3
2	Kt—KB3	P—K3
3	P—B4	P—B4
4	P—Q5	P—QKt4
5	P x KP	BP x P
6	P x P	P—Q4
7	P—K3	B—Q3
8	Kt—B3	O—O
9	B—K2	B—Kt2
10	P—QKt3	QKt—Q2
11	B—Kt2	Q—K2
12	O—O	QR—Q1
13	Q—B2	P—K4
14	KR—K1	P—K5
15	Kt—Q2	Kt—K4
16	Kt—Q1	Kt(B3)—Kt5
17	KB x Kt	Kt x B
18	Kt—B1	Q—Kt4!
19	P—KR3	Kt—R3
20	K—R1	Kt—B4
21	Kt—R2	P—Q5!
22	B—B1	P—Q6
23	Q—B4ch	K—R1
24	B—Kt2	Kt—Kt6ch
25	K—Kt1	B—Q4
26	Q—R4	Kt—K7ch
27	K—R1	R—B2
28	Q—R6	P—R4!
29	P—Kt6	Kt—Kt6ch
30	K—Kt1	P x P
31	Q x KtP	P—Q7
32	R—KB1	Kt x R
33	Kt x Kt	B—K3
34	K—R1	B x P!
35	P x B	R—B6
36	Kt—Kt3	P—R5
37	B—B6	Q x B
38	Kt x P	R x Pch
	Resigns	

Much can be derived from the study of this beautiful game.

---

211. Teplitz-Schoenau, 1922.

Tartakower's Masterpiece.

It deservedly carried off a brilliancy prize.

DUTCH DEFENSE

G. MAROCZY DR. S. TARTAKOWER

	White	Black
1	P—Q4	P—K3
2	P—QB4	P—KB4
3	Kt—QB3	Kt—KB3
4	P—QR3	B—K2
5	P—K3	O—O
6	B—Q3	P—Q4
7	Kt—B3	P—B3
8	O—O	Kt—K5
9	Q—B2	B—Q3
10	P—QKt3	Kt—Q2
11	B—Kt2	R—B3
12	KR—K1	R—R3
13	P—Kt3	Q—B3
14	B—KB1	P—KKt4
15	QR—Q1	P—Kt5
16	Kt x Kt	BP x Kt
17	Kt—Q2	. . . .

17	. . . .	R x P!!
18	K x R	Q x Pch
19	K—R1	Kt—B3
20	R—K2	Q x KtP
21	Kt—Kt1	Kt—R4
22	Q—Q2	B—Q2!

23	R—B2	Q—R5ch
24	K—Kt1	B—Kt6!
25	B—B3	B x Rch
26	Q x B	P—Kt6
27	Q—KKt2	R—KB1
28	B—K1	R x Bch!!
29	K x R	P—K4!
30	K—Kt1	B—Kt5
31	B x P	Kt x B
32	R—K1	Kt—B4!
33	Q—KB2	Q—Kt4
34	QP x P	B—B6ch
35	K—B1	Kt—Kt6ch
	Resigns	

---

212. London Congress, 1922.

First Brilliancy Prize

QUEEN'S GAMBIT DECLINED

R. RETI — E. ZNOSKO-BOROVSKY

	White	Black
1	P—Q4	P—Q4
2	P—QB4	P—K3
3	Kt—QB3	Kt—KB3
4	B—Kt5	QKt—Q2
5	P—K3	B—K2
6	Kt—B3	O—O
7	Q—B2	P—B4
8	R—Q1	P x QP
9	KP x P	P x P
10	B x P	P—KR3
11	B—R4	Kt—Kt3
12	B—QKt3	B—Q2
13	O—O	R—B1
14	Q—K2	P—R3
15	KR—K1	B—Kt5
16	Kt—K5!	B x Kt
17	P x B	P—Kt4
18	B—Kt3	R x P
19	P—KR4	KKt—Q4
20	Q—R5	K—Kt2
21	B x Kt	P x B
22	Kt x P!	R x Kt
23	B—K5ch	R—B3
24	P x P	P x P
25	Q x Pch	K—B2
26	Q—R5ch	K—Kt1
27	R—Kt1!	R(6)—B3
28	R—Kt3	B—K1
29	R—Kt3ch	B—Kt3
30	R x Bch	R x R
31	Q—R8ch	K—B2
32	Q x Q	R—B1
33	Q—R4	Resigns

---

213. June, 1922.

Exhibition Game at Seville

RUY LOPEZ

DR. TORRES — A. ALEKHINE

	White	Black
1	P—K4	P—K4
2	Kt—KB3	Kt—QB3
3	B—Kt5	P—QR3
4	B—R4	Kt—B3
5	O—O	P—Q3
6	B x Ktch	P x B
7	P—Q4	Kt x P
8	R—K1	P—KB4
9	P x P	P—Q4
10	Kt—Q4	B—B4
11	P—QB3	O—O
12	P—KB4	Q—K1
13	B—K3	B—Kt3
14	Kt—Q2	B—Kt2
15	Kt(2)—B3	QR—Q1
16	Q—B2	P—B4
17	Kt—Kt3	P—B5!
18	Kt(Kt3)—Q4	P—B4
19	Kt—K2	Q—B3
20	QR—Q1	P—R3!
21	R—KB1	K—R1
22	K—R1	Q—Kt3
23	Kt(2)—Kt1	Q—R4
24	Kt—R3	P—Q5!
25	P x P	P x P
26	B x P	B x B
27	R x B	R x R

28	Kt x R	Q x Kt!
29	P x Q	Kt—B7ch
30	K—Kt1	Kt x P mate

---

214. Kristianstad, 1922.

Another amazing Nimzovich finish. It is piquant . . . and pitiful!

FRENCH DEFENSE

A. NIMZOVICH		HAKANSSON
	White	Black
1	P—K4	P—K3
2	P—Q4	P—Q4
3	P—K5	P—QB4
4	Q—Kt4	P x P
5	Kt—KB3	Kt—QB3
6	B—Q3	P—B4
7	Q—Kt3	KKt—K2
8	O—O	Kt—Kt3
9	P—KR4	Q—B2
10	R—K1	B—Q2
11	P—R3	O—O—O
12	P—Kt4	P—QR3
13	P—R5	KKt—K2
14	B—Q2	P—R3
15	P—R4	P—KKt4
16	P—Kt5	P—B5
17	Q—Kt4	Kt—QKt1
18	P—B3	R—K1
19	P x QP	K—Q1
20	R—QB1	Q—Kt3

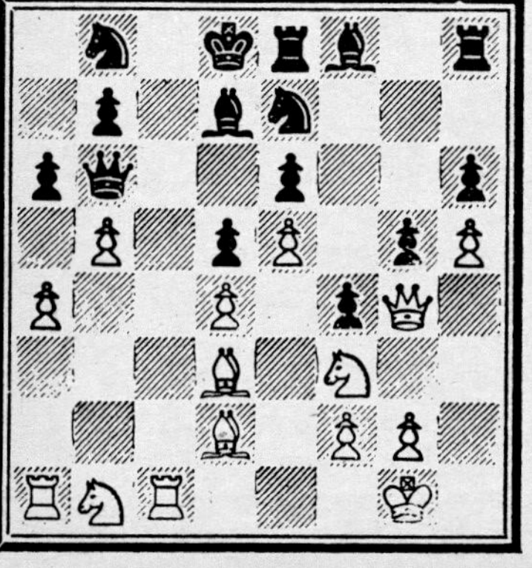

21	P—R5	Q—R2
22	P—Kt6	Q—R1
23	R—B7	Kt—B4
24	Kt—B3	B—K2
25	Kt x QP	Kt x P
26	Kt x Kt	P x Kt
27	Q x Bch!	

and mate next move.

---

215. Hastings, 1922.

The finish is played with that crisp elegance for which Rubinstein is famous.

RUY LOPEZ

SIR GEO. THOMAS		A. RUBINSTEIN
	White	Black
1	P—K4	P—K4
2	Kt—KB3	Kt—QB3
3	B—Kt5	P—QR3
4	B—R4	Kt—B3
5	Q—K2	P—QKt4
6	B—Kt3	B—B4
7	P—B3	O—O
8	O—O	P—Q3
9	P—Q3	Kt—K2
10	B—Kt5	Kt—Kt3
11	Kt—R4	Kt x Kt
12	B x QKt	P—R3
13	K—R1	P—Kt4
14	B—Kt3	K—Kt2
15	Kt—Q2	Q—K2
16	B—B2	B—Q2
17	KR—K1	QR—K1
18	P—QR4	KR—R1
19	P x P	P x P
20	Kt—B1	P—R4
21	P—B3	P—R5
22	B—B2	B x B
23	Q x B	P—KKt5
24	P x P	Kt x KtP
25	Q—B3	P—R6
26	P—KKt3	Q—Kt4
27	Kt—K3	R—R1
28	Kt x Kt	B x Kt

29 Q—B2	R x R
30 R x R	R—R1!!
31 R—QKt1	P—Kt5!
32 B—Kt3	P—KB3
33 P—B4	P—KB4
34 K—Kt1	P x P
35 R—KB1	P—K6
36 Q—B7ch	K—R1
37 Q—Q5	P—B3!
38 Q x BP	R—QB1
39 Q—K4	P—K7
40 R—K1	P—Q4!
41 P x P	R—B8
Resigns	

---

216. London, March 22, 1923.

Janowski used to call Rooks on the seventh rank, "blind pigs." They wreak havoc!

QUEEN'S GAMBIT DECLINED

B. E. SIEGHEIM (Metropolitan C. C.)	BUTTFIELD (N. London C. C.)
White	**Black**
1 P—Q4	P—Q4
2 P—QB4	P—K3
3 Kt—QB3	Kt—KB3
4 Kt—B3	QKt—Q2
5 B—Kt5	B—K2
6 P—K3	O—O
7 R—B1	P—B3
8 Q—B2	P x P
9 B x P	Kt—Q4
10 Kt—K4	P—KB4?
11 B x B	Q x B
12 Kt(4)—Q2	**K—R1**
13 O—O	P—QKt4?
14 B x Kt	BP x B
15 Q—B7	Q—Q1
16 Q—B6	Q—Kt3
17 Q x R	B—Kt2
18 Q x Rch	Kt x Q
19 Kt—K5	K—Kt1
20 Kt—Kt3	P—QR4
21 R—B5	P—R5
22 Kt—Q2	P—Kt5
23 KR—B1	P—R3
24 R—B7	P—Kt6
25 P—QR3	Q—Kt4
26 P—R3	Q—K7
27 R x B	Q x Kt
28 R(1)—B7	Q x KtP
29 R x Pch	K—R1
30 R(KKt7)—K7!	Q x RP

31 Kt—Kt6ch

and mates in two.

---

217. Carlsbad Congress, 1923.

First Brilliancy Prize.

The waiting moves in Black's combination give it rare artistic charm.

A. ALEKHINE	F. D. YATES
White	**Black**
1 P—Q4	Kt—KB3
2 P—QB4	P—KKt3
3 P—KKt3	B—Kt2
4 B—Kt2	O—O
5 Kt—QB3	P—Q3
6 Kt—B3	Kt—B3
7 P—Q5	Kt—Kt1
8 P—K4	QKt—Q2
9 O—O	P—QR4
10 B—K3	Kt—Kt5
11 B—Q4	KKt—K4

12	Kt x Kt	Kt x Kt
13	P—B5	P x P
14	B x P	P—Kt3
15	B—Q4	B—QR3
16	R—K1	Q—Q3
17	B—B1	B x B
18	R x B	P—QB4!
19	B x Kt	Q x B
20	Q—Kt3	QR—Kt1
21	Q—Kt5	P—B4!
22	QR—K1	P—KB5!
23	Q—Q7	QR—Q1
24	P x P	Q x BP
25	Q—K6ch	K—R1
26	P—B3	Q—Kt4ch
27	K—R1	R—Q3
28	Q—R3	B—K4!
29	R—K2	QR—KB3
30	Kt—Q1	R—B5
31	Kt—K3	R—R5
32	Q—K6	Q—R4
33	Kt—Kt4	R x Kt!!

34	P x R	R x Rch
35	K—Kt2	Q x RPch
36	K x R	Q—R8ch
37	K—B2	B—Q5ch
38	K—Kt3	Q—Kt8ch
39	K—R3	Q—B8ch
40	R—Kt2	Q—R8ch
41	K—Kt3	Q—K8ch
42	K—R3	P—KKt4!!
43	R—QB2	Q—B8ch
44	K—R2	Q—Kt8ch
45	K—R3	Q—R8ch
46	K—Kt3	Q—Q8!!
47	R—B3	Q—Kt8ch
48	K—R3	Q—B8ch
49	K—Kt3	B—B7ch
50	K—B3	B—Kt8ch
51	K—Kt3	Q—B7ch
52	K—R3	Q—R7 mate

Yates wins over his powerful adversary, even more brilliantly than he did in 1922 at Hastings and exactly in the same number of moves; i. e. 52.

---

218. Carlsbad Congress, 1923.

Brilliancy Prize: Black's decisive combination is admirably calculated.

RETI OPENING

	F. D. YATES White	A. NIMZOVICH Black
1	Kt—KB3	P—K3
2	P—KKt3	P—Q4
3	B—Kt2	P—QB3
4	P—Q3	B—Q3
5	Kt—B3	Kt—K2
6	O—O	O—O
7	P—K4	P—QKt4
8	Kt—K1	P—KB4
9	P x QP	KP x P
10	Kt—K2	Kt—Q2
11	B—B4	Kt—QKt3
12	Q—Q2	Kt—Kt3
13	P—KR4	Kt x B
14	Kt x Kt	Q—B3
15	P—QB3	B x Kt
16	Q x B	Kt—R5
17	R—Kt1	Kt—B4
18	Q—K3	Q—Q3
19	P—KB4	B—R3
20	Kt—B3	P—Kt5
21	KR—Q1	P x P
22	P x P	Kt—R5
23	Q—Q4	Q—R6
24	Kt—K5	Kt x P

25 R—K1	Kt x R
26 R x Kt	K—R1
27 P—R5	Q—Q3
28 K—B2	QR—K1
29 P—R6	Q x P
30 R—KR1	Q—B3
31 Q x RP	R x Kt!
32 P x R	Q x P
33 Q x B	Q—Q5ch!
34 K—B1	P—B5
35 Q—R3	K—Kt1
36 R—R4	P—Kt4
37 R—Kt4	Q—R8ch
38 K—B2	P x Pch
39 K x P	Q—K4ch
40 K—R3	P—R4
41 R—QR4	P—Kt5ch
42 K—R4	R—B4
43 R—R8ch	K—Kt2
44 Q—R7ch	K—R3
45 Q—Kt1	Q—B3ch
Resigns	

---

219. Carlsbad Congress, 1923.

Alekhine's Immortal.
Brilliancy Prize.

QUEEN'S GAMBIT DECLINED

E. GRUENFELD	A. ALEKHINE
White	Black
1 P—Q4	Kt—KB3
2 P—QB4	P—K3
3 Kt—KB3	P—Q4
4 Kt—B3	B—K2
5 B—Kt5	QKt—Q2
6 P—K3	O—O
7 R—B1	P—B3
8 Q—B2	P—QR3!
9 P—QR3	P—R3
10 B—R4	R—K1!
11 B—Q3	P x P
12 B x P	P—QKt4
13 B—R2	P—B4
14 R—Q1	P x P
15 Kt x QP	Q—Kt3
16 B—Kt1	B—Kt2!
17 O—O	QR—B1
18 Q—Q2	Kt—K4!
19 B x Kt	B x B
20 Q—B2	P—Kt3
21 Q—K2	Kt—B5
22 B—K4!	B—Kt2
23 B x B	Q x B
24 R—B1	P—K4!
25 Kt—Kt3	P—K5
26 Kt—Q4	KR—Q1
27 KR—Q1	Kt—K4
28 Kt—R2	Kt—Q6
29 R x R	Q x R
30 P—B3	....

30	R x Kt!
31 P x P	Kt—B5!
32 P x Kt	Q—B5!
33 Q x Q	R x Rch
34 Q—B1	B—Q5ch

and mates next move.

---

220. Manhattan Chess Club,
New York, 1923.

Ten Seconds a Move!

TWO KNIGHTS' DEFENSE

OTIS FIELD	OSCAR TENNER
White	Black
1 P—K4	P—K4
2 Kt—KB3	Kt—QB3
3 B—B4	Kt—B3
4 Kt—Kt5	P—Q4
5 P x P	Kt—QR4
6 P—Q3	P—KR3
7 Kt—B3	P—K5
8 Q—K2	Kt x B
9 P x Kt	B—QB4
10 KKt—Q2	O—O
11 O—O?	B—KKt5
12 Q—K1	Q—Q2!
13 Kt—Kt3	B—B6!
14 B—B4	Q—Kt5
15 B—Kt3	Kt—R4!
16 Kt x B	Kt—B5
17 Kt x KP	Q—R6!

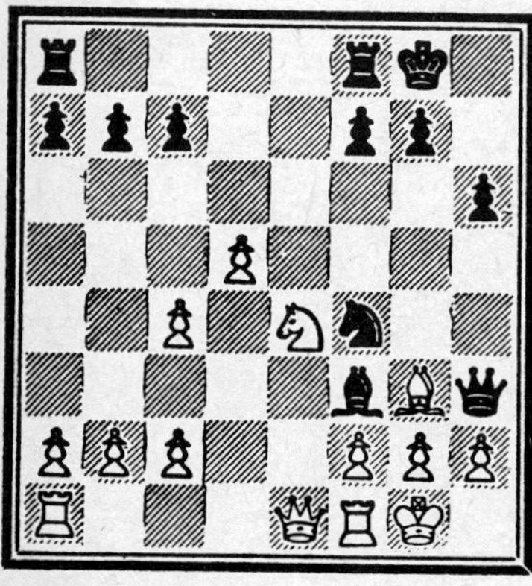

White resigns!!

---

221. Trieste Congress, 1923.

The young Peruvian master makes his debut by winning the Second Brilliancy Prize.

TWO KNIGHTS' DEFENSE

E. CANAL	P. JOHNER
White	Black
1 P—K4	P—K4
2 Kt—KB3	Kt—QB3
3 B—B4	Kt—B3
4 P—Q4	P x P
5 O—O	Kt x P
6 R—K1	P—Q4
7 Kt—B3	P x B
8 R x Ktch	B—K3
9 Kt x P	Kt x Kt
10 R x Kt	Q—B1
11 B—Kt5	B—Q3
12 Kt—K4	O—O

13 Kt—B6ch	P x Kt
14 B x P	B—K4
15 B x B	P—KB3
16 B—Kt3	R—Q1
17 B—R4	P—QB4
18 R x Rch	Q x R
19 Q—B3	K—Kt2
20 Q x KtPch	B—B2
21 Q—B3	R—Kt1
22 R—Q1	Q—Kt3
23 Q—Kt3ch	B—Kt3
24 R—Q7ch	K—B1
25 B x P	R—Kt2
26 R—Q8ch	K—B2
27 Q—B4	Q—K3
28 B—B3ch	Q—B4
29 Q x Pch	Q—K3
30 R—B8ch	Resigns

---

222. Copenhagen, 1923.

"The Evergreen Zugzwang Game."

INDIAN DEFENSE

F. SAEMISCH White	A. NIMZOVICH Black
1 P—Q4	Kt—KB3
2 P—QB4	P—K3
3 Kt—KB3	P—QKt3
4 P—KKt3	B—Kt2
5 B—Kt2	B—K2
6 Kt—B3	O—O
7 O—O	P—Q4
8 Kt—K5	P—B3
9 P x P	BP x P
10 B—B4	P—QR3!
11 R—B1	P—QKt4
12 Q—Kt3	Kt—B3
13 Kt x Kt	B x Kt
14 P—KR3	Q—Q2
15 K—R2	Kt—R4!
16 B—Q2	P—B4!
17 Q—Q1	P—Kt5
18 Kt—Kt1	B—QKt4
19 R—Kt1	B—Q3!!
20 P—K4	BP x P!
21 Q x Kt	R x P
22 Q—Kt5	QR—KB1
23 K—R1	QR—B4
24 Q—K3	B—Q6!
25 QR—K1	P—R3!
Resigns	

223. Exhibition Game, Berlin, February, 1923.

White tips over the apple-cart with a neat Queen sacrifice.

SICILIAN DEFENSE

A. ALEKHINE White	F. SAEMISCH Black
1 P—K4	P—QB4
2 Kt—KB3	Kt—QB3
3 B—K2	P—K3
4 O—O	P—Q3
5 P—Q4	P x P
6 Kt x P	Kt—B3
7 B—B3!	Kt—K4
8 P—B4!	Kt x Bch
9 Q x Kt	B—K2
10 Kt—B3	O—O
11 P—QKt3	Kt—Q2
12 B—Kt2	B—B3
13 QR—Q1	P—QR3
14 Q—Kt3	Q—B2
15 K—R1!	R—Q1
16 P—B4	P—QKt3
17 P—B5!	B—K4
18 P x P!!	B x Q
19 P x Pch	K—R1
20 Kt—Q5	Resigns

---

224. Mahrisch-Ostrau, 1923.

First Brilliancy Prize. Black must have been bowled over by Rubinstein's 25th move!

KING'S GAMBIT DECLINED

A. RUBINSTEIN White	K. HROMADKA Black
1 P—K4	P—K4
2 P—KB4	B—B4
3 Kt—KB3	P—Q3
4 Kt—B3	Kt—KB3
5 B—B4	Kt—B3
6 P—Q3	B—KKt5
7 P—KR3	B x Kt

8	Q x B	Kt—Q5
9	Q—Kt3!?	Q—K2
10	P x P	P x P
11	K—Q1	P—B3
12	P—QR4	R—KKt1
13	R—B1	P—KR3
14	Kt—K2	O—O—O
15	Kt x Kt	B x Kt
16	P—B3	B—Kt3
17	P—R5	B—B2
18	B—K3	K—Kt1
19	K—B2	K—R1
20	R—B3	Kt—Q4
21	B—Kt1	Kt—B5
22	Q—B2	B—Kt1
23	P—KKt3!	Kt x RP
24	R x P	Q—Q3

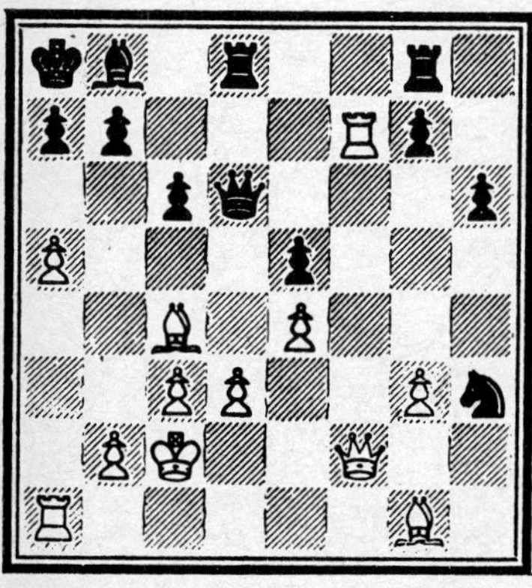

25	Q—Kt6!!	R—Q2
26	B—B5!	R x R
27	B x Q	R—B7ch
28	Q x R	Kt x Q
29	B—B5!	Resigns

225. Paris, 1924.

Here is the shortest game on record from master tourney play.

QUEEN PAWN GAME

A. GIBAUD — M. LAZARD

	White	Black
1	P—Q4	Kt—KB3
2	Kt—Q2	P—K4
3	P x P	Kt—Kt5
4	P—KR3?	Kt—K6!!
	Resigns	

226. New York, 1924.

First Brilliancy Prize.

RETI OPENING

R. RETI — E. BOGOLYUBOV

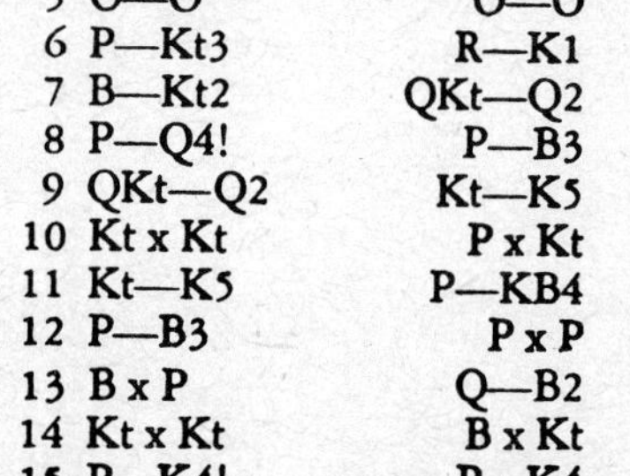

	White	Black
1	Kt—KB3	Kt—KB3
2	P—B4	P—K3
3	P—KKt3	P—Q4
4	B—Kt2	B—Q3
5	O—O	O—O
6	P—Kt3	R—K1
7	B—Kt2	QKt—Q2
8	P—Q4!	P—B3
9	QKt—Q2	Kt—K5
10	Kt x Kt	P x Kt
11	Kt—K5	P—KB4
12	P—B3	P x P
13	B x P	Q—B2
14	Kt x Kt	B x Kt
15	P—K4!	P—K4
16	P—B5	B—KB1
17	Q—B2!	P x QP
18	P x P	QR—Q1

19 B—R5!	R—K4
20 B x P	R x KBP
21 R x R	B x R
22 Q x B	R x B
23 R—KB1	R—Q1

Now comes an exquisite finish.

24 B—B7ch	K—R1
25 B—K8!!	Resigns

After White's last move you could hear a pin drop!

---

227. New York, 1924.

Second Brilliancy Prize

QUEEN'S GAMBIT DECLINED

F. J. MARSHALL White	E. BOGOLYUBOV Black
1 P—Q4	Kt—KB3
2 Kt—KB3	P—K3
3 B—Kt5	P—Q4
4 P—K3	QKt—Q2
5 P—B4	P—B3
6 P x P	KP x P
7 Kt—B3	Q—R4
8 B—Q3	Kt—K5
9 Q—B2	Kt x B
10 Kt x Kt	P—KR3
11 Kt—B3	B—K2
12 O—O	O—O
13 P—QR3	Q—Q1
14 QR—K1	P—QR4
15 Q—K2	Kt—B3
16 Kt—K5	B—Q3
17 P—B4	P—B4
18 B—Kt1	B—Q2
19 Q—QB2	B—B3
20 P x P!	B x P
21 K—R1	R—K1
22 P—K4	B—Q5
23 Kt x B	P x Kt
24 P—K5	Kt—Kt5
25 Q—R7ch	K—B1
26 P—KKt3	Q—Kt3
27 B—B5	Kt—B7ch
28 R x Kt!	B x R
29 Q—R8ch	K—K2
30 Q x KtP	K—Q1
31 Q—B6ch	R—K2
32 P—K6!	B—Q5
33 P x P	B x Q
34 P—B8 (Q) ch	K—B2
35 R x Rch	B x R
36 Q x R	K—Q3
37 Q—R8	Q—Q1
38 Q—K5ch	

and Marshall declared mate in five. 38 . . . K—B4; 39 Kt—R4ch, K—Kt4; 40 Q—K2ch, K x Kt; 41 B—B2 mate.
Marshall considers this his best game.

---

228. New York, 1924.

Magnificent Timing.

QUEEN'S GAMBIT DECLINED

A. ALEKHINE White	DR. EM. LASKER Black
1 P—Q4	P—Q4
2 P—QB4	P—K3
3 Kt—KB3	Kt—KB3
4 Kt—B3	QKt—Q2
5 P x P	P x P
6 B—B4	P—B3
7 P—K3	Kt—R4
8 B—Q3	Kt x B
9 P x Kt	B—Q3
10 P—KKt3	O—O
11 O—O	R—K1
12 Q—B2	Kt—B1
13 Kt—Q1	P—B3
14 Kt—K3	B—K3
15 Kt—R4	B—QB2!
16 P—QKt4	B—Kt3
17 Kt—B3	B—KB2!
18 P—Kt5	B—KR4
19 P—Kt4	B—KB2

20	P x P	R—B1
21	Q—Kt2	P x P
22	P—B5	Q—Q3
23	Kt—Kt2	B—B2
24	KR—K1	P—KR4!
25	P—KR3	Kt—R2!
26	R x Rch	R x R
27	R—K1	R—Kt1
28	Q—B1	Kt—Kt4
29	Kt—K5	P x Kt
30	Q x Kt	P—K5
31	P—B6	P—Kt3
32	P—B4	P x KtP
33	B—K2	P x P
34	B—R5	R—Kt7!
35	Kt—R4	Q x P(B5)
36	Q x Q	B x Q
37	Resigns	

---

229. New York, 1924.

One of the immortal games of chess history.

RETI OPENING

	R. RETI White	DR. E. LASKER Black
1	Kt—KB3	P—Q4
2	P—B4	P—QB3
3	P—QKt3	B—B4
4	P—Kt3	Kt—B3
5	B—KKt2	QKt—Q2
6	B—Kt2	P—K3
7	O—O	B—Q3
8	P—Q3	O—O
9	QKt—Q2	P—K4
10	P x P	P x P
11	R—B1	Q—K2
12	R—B2	P—QR4
13	P—QR4	P—R3
14	Q—R1!	KR—K1
15	KR—B1	B—R2
16	Kt—B1	Kt—B4
17	R x Kt!	B x R
18	Kt x P	QR—B1
19	Kt—K3	Q—K3
20	P—R3	B—Q3?
21	R x R	R x R
22	Kt—B3?	B—K2
23	Kt—Q4	Q—Q2
24	K—R2	P—R4
25	Q—R1!	P—R5!!
26	Kt x P	P x Pch
27	P x P	Kt x Kt
28	B x Kt	B—B3!
29	B x P	R—B4
30	B—R6	B—Kt3
31	Q—Kt7	Q—Q1
32	P—QKt4	R—B2
33	Q—Kt6	R—Q2!
34	Q x Qch	R x Q
35	P—K3	P x P
36	K—Kt2	B x Kt!
37	P x B	B—B4
38	B—Kt7	B—K3!
39	K—B3	B—Kt6
40	B—B6	R—Q3
41	B—Kt5	R—B3ch
42	K—K3	R—K3ch!
43	K—B4	R—K7
44	B—B1	R—QB7
45	B—K3	B—Q4
	Resigns	

---

230. New York, January, 1924.

A Perfect Gem of a Simultaneous Game, and a field day for the White Knights.

QUEEN'S GAMBIT DECLINED

	A. ALEKHINE White	A. KUSSMAN Black
1	P—Q4	P—Q4
2	Kt—KB3	Kt—KB3
3	P—B4	P—K3
4	Kt—B3	P—B4
5	BP x P	KP x P
6	B—Kt5!	B—K3
7	B x Kt	Q x B
8	P—K4!	P x KP
9	B—Kt5ch	B—Q2

10 Kt x P	Q—QKt3
11 B x Bch	Kt x B
12 O—O	P x P
13 Kt x P	R—Q1
14 Kt—KB5!	Kt—K4
15 Q—K2	P—Kt3

16 Q—Kt5ch	Kt—Q2
17 KR—K1	B—Kt5
18 Kt—B6ch	K—B1
19 Kt x Ktch	R x Kt
20 Q—K5	Resigns

Mate is now threatened in three different ways.

---

231. New Orleans, 1925.

The mad gyrations of White's Queen stamp this game as one of the finest ever played.

PHILIDOR DEFENSE

E. Z. ADAMS	C. TORRE
White	Black
1 P—K4	P—K4
2 Kt—KB3	P—Q3
3 P—Q4	P x P
4 Q x P	Kt—QB3
5 B—QKt5	B—Q2
6 B x Kt	B x B
7 Kt—B3	Kt—B3
8 O—O	B—K2
9 Kt—Q5	B x Kt
10 P x B	O—O
11 B—Kt5	P—B3
12 P—B4	P x P
13 P x P	R—K1
14 KR—K1	P—QR4
15 R—K2	R—QB1
16 QR—K1!	Q—Q2
17 B x Kt!	B x B

18 Q—KKt4!	Q—Kt4
19 Q—QB4!	Q—Q2
20 Q—B7!	Q—Kt4
21 P—QR4!	Q x RP
22 R—K4!!	Q—Kt4
23 Q x KtP!	Resigns

---

232. Baden-Baden, 1925.

Black recovers miraculously from an inferior position.

IRREGULAR OPENING

RICHARD RETI	A. ALEKHINE
White	Black
1 P—KKt3	P—K4
2 Kt—KB3	P—K5
3 Kt—Q4	P—Q4
4 P—Q3	P x P
5 Q x P	Kt—KB3
6 B—Kt2	B—Kt5ch
7 B—Q2	B x Bch
8 Kt x B	O—O

9	P—QB4	Kt—R3
10	P x P	Kt—QKt5
11	Q—B4	QKt x QP
12	QKt—Kt3	P—B3
13	O—O	R—K1
14	KR—Q1	B—Kt5
15	R—Q2	Q—B1
16	Kt—QB5	B—R6
17	B—B3	B—Kt5
18	B—Kt2	B—R6
19	B—B3	B—Kt5
20	B—R1	P—KR4
21	P—Kt4	P—R3
22	R—QB1	P—R5
23	P—R4	P x P
24	RP x P	Q—B2
25	P—Kt5	RP x P
26	P x P	R—K6!!
27	Kt—B3	P x P
28	Q x P	Kt—B6
29	Q x P	Q x Q
30	Kt x Q	Kt x Pch!
31	K—R2	Kt—K5

32	R—B4	Kt x BP
33	B—Kt2	B—K3
34	R(4)—B2	Kt—Kt5ch
35	K—R3	Kt—K4ch
36	K—R2	R x Kt
37	R x Kt	Kt—Kt5ch
38	K—R3	Kt—K6ch
39	K—R2	Kt x R
40	B x R	Kt—Q5
	Resigns	

233. Marienbad, 1925.

First Brilliancy Prize.

QUEEN'S PAWN GAME

D. JANOWSKI — F. SAEMISCH

	White	Black
1	P—Q4	Kt—KB3
2	Kt—KB3	P—K3
3	B—Kt5	P—B4
4	P—K3	Kt—B3
5	QKt—Q2	P—QKt3
6	P—B3	B—Kt2
7	B—Q3	P x P
8	KP x P	B—K2
9	Kt—B4	O—O
10	Q—K2	Q—B2
11	P—KR4	P—KR3?
12	Q—Q2!	Kt—KKt5
13	B—B4	P—Q3
14	Kt—K3	Kt x Kt
15	Q x Kt	P—KR4
16	R—R3	P—K4?
17	P x P	Kt x P
18	Kt x Kt	P x Kt
19	B x P	B—Q3
20	Q—R6!	Resigns

Dynamically magnificent!

---

234. Moscow, 1925.

The champion is outplayed in magnificent style.

SICILIAN DEFENSE

J. R. CAPABLANCA — L. ILJIN-GENEVSKY

	White	Black
1	P—K4	P—QB4
2	Kt—QB3	Kt—QB3
3	P—KKt3	P—KKt3
4	B—Kt2	B—Kt2
5	KKt—K2	P—Q3
6	P—Q3	Kt—B3
7	O—O	O—O

8	P—KR3	P—QR3
9	B—K3	B—Q2
10	Q—Q2	R—K1
11	Kt—Q1	QR—B1
12	P—QB3	Q—R4
13	P—KKt4	KR—Q1
14	P—KB4	B—K1
15	P—Kt5	Kt—Q2
16	P—B5	P—Kt4
17	Kt—B4	P—Kt5
18	P—B6	B—B1
19	Kt—B2	P x QBP
20	P x BP	P—K3
21	P—KR4	R—Kt1
22	P—R5	R—Kt3
23	P x P	RP x P
24	Kt—Q1	Kt(2)—K4
25	Q—KB2	Kt—KKt5
26	Q—R4	Kt(3)—K4
27	P—Q4? (B—Q2!!)	Kt x B
28	Kt x Kt	Q x BP
29	P x Kt	Q x Ktch
30	K—R1	P x P
31	R—B3	. . . .

31	. . . .	P x Kt!!
32	R x Q	P x R
33	Q—K1	R—Kt7
34	Q x P	R(1)—Q7
35	B—B3	P—B5
36	P—QR3	B—Q3
37	Q—R7	P—B6
	Resigns	

235. Moscow Congress, 1925,

White's windmill checks are amusing.

INDIAN DEFENSE

C. TORRE — DR. E. LASKER

	White	Black
1	P—Q4	Kt—KB3
2	Kt—KB3	P—K3
3	B—Kt5	P—B4
4	P—K3	P x P
5	P x P	B—K2
6	QKt—Q2	P—Q3
7	P—B3	QKt—Q2
8	B—Q3	P—QKt3
9	Kt—B4	B—Kt2
10	Q—K2	Q—B2
11	O—O	O—O
12	KR—K1	KR—K1
13	QR—Q1	Kt—B1
14	B—B1	Kt—Q4
15	Kt—Kt5	P—Kt4
16	Kt—R3	P—Kt5
17	P x P	Kt x P
18	Q—R5	B x Kt
19	B x B	Kt x B
20	R x Kt	Q—R4
21	P—QKt4	Q—KB4
22	R—KKt3	P—KR3
23	Kt—B4	Q—Q4
24	Kt—K3	Q—Kt4
25	B—B6!	Q x Q
26	R x Pch	K—R1
27	R x Pch	K—Kt1
28	R—Kt7ch	K—R1
29	R x Bch	K—Kt1
30	R—Kt7ch	K—R1
31	R—Kt5ch	K—R2
32	R x Q	K—Kt3
33	R—R3	K x B
34	R x Pch	K—Kt4
35	R—R3	KR—Kt1
36	R—Kt3ch	K—B3
37	R—B3ch	K—Kt3
38	P—QR3	P—R4
39	P x P	R x P

40	Kt—B4	R—Q4
41	R—B4	Kt—Q2
42	R x Pch	K—Kt4
43	P—Kt3	Resigns

---

236. Match, Amsterdam, 1922.

An old theme, but its execution is very attractive.

TWO KNIGHTS' DEFENSE

DR. M. EUWE — R. RETI

	White	Black
1	P—K4	P—K4
2	Kt—KB3	Kt—QB3
3	B—B4	Kt—B3
4	P—Q4	P x P
5	O—O	Kt x P
6	R—K1	P—Q4
7	B x P	Q x B
8	Kt—B3	Q—QR4
9	Kt x P?	Kt x Kt
10	Q x Kt	P—KB4
11	B—Kt5	Q—B4!
12	Q—Q8ch	K—B2
13	Kt x Kt	P x Kt
14	QR—Q1	B—Q3!
15	Q x R	Q x B
16	P—KB4	Q—R5
17	R x P	. . . .

17	. . . .	B—KR6!
18	Q x R	B—B4ch
19	K—R1	B x Pch
20	K x B	Q—Kt5ch
	Resigns	

---

237. Semmering, 1926.

A victory that the great Nimzovich must have relished.

ALEKHINE'S DEFENSE

A. NIMZOVICH — DR. A. ALEKHINE

	White	Black
1	P—K4	Kt—KB3
2	Kt—QB3	P—Q4
3	P—K5	KKt—Q2
4	P—B4	P—K3
5	Kt—B3	P—QB4
6	P—KKt3	Kt—QB3
7	B—Kt2	B—K2
8	O—O	O—O
9	P—Q3	Kt—Kt3
10	Kt—K2	P—Q5
11	P—KKt4	P—B3
12	P x P	P x P
13	Kt—Kt3	Kt—Q4
14	Q—K2	B—Q3
15	Kt—R4	Kt(3)—K2
16	B—Q2	Q—B2
17	Q—B2	P—B5!
18	P x P	Kt—K6!
19	B x Kt	P x B
20	Q—B3	Q x P
21	Kt—K4!	B—B2
22	P—Kt3	Q—Q5
23	P—B3	Q—Kt3
24	K—R1	Kt—Q4
25	P—B5	Kt—B5!
26	KR—Q1	K—R1
27	B—B1	P x P
28	P x P	B—K4
29	R—K1	B—Q2
30	R x P	B—B3
31	QR—K1	Kt—Q4
32	R—Q3	Kt x P

33	Kt—Kt6ch!	P x Kt
34	Q—Kt4!	R—B2
35	R—R3ch	K—Kt2
36	B—B4!	B—Q4
37	P x P	Kt x Kt
38	P x Rch	K—B1
39	R x Kt	B x Rch
40	Q x B	K—K2
41	P—B8 (Q) ch!	R x Q
42	Q—Q5	Q—Q3
43	Q x Pch	K—Q1
44	R—Q3	B—Q5
45	Q—K4	R—K1
46	R x B	Resigns

---

238. Dresden, 1926.

First Brilliancy Prize

One of the best examples of blockading tactics.

INDIAN DEFENSE

P. JOHNER		A. NIMZOVICH
White		Black
1	P—Q4	Kt—KB3
2	P—QB4	P—K3
3	Kt—QB3	B—Kt5
4	P—K3	O—O
5	B—Q3	P—B4
6	Kt—B3	Kt—B3
7	O—O	B x Kt
8	P x B	P—Q3
9	Kt—Q2	P—QKt3
10	Kt—Kt3	P—K4
11	P—B4	P—K5
12	B—K2	Q—Q2
13	P—KR3	Kt—K2
14	Q—K1	P—KR4!
15	B—Q2	Q—B4!
16	K—R2	Q—R2!
17	P—QR4	Kt—B4
18	P—Kt3	P—R4!
19	R—KKt1	Kt—R3
20	B—KB1	B—Q2
21	B—B1	QR—B1
22	P—Q5	K—R1
23	Kt—Q2	R—KKt1
24	B—KKt2	P—KKt4
25	Kt—B1	R—Kt2
26	R—R2	Kt—B4
27	B—R1	QR—KKt1
28	Q—Q1	P x P
29	KP x P	B—B1
30	Q—Kt3	B—R3
31	R—K2	Kt—R5

32	R—K3	B—B1
33	Q—B2	B x P!
34	B x P	B—B4
35	B x B	Kt x B
36	R—K2	P—R5
37	R (1)—Kt2	P x Pch
38	K—Kt1	Q—R6
39	Kt—K3	Kt—R5

40	K—B1	R—K1!
	Resigns	

---

239. Dresden Tournament, 1926.

Second Brilliancy Prize — an instructive lesson in the cumulative increase of positional pressure.

ENGLISH OPENING

	A. NIMZOVICH White	A. RUBINSTEIN Black
1	P—QB4	P—QB4
2	Kt—KB3	Kt—KB3
3	Kt—B3	P—Q4
4	P x P	Kt x P
5	P—K4	Kt—Kt5
6	B—B4	P—K3
7	O—O	Kt(1)—B3
8	P—Q3	Kt—Q5
9	Kt x Kt	P x Kt
10	Kt—K2	P—QR3
11	Kt—Kt3	B—Q3
12	P—B4	O—O
13	Q—B3	K—R1
14	B—Q2	P—KB4
15	QR—K1	Kt—B3
16	R—K2	Q—B2
17	P x P	P x P
18	Kt—R1	B—Q2
19	Kt—B2	QR—K1
20	R(1)—K1	R x R
21	R x R	Kt—Q1
22	Kt—R3	B—B3
23	Q—R5	P—KKt3
24	Q—R4	K—Kt2
25	Q—B2!	B—B4
26	P—QKt4	B—Kt3
27	Q—R4	R—K1
28	R—K5!	Kt—B2
29	B x Kt	Q x B
30	Kt—Kt5	Q—Kt1
31	R x R	B x R
32	Q—K1!	. . . .
32	. . . .	B—B3
33	Q—K7ch	K—R1

34	P—Kt5!	Q—Kt2

If 34 . . . P x P; 35 B—Kt4!

35	Q x Qch	K x Q
36	P x B and wins.	

---

240. Berlin, 1926.

Brilliancy Prize. Undoubtedly one of the most brilliant games ever played.

QUEEN'S PAWN GAME

	E. COLLE White	E. GRUENFELD Black
1	P—Q4	Kt—KB3
2	Kt—KB3	P—K3
3	P—K3	P—QKt3
4	B—Q3	B—Kt2
5	QKt—Q2	P—B4
6	O—O	B—K2
7	P—QKt3	P x P
8	P x P	P—Q3
9	B—Kt2	QKt—Q2
10	P—B4	O—O
11	R—B1	R—K1
12	R—K1	Q—B2
13	Q—K2	QR—B1
14	Kt—B1	Q—Kt1
15	Kt—Kt3	Q—R1
16	Kt—Kt5	P—Kt3

17 Kt x BP!	K x Kt
18 Q x Pch	K—Kt2
19 P—Q5	Kt—B4
20 Kt—B5ch!	. . . .

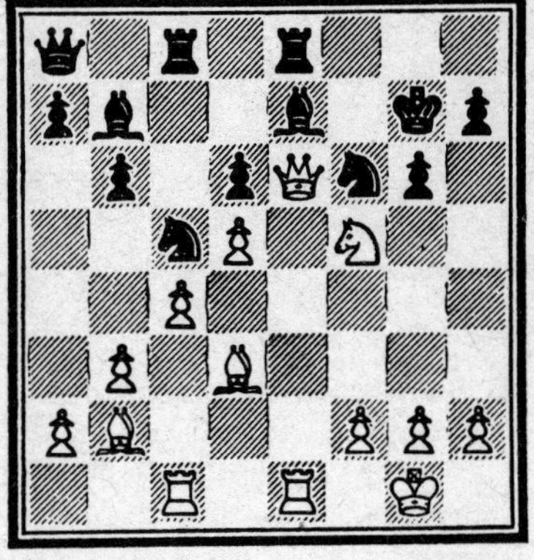

20	K—B1
21 Q—K3	P x Kt
22 Q—R6ch	K—B2
23 B x P	B x P
24 R x Bch!	R x R
25 Q x Ktch	K—K1
26 Q—R8ch	K—B2
27 B x R	Resigns

---

241. Meran, 1926

Just one sacrifice after another!

KING'S FIANCHETTO DEFENSE

D. PRZEPIORKA	J. VON PATAY
White	Black
1 P—K4	P—KKt3
2 P—Q4	P—Q3
3 Kt—KB3	B—Kt2
4 B—Q3	P—K3
5 O—O	Kt—K2
6 B—K3	O—O
7 Q—Q2	R—K1
8 B—KR6	B—R1
9 Kt—B3	QKt—B3
10 Kt—K2	P—Q4?
11 P—K5	Kt—B4
12 B—KB4	P—B3
13 P—B3	P—KKt4?
14 Kt x P!	P x Kt
15 B x P	Q—Q2
16 P—KKt4	P—KR3
17 P x Kt	P x B
18 P—B6	K—B2
19 B—Kt6ch!!	K x B
20 Q—Q3ch	K—R3
21 Q—R3ch	K—Kt3
22 Kt—B4ch!	P x Kt
23 K—R1	B x P
24 R—Kt1ch	B—Kt4
25 R x Bch!	K x R
26 R—Kt1 mate	

---

242. New York, 1927.

2nd Brilliancy Prize

DUTCH DEFENSE (in effect)

A. ALEKHINE	F. J. MARSHALL
White	Black
1 P—Q4	Kt—KB3
2 P—QB4	P—K3
3 Kt—KB3	Kt—K5
4 KKt—Q2	B—Kt5
5 Q—B2	P—Q4
6 QKt—B3	P—KB4
7 Kt(2) x Kt	BP x Kt
8 B—B4	O—O
9 P—K3	P—B3
10 B—K2	Kt—Q2
11 P—QR3	B—K2
12 O—O	B—Kt4
13 P—B3	B x B
14 P x B	R x P
15 P x KP	R x Rch
16 R x R	P—K4
17 Q—Q2	P—B4
18 P x KP!	P—Q5
19 Q—B4!	P x Kt

20	Q—B7ch	K—R1
21	P x P!	Q—Kt1
22	Q—K7	P—KR3
23	B—R5!!	P—QR4
24	P—K6	P—KKt3
25	P x Kt	B x P
26	R—B7	Resigns

---

243. Kecskemet, Hungary, 1927.

White's deep combination has pretty points.

SICILIAN DEFENSE

F. D. YATES — A. TAKACS

	White	Black
1	P—K4	P—QB4
2	Kt—KB3	Kt—QB3
3	P—Q4	P x P
4	Kt x P	Kt—B3
5	Kt—QB3	P—Q3
6	B—K2	P—K3
7	O—O	B—K2
8	K—R1	P—QR3
9	B—K3	Q—B2
10	P—B4	B—Q2
11	Q—K1	P—QKt4
12	P—QR3	O—O
13	R—Q1	Kt—QR4
14	Q—Kt3	Kt—B5
15	B—B1	KR—B1
16	P—Kt3	Kt x RP
17	P—K5	Kt—K1
18	Kt—K4	P—Q4
19	Kt—B6ch	K—R1
20	Q—R4	Kt x Kt
21	B—Q3	P—Kt3
22	P x Kt	B—B1
23	Kt—B3	K—Kt1
24	Kt—Kt5	P—R3
25	B x Kt	P x Kt
26	P x P	B x B
27	B x KKtP	P x B
28	R—Q3	R—B1
29	P—QKt4!!	B x P
30	R—KR3	Resigns

---

244. Twenty-first Match Game, October, 1927.

White's game crumbles before Joshua's trumpet.

QUEEN'S GAMBIT DECLINED

J. R. CAPABLANCA — A. ALEKHINE

	White	Black
1	P—Q4	P—Q4
2	P—QB4	P—K3
3	Kt—QB3	Kt—KB3
4	B—Kt5	QKt—Q2
5	P—K3	B—K2
6	Kt—B3	O—O
7	R—B1	P—QR3
8	P—QR3	P—R3
9	B—R4	P x P
10	B x P	P—QKt4!
11	B—K2	B—Kt2
12	O—O	P—B4
13	P x P	Kt x P
14	Kt—Q4	R—B1
15	P—QKt4	QKt—Q2
16	B—Kt3	Kt—Kt3
17	Q—Kt3	KKt—Q4
18	B—B3	R—B5!
19	Kt—K4	Q—B1
20	R x R	Kt x R
21	R—B1	Q—R1!!
22	Kt—B3	R—B1
23	Kt x Kt	B x Kt
24	B x B	Q x B
25	P—QR4	B—B3
26	Kt—B3	B—Kt7!
27	R—K1	R—Q1
28	P x P	P x P
29	P—R3	P—K4
30	R—Kt1	P—K5!
31	Kt—Q4	B x Kt
32	R—Q1	Kt x P!
	Resigns	

---

245. U. S. S. R., 1927.

An interesting portent of Botvinnik's later fame.

DUTCH DEFENSE

E. RABINOVICH	M. BOTVINNIK
White	Black
1 P—Q4	P—K3
2 P—QB4	P —KB4
3 P—KKt3	Kt—KB3
4 B—Kt2	B—K2
5 Kt—QB3	O—O
6 Kt—B3	P—Q4
7 O—O	P—B3
8 Q—B2	Q—K1
9 B—B4	Q—R4
10 QR—Q1	QKt—Q2
11 P—Kt3	Kt—K5
12 Kt—K5	Kt—Kt4!?
13 P—KR4?	Kt—K5!
14 B—B3	Q—K1
15 Kt x QKt	B x Kt
16 K—Kt2	B—Kt5!
17 B x Kt?	BP x B
18 R—KR1	Q—R4
19 P—B3?	Q—Kt3!
20 K—B1	P—K4!
21 QP x P	R x B!
22 P xR	Q—Kt6!
23 Kt x KP	P x Kt
24 R x B	B—B4
25 P—K3	Q x Pch
26 Q—B2	Q x Rch
27 K—K2	Q—R6!
28 P—B5	Q—Kt5ch
29 K—Q2	R—KB1
30 P—K6	Q x BP
31 Q x Q	R x Q and wins

---

246. Los Angeles, 1928.

A lively variation leads to a bright finish.

TWO KNIGHTS' DEFENSE

K. F. WILLIAMS	K. L. HAEGG
White	Black
1 P—K4	P—K4
2 Kt—KB3	Kt—QB3
3 B—B4	Kt—B3
4 Kt—Kt5	B—B4(?!)
5 Kt x BP	B x Pch
6 K x B	Kt x Pch
7 K—K3	Q—K2
8 K x Kt	P—Q4ch
9 B x P	Q—R5ch
10. P—KKt4	B x P
11 Q—K1	B—B4ch

and Black mates in three moves.

---

247. Trenchin-Teplitz, 1928.

A problem mate in actual play!

CARO-KANN DEFENSE

R. SPIELMANN	M. WALTER
White	Black
1 P—K4	P—QB3
2 Kt—QB3	P—Q4
3 Kt—B3	Kt—B3
4 P—K5	Kt—K5
5 Q—K2	Kt x Kt
6 QP x Kt	P—QKt3
7 Kt—Q4	P—QB4?
8 P—K6!	P x P
9 Q—R5ch	K—Q2
10 Kt—B3	K—B2
11 Kt—K5	B—Q2
12 Kt—B7	Q—K1

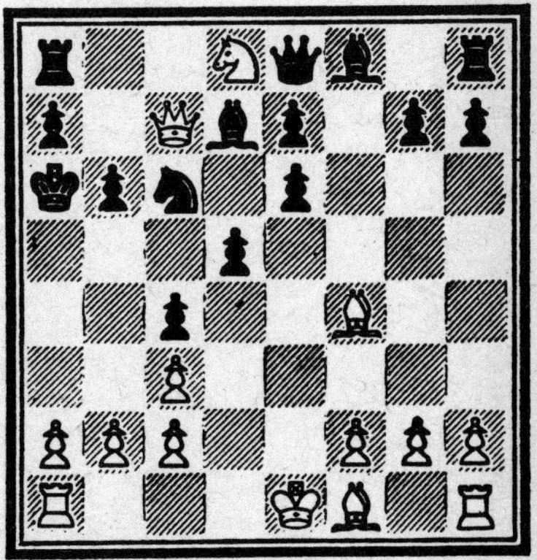

13	Q—K5ch	K—Kt2
14	B—KB4	P—B5
15	Q—B7ch	K—R3
16	Kt—Q8!	Kt—B3
17	Q—Kt7ch	K—Kt4
18	P—R4ch	K—B4
19	Q x Ktch	B x Q
20	Kt x P mate!	

---

248. Match, 1928.

Colle works up a murderous attack with his customary ingenuity.

INDIAN DEFENSE

	E. COLLE White	S. LANDAU Black
1	P—Q4	Kt—KB3
2	Kt—KB3	P—QKt3
3	P—K3	B—Kt2
4	B—Q3	P—Q3
5	O—O	QKt—Q2
6	QKt—Q2	P—K4
7	P—K4	P x P?
8	Kt x P	P—Kt3
9	B—Kt5!	P—QR3
10	B—B6	Q—B1
11	P—K5!!	P x P
12	Q—B3!	B x B
13	Kt x B	B—Q3
14	Kt—B4!	P—K5
15	R—K1	P—R3
16	Q—B3!	Q—Kt2
17	Kt x Bch	P x Kt
18	R x Pch!	K—B1
19	R—K7!	K—Kt2
20	B—B4	QR—QB1
21	Q—QKt3	P—Q4
22	Kt—K5	QR—K1
23	R x Pch	K—Kt1
24	Q—Kt3	P—KKt4
25	B x P!	R x Kt
26	B x Ktch	K x R
27	Q—Kt7ch	K—K3
28	B x R	Resigns

---

249. Rogaska-Slatina, 1929.

The game that made Flohr famous.

QUEEN'S GAMBIT DECLINED

	SALO FLOHR White	F. SAEMISCH Black
1	P—Q4	Kt—KB3
2	P—QB4	P—K3
3	P—QR3	P—Q4
4	Kt—QB3	B—K2
5	B—Kt5	O—O
6	P—K3	P—QKt3
7	P x P	P x P
8	B—Q3	B—Kt2
9	KKt—K2	QKt—Q2
10	Kt—Kt3	Kt—K1?
11	P—KR4!	P—Kt3?
12	B—KR6	Kt—Kt2
13	P—R5	P—KB4
14	P x P	P x P
15	Q—B3	P—B3
16	QKt—K2	B—Q3
17	O—O—O	Q—B3
18	R—R3	K—B2
19	B x Kt	Q x B
20	B x P!	Kt—B3
21	Kt—B4	B x Kt
22	Q x B	QR—K1
23	QR—R1	K—Kt1

24	R—R8ch	Q x R
25	R x Qch	K x R
26	Q—R6ch	K—Kt1

27 Q x Pch	K—R1
28 Q—R6ch	K—Kt1
29 Kt—R5 and wins	

---

250. Carlsbad, 1929.

Brilliancy Prize

QUEEN'S GAMBIT DECLINED

E. COLLE F. D. YATES

White	Black
1 P—Q4	Kt—KB3
2 Kt—KB3	P—QKt3
3 P—K3	B—Kt2
4 B—Q3	P—K3
5 QKt—Q2	P—Q4
6 O—O	B—Q3
7 P—B4	O—O
8 P—QKt3	QKt—Q2
9 B—Kt2	Q—K2
10 R—B1	QR—Q1
11 Kt—K5	P—B4
12 Q—K2	Kt—K5
13 BP x P	KP x P
14 P—B4	Kt x Kt
15 Q x Kt	P—B3
16 Kt—Kt4	KR—K1
17 R—B3!	Q—K3
18 R—Kt3	K—R1
19 Q—QB2	Kt—B1
20 B—B5	Q—B2
21 R—R3	P—KR4
22 R—B1!	K—Kt1
23 Kt—K5!	B x Kt
24 BP x B	P x QP
25 B x P!	B—R3
26 R—B2	R—B1
27 B x R	R x B
28 Q—Q1	P—B4
29 B—Kt2	P—Kt3
30 P—KKt4!	P—Q5
31 P x BP	P x KP
32 R x KP	B—Kt2
33 P—K6	Q—K2
34 R—Kt3	R—Q1
35 Q x P	Resigns

---

251. Antwerp, 1929.

One of ten blindfold games

MAX LANGE ATTACK

G. KOLTANOWSKI P. DUNKELBLUM

White	Black
1 P—K4	P—K4
2 Kt—KB3	Kt—QB3
3 B—B4	B—B4
4 O—O	Kt—B3
5 P—Q4	P x P
6 P—K5	P—Q4
7 P x Kt	P x B
8 R—K1ch	B—K3
9 Kt—Kt5	Q—Q4
10 Kt—QB3	Q—B4
11 QKt—K4	B—Kt5?
12 P—QB3	P x P
13 P x P	B—R4
14 P—Kt4	Q—Kt3
15 Kt x B	P x Kt
16 P—B7ch	K x P
17 Kt—Kt5ch	K—Kt1
18 R x P	Q—Q6

19	Q—K1!	R—KB1
20	R—K8!	Q—Q2
21	R x Rch	K x R
22	B—R3ch	Kt—K2
23	R—Q1!!	Q x Pch
24	K—B1!	Q x Kt
25	R—Q5!	Q—R5
26	R—R5	Q—B3
27	R—KB5!	Resigns

---

252. Manhattan Chess Club, Spring, 1930.

White gives odds of QR.
The kind of mate that odds-givers pray for.

I. Kashdan		B. Horneman
White		Black
1	P—K4	P—K3
2	P—Q4	P—Q4
3	P—K5	P—QB4
4	Q—Kt4	P x P
5	Kt—KB3	Kt—KR3
6	Q—R3	B—K2
7	B—Q3	P—QKt3
8	Q—Kt3	Kt—B4
9	B x Kt	P x B
10	Q x P	R—B1
11	Kt x P	B—R3?
12	Kt x P	Kt—Q2
13	B—Kt5	P—B3?
14	P—K6!	P x B
15	Q—Kt6ch!!	P x Q
16	Kt—Kt7 mate	

---

253. Nice, 1930.

First Brilliancy Prize

QUEEN'S PAWN OPENING

E. Colle		J. J. O'Hanlon
White		Black
1	P—Q4	P—Q4
2	Kt—KB3	Kt—KB3
3	P—K3	P—B4
4	P—B3	P—K3
5	B—Q3	B—Q3
6	QKt—Q2	QKt—Q2
7	O—O	O—O
8	R—K1	R—K1
9	P—K4	QP x P
10	Kt x P	Kt x Kt
11	B x Kt	P x P

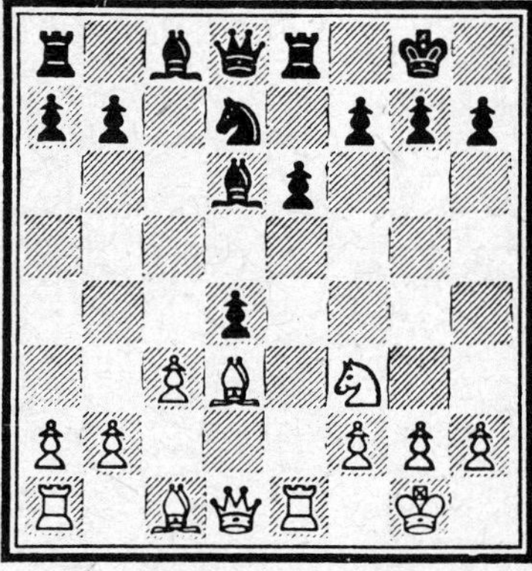

12	B x Pch!!	K x B
13	Kt—Kt5ch	K—Kt3
14	P—KR4!	R—R1
15	R x Pch!!	Kt—B3
16	P—R5ch	K—R3
17	R x B	Q—R4
18	Kt x Pch	K—R2
19	Kt—Kt5ch	K—Kt1
20	Q—Kt3ch	Resigns

---

254. San Remo, 1930.

Black concludes with one of the most beautiful mates ever seen in actual play.

INDIAN DEFENSE

E. Bogolyubov		M. Monticelli
White		Black
1	P—Q4	Kt—KB3
2	P—QB4	P—K3

3	Kt—QB3	B—Kt5
4	Kt—B3	P—QKt3
5	B—Kt5	B x Ktch
6	P x B	B—Kt2
7	P—K3	P—Q3
8	B—Q3	QKt—Q2
9	O—O	Q—K2
10	Kt—Q2	P—KR3
11	B—R4	P—KKt4
12	B—Kt3	O—O—O
13	P—QR4	P—QR4
14	R—Kt1	QR—Kt1
15	P—B3	P—R4
16	P—K4	P—R5
17	B—K1	P—K4
18	P—R3	Kt—R4
19	P—B5!	QP x P
20	P—Q5	Kt—B5
21	Kt—B4	R—R3!
22	R—B2	P—B4!
23	P—Q6!	R x P!
24	Kt x Rch	Q x Kt
25	B—B4	R—B1
26	P x P	R x P
27	R—Q2?	Q—K2
28	Q—Kt3	R—B1
29	B—Q3	P—K5!
30	B x P	B x B
31	P x B	Q x P
32	Q—B2	Q—B3
33	P—B4	P—Kt5
34	B x P	P x P
35	P—Kt3	Kt—K4!
36	R—Kt3	

Black calls mate in 4.

36	....	Kt—K7ch!!
37	R x Kt	R—B8ch!
38	K x R	Q—R8ch
39	K—B2	Kt—Kt5 mate

---

255. Hamburg, July, 1930.

Brilliancy Prize

INDIAN DEFENSE

	G. STAHLBERG White	A. ALEKHINE Black
1	P—Q4	Kt—KB3
2	P—QB4	P—K3
3	Kt—QB3	B—Kt5
4	Q—Kt3	P—B4
5	P x P	Kt—B3
6	Kt—B3	Kt—K5
7	B—Q2	Kt x QBP
8	Q—B2	P—B4
9	P—QR3	B x Kt
10	B x B	O—O
11	P—QKt4	Kt—K5
12	P—K3	P—QKt3
13	B—Q3	Kt x B
14	Q x Kt	B—Kt2
15	O—O	Kt—K2
16	B—K2	Q—K1
17	KR—Q1	R—Q1
18	P—QR4	P—B5!
19	P—R5	P x KP
20	Q x P	Kt—B4
21	Q—B3	P—Q3!
22	P x P	P x P
23	Kt—K1	P—K4
24	R—R7	Kt—Q5!
25	Q—K3	R—Q2
26	R—R2	R(2)—KB2
27	P—B3	R—B5
28	B—Q3	Q—R4
29	B—B1	Q—Kt4!
30	R—KB2	....

30	P—R3!
31 K—R1	R x P!!
Resigns	

If 32 Q x Q, R x R; etc.

---

256. Hamburg, 1930.

Exemplary precision

INDIAN DEFENSE

G. STAHLBERG White	I. KASHDAN Black
1 P—Q4	Kt—KB3
2 P—QB4	P—K3
3 Kt—QB3	B—Kt5
4 Q—Kt3	P—B4
5 P x P	Kt—B3
6 Kt—B3	Kt—K5
7 B—Q2	Kt x QBP
8 Q—B2	O—O
9 P—K4	Q—B3!
10 O—O—O	P—QKt3!
11 B—Q3	P—QR4!
12 K—Kt1	Q—Kt3
13 KR—Kt1	B—R3
14 B—K3	Kt x B
15 Q x Kt	B x Kt
16 P x B	P—Q4!
17 KP x P	Q x Qch
18 R x Q	B x P
19 R—Q2	B x QP
20 B x P	KR—Kt1
21 R—Kt2	P—R5
22 B—B7	R—QB1
23 B—B4	Kt—R4
24 R—QB1	B—K5ch
25 K—R1	Kt—Kt6ch!
26 Resigns	

---

257. Zwickau, 1930.

Black's play is studded with sacrifices.

ENGLISH OPENING

P. BLECHSCHMIDT White	S. FLOHR Black
1 P—QB4	Kt—KB3
2 P—KKt3	P—B4
3 B—Kt2	P—KKt3
4 Kt—QB3	B—Kt2
5 Kt—B3	Kt—B3
6 O—O	P—Q3
7 P—KR3	B—Q2
8 P—K3?	Q—B1
9 K—R2	P—KR4!
10 P—Q4	P—R5!!
11 P x RP	P—KKt4!
12 R—R1	P—Kt5!
13 RP x P	B x P!
14 K—Kt1	Q—B4
15 P—Q5	Kt—K4
16 Q—R4ch	KKt—Q2
17 Kt x Kt	B x Kt
18 P—K4	Q—Kt3
19 K—B1	B x Kt
20 P x B	B—K7ch
21 K x B	Q x B
22 B—K3	Q x P
23 QR—QKt1	P—Kt4!!
24 Q x KtP	R—QKt1!
25 Q—B6!	Q x Pch
26 K—B3	P—B4!!
27 R x Rch	K—B2
28 B—Q4!	Kt—K4ch!
29 B x Kt	Q—K5ch!
30 K—Kt3	Q—Kt5ch
31 K—R2	R x P mate

258. Los Angeles-San Francisco Match, San Luis Obispo, May, 1931 (Board No. 17)

White saves himself with an amazing resource.

GIUOCO PIANO

VAN ESSEN White	WOSKOFF Black
1 P—K4	P—K4
2 Kt—KB3	Kt—QB3
3 B—B4	B—B4
4 P—B3	B—Kt3
5 P—Q4	Q—K2
6 O—O	P—Q3
7 P—KR3	Kt—B3
8 R—K1	P—KR3
9 Q—Q3	Kt—KR4
10 B—Q5	B—Q2
11 B—K3	P—Kt4
12 P x P	P x P
13 Kt—R2	Kt—B5
14 QB x Kt	KtP x B
15 Kt—Q2	R—KKt1
16 QKt—B1	Q—R5
17 B x Pch	K x B
18 Q x Bch	Kt—K2
19 R—K2	QR—Q1
20 Kt—B3	Q—R4

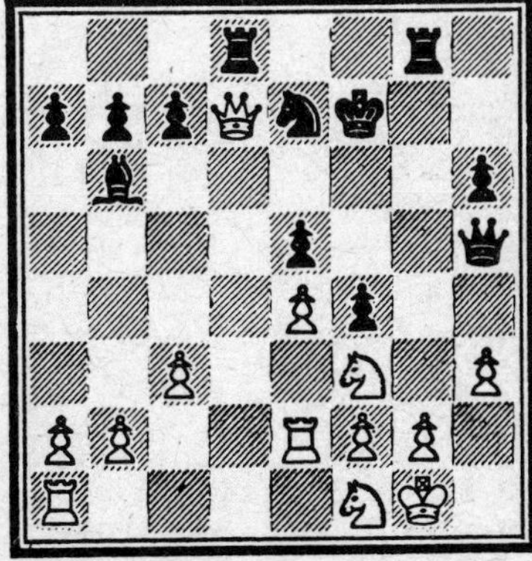

How does White save himself?!

21 Q—Kt4	R x Q
22 P x R	Q—Kt4
23 Kt x Qch	RP x Kt
24 R—Q2 and wins	

---

259. Prague, 1931.

Wild and woolly!

QUEEN'S GAMBIT DECLINED

DR. M. VIDMAR White	V. MIKENAS Black
1 P—Q4	P—Q4
2 P—QB4	P—QB3
3 Kt—KB3	Kt—B3
4 Kt—B3	P x P
5 P—QR4	B—B4
6 Kt—K5	P—K3
7 P—B3	B—QKt5
8 P—K4	B x P!!
9 P x B	Kt x P
10 Q—B3	Q x P
11 Q x Pch	K—Q1
12 B—Kt5ch!	K—B1
13 B x P	Kt x B
14 Q x KtP	Q—K6ch
15 K—Q1	R—Q1ch
16 K—B2	R—Q7ch
17 K—Kt3	R x Pch!!
18 K x R	B x Ktch
19 K—Kt1	B x Kt
20 Q—B8ch	K—B2
21 R—R3	Q—Q5
22 R—R2	Q x B
23 R—Q1!	Kt—Q2!
24 R x Ktch	K x R
25 R—Q2ch	K—B2
26 Q x R	Kt—B2
27 Q—Kt8	Q—KB8ch
28 K—B2	Q—B4ch
29 K—Q1	Kt—Q3
30 P—R5	B—B6
31 R x Kt	K x R
32 Q—Q8ch	K—B4
33 Q—K7ch	K—B5
34 Q x KtP	Q—B8ch
35 K—B2	Q—Q6ch

36 K—B1	Q—Q7ch
Resigns	

---

260. New York, 1931.

White announces mate out of a clear sky!

INDIAN DEFENSE

I. A. HOROWITZ White	A. KEVITZ Black
1 Kt—KB3	Kt—KB3
2 P—B4	P—QKt3
3 P—Q4	B—Kt2
4 Kt—B3	P—K3
5 P—K3	B—Kt5
6 B—Q3	O—O
7 O—O	P—Q4
8 P x P	P x P
9 P—QR3	B x Kt
10 P x B	QKt—Q2
11 P—B4	P—B4
12 B—Kt2	R—B1
13 R—B1	P—QR3
14 Kt—K5	P x QP
15 KP x P	P x P
16 Kt x QBP	P—QKt4
17 Kt—Q6	R x R
18 Q x R	B—R1
19 Kt—B5	Kt—Q4
20 R—K1	QKt—Kt3
21 R—K4	R—K1

White announced mate in seven(!) beginning with 22 Q—Kt5!!

---

261. Pasadena, 1932.

How to beat a champion.

CARO-KANN DEFENSE

A. DAKE White	A. ALEKHINE Black
1 P—K4	P—QB3
2 P—Q4	P—Q4
3 P x P	P x P
4 P—QB4	Kt—KB3
5 Kt—QB3	Kt—B3
6 Kt—B3	B—K3
7 P—B5	P—KKt3
8 B—QKt5	B—Kt2
9 Kt—K5	Q—B1
10 Q—R4	B—Q2
11 O—O	O—O
12 B—KB4	P—QR3
13 B x Kt	P x B
14 KR—K1	Kt—R4
15 B—Q2	R—R2
16 R—K2	B—K1
17 QR—K1	P—B4
18 Kt—B3	Kt—B3
19 R x P	R x R
20 R x R	P—B5
21 B x P	Kt—K5
22 B—K5	B—R3
23 Kt x Kt	P x Kt

24 Kt—Kt5!	Q—B4
25 Q—Kt3ch	B—B2
26 Kt x B	R x Kt
27 R x R	Q x R
28 Q—Kt8ch	Q—B1
29 P—Q5!	P—K6
30 P—B4	Q x Q
31 B x Q	K—B2
32 P x P	K—K1
33 P—QKt4	P—Kt4
34 P—Kt3	P x P
35 P x P	K—Q1
36 P—QR4	K—B1
37 B—Q6	B—Kt2
38 K—B1	Resigns

262. Pasadena, 1932.

A Steiner Brilliancy

QUEEN'S GAMBIT DECLINED

R. FINE White	H. STEINER Black
1 Kt—KB3	P—Q4
2 P—Q4	Kt—KB3
3 P—B4	P—K3
4 Kt—B3	B—K2
5 B—Kt5	O—O
6 P—K3	QKt—Q2
7 R—B1	P—B3
8 B—Q3	P x P
9 B x P	Kt—Q4
10 B x B	Q x B
11 O—O	Kt x Kt
12 P x Kt	P—K4
13 Q—B2	P—K5
14 Kt—Q2	Kt—B3
15 QR—K1	B—B4
16 P—KB3	B—Kt3
17 P x P	Kt x P
18 Kt x Kt	B x Kt
19 Q—Q2	K—R1
20 R—B4	P—B4
21 B—Q3	P—KKt4
22 R—B2	QR—K1
23 B—B4	R—B3
24 QR—KB1	R—R3
25 B—Q3	Q—Q3!
26 P—Kt3	Q x Pch!!
27 R—Kt2	Q x Rch
28 Q x Q	B x Q
29 K x B	R x P
Resigns	

263. London Congress, 1932.

The following snappy game is a fair specimen of the convincing style of the world's woman champion.

INDIAN DEFENSE

MRS V. MENCHIK STEVENSON White	SIR G. A. THOMAS Black
1 P—Q4	Kt—KB3
2 P—QB4	P—KKt3
3 Kt—QB3	B—Kt2
4 P—K4	P—Q3
5 P—B3	O—O
6 B—K3	P—K4
7 KKt—K2!	P—Kt3
8 Q—Q2	Kt—B3
9 P—Q5	Kt—K2
10 P—KKt4	Kt—Q2
11 R—KKt1	P—QR4
12 O—O—O	Kt—QB4

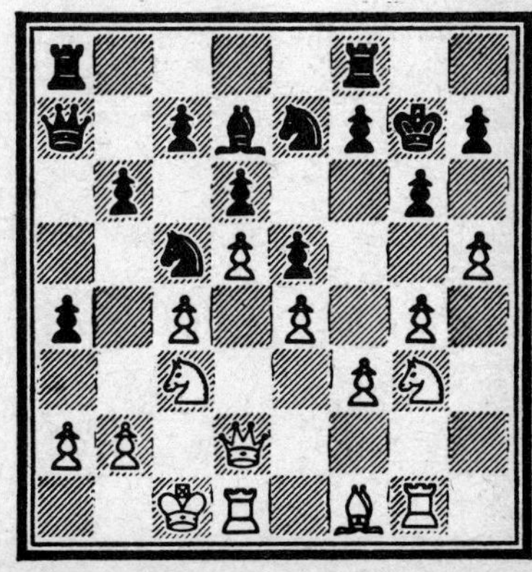

13 Kt—Kt3	B—Q2
14 P—KR4	P—R5
15 P—R5	Q—Kt1
16 B—R6	Q—R2
17 B x B	K x B
18 Kt—B5ch	Kt x Kt
19 KtP x Kt	P—R6
20 P—B6ch!	K—R1
21 Q—R6	P x Pch
22 K—Kt1	R—KKt1
23 P x P	P x P
24 Q x Pch!	Resigns

---

264. Tokio, January, 1933.

One of fifteen blindfold games.

RUY LOPEZ

A. ALEKHINE	KIMURA
White	Black
1 P—K4	P—K4
2 Kt—KB3	Kt—QB3
3 B—Kt5	P—QR3
4 B x Kt	KtP x B
5 P—Q4	P x P
6 Q x P	P—Q3
7 O—O	B—K3
8 Kt—B3	Kt—B3
9 B—Kt5	B—K2
10 Q—R4	B—Q2
11 QR—Q1	O—O
12 P—K5!	Kt—K1
13 B x B	Q x B
14 P x P	P x P
15 KR—K1	Q—Q1
16 Kt—Q4	Q—B2
17 R—K7	Kt—B3
18 Kt—B5	Q—Q1
19 R x QP	R—K1

(see diagram next column)

20 Kt—K4!	R x R
21 Kt x Ktch	K—R1
22 Kt x R	Q x Kt
23 Q—K4!	Q x Q
24 Kt x Q	B—K3
25 P—QKt3	P—Kt3
26 Kt—B5	B—B4
27 R x BP	R—K1
28 P—KB3	R—K7
29 R x RP	R x P
30 Kt—K4	B—K3
31 P—KR4	K—Kt2
32 K—R2	K—R3
33 K—Kt3	B—Q2
34 P—R4	P—B4
35 Kt—Kt5	R—B6
36 R—R7	R—Q6
37 P—QR5	K—R4
38 Kt x P	Resigns

---

265. Folkestone, 1933.

A pretty finish.

FRENCH DEFENSE

A. W. DAKE (Portland, Ore.)	CRANSTON (Ireland)
White	Black
1 P—K4	P—K3
2 P—Q4	P—Q4
3 Kt—QB3	Kt—KB3
4 B—Kt5	P x P
5 Kt x P	B—K2
6 B x Kt	B x B
7 Kt—KB3	Kt—Q2
8 P—B3	O—O
9 Q—B2	B—K2

10 O—O—O	P—QB3
11 P—KR4	Kt—B3
12 Kt x Ktch	B x Kt
13 B—Q3	P—KKt3
14 P—R5	K—Kt2
15 R—R2	R—KKt1
16 Q—Q2	K—R1
17 Q—R6	B—Kt2
18 Q x Pch!	Resigns

---

266. New York, 1933.

A magnificent display of combinative skill.

QUEEN'S GAMBIT DECLINED

R. FINE White	N. GROSSMAN Black
1 P—Q4	Kt—KB3
2 P—QB4	P—K3
3 Kt—QB3	P—Q4
4 B—Kt5	B—Kt5
5 P—K3	P—B3
6 Q—Kt3!	B x Ktch
7 P x B	QKt—Q2
8 P x P	BP x P
9 B—Q3	O—O
10 Kt—K2	Q—R4
11 P—B3	P—QKt3
12 O—O	B—R3
13 Q—B2	B x B
14 Q x B	KR—B1
15 B—R4	P—QKt4
16 P—K4	R—B5
17 P—K5	Kt—K1
18 P—B4	P—Kt3
19 P—Kt4	Q—Kt3
20 K—R1	Kt—Kt2
21 P—B5!	KP x P
22 P x P	Kt x KP
23 Q—R3	Kt—B3
24 B—B6	Kt—R4
25 P x P	RP x P

(see diagram next page)

26 Kt—B4!	Kt x B
27 Kt x KtP!	K—Kt2
28 R—KKt1!!	P x Kt
29 R x Pch	K x R
30 Q—K6!	Kt x P?
31 R—Kt1ch	K—R3
32 Q—K3ch	K—R2

33 Q—K7ch	K—R3
34 Q—Kt7ch	Resigns

30 . . . Kt—K4!! draws. Hard game!

---

267. Leningrad, 1933.

Watch the wanderings of Black's Queen!

SICILIAN DEFENSE

W. A. RAUSER White	M. BOTVINNIK Black
1 P—K4	P—QB4
2 Kt—KB3	Kt—QB3
3 P—Q4	P x P
4 Kt x P	Kt—B3
5 Kt—QB3	P—Q3
6 B—K2	P—KKt3
7 B—K3	B—Kt2
8 Kt—Kt3	B—K3
9 P—B4	O—O
10 O—O	Kt—QR4!

11	Kt x Kt	Q x Kt
12	B—B3	B—B5
13	KR—K1	KR—Q1
14	Q—Q2	Q—B2
15	QR—B1	P—K4
16	P—QKt3	P—Q4!!
17	KP x P	P—K5!
18	P x B	P x B
19	P—B5	Q—R4
20	KR—Q1	Kt—Kt5
21	B—Q4	P—B7ch!
22	K—B1	Q—R3ch
23	Q—K2	B x B
24	R x B	Q—KB3!
25	QR—Q1	Q—R5
26	Q—Q3	R—K1!
27	R—K4	P—B4!
28	R—K6	Kt x Pch
29	K—K2	Q x P
30	Resigns	

---

268. Munich, 1933(?)

Dr. Tarrasch was over seventy when this game was played!

RUY LOPEZ

AMATEUR — DR. S. TARRASCH

	White	Black
1	P—K4	P—K4
2	Kt—KB3	Kt—QB3
3	B—Kt5	P—QR3
4	B—R4	Kt—B3
5	O—O	B—B4
6	Kt x P	Kt x P
7	Kt x Kt	QP x Kt
8	Q—B3	Q—R5
9	Kt—B3	Kt x Kt
10	B x Pch	P x B!
11	Q x QBPch	B—Q2
12	Q x Rch	K—K2
13	Q x R	Kt—K7ch
14	K—R1	B x P
15	P—KR3	Q x Pch!
16	P x Q	B—B3ch
17	K—R2	B—Kt6 mate

269. Sitges, 1934.

Tartakower is trounced in the opening.

QUEEN'S GAMBIT DECLINED

DR. S. TARTAKOWER — DR. R. REY-ARDID

	White	Black
1	P—Q4	P—Q4
2	P—QB4	P—K3
3	Kt—KB3	Kt—KB3
4	Kt—B3	P—B4
5	BP x P	Kt x P
6	P—KKt3	P x P
7	Kt x P?	Kt x Kt
8	P x Kt	P—K4
9	Kt—Kt5	Q—R4!
10	Q—Q5	Kt—B3
11	R—QKt1	B—K3
12	Kt—Q6ch	B x Kt
13	Q x B	R—Q1
14	Q—R3	Kt—Q5!
15	Q—Kt2	B—B4
16	B—Q2	Kt—B7ch
17	K—Q1	Kt—R6
18	Q—Kt4	Q—Q4
19	R—Kt2	Q x R
	Resigns	

270. About 1934.

The "stairway" mate is interesting.

PETROFF DEFENSE

E. NORMAN-HANSEN — E. ANDERSON

	White	Black
1	P—K4	P—K4
2	Kt—KB3	Kt—KB3
3	Kt x P	P—Q3
4	Kt—KB3	Kt x P
5	P—Q4	P—Q4

6 B—Q3	B—KKt5
7 O—O	B—Q3
8 P—B4	O—O
9 P x P	P—KB4
10 Kt—B3	Kt—Q2
11 P—KR3	B—R4
12 Kt x Kt	P x Kt
13 B x P	Kt—B3
14 B—B5	K—R1
15 B—K6	Kt—K5
16 P—KKt4	B—Kt3
17 K—Kt2	Q—B3
18 B—K3	QR—K1
19 P—KR4	R x B!
20 P x R	Kt—B6!!
21 P x Kt	B—K5

Black now wins by force in all variations.

22 K—R3	Q x Ktch
23 Q x Q	R x Qch
24 K—Kt2	R—Kt6ch
25 K—R2	R—Kt7ch
26 K—R1	R—R7ch
27 K—Kt1	R—R8 mate

A Pure Mate.

---

271. World Championship Match, 1935.

(Twenty-sixth game)

The famous game (known as "The Pearl of Zandvoort") which virtually decided the match.

DUTCH DEFENSE

DR. M. EUWE	A. ALEKHINE
White	Black
1 P—Q4	P—K3
2 P—QB4	P—KB4
3 P—KKt3	B—Kt5ch
4 B—Q2	B—K2
5 B—Kt2	Kt—KB3
6 Kt—QB3	O—O
7 Kt—B3	Kt—K5
8 O—O	P—QKt3
9 Q—B2	B—Kt2
10 Kt—K5	Kt x Kt
11 B x Kt	B x B
12 K x B	Q—B1
13 P—Q5!	P—Q3
14 Kt—Q3	P—K4
15 K—R1	P—B3
16 Q—Kt3	K—R1
17 P—B4	P—K5
18 Kt—Kt4!	P—B4
19 Kt—B2	Kt—Q2
20 Kt—K3	B—B3?
21 Kt x P!	B x B
22 Kt x QP	Q—Kt1
23 Kt x P	B—B3
24 Kt—Q2!	P—KKt4!
25 P—K4	P x P
26 P x P	B—Q5
27 P—K5	Q—K1
28 P—K6	KR—Kt1
29 Kt—B3	Q—Kt3
30 R—KKt1	B x R
31 R x B	Q—B3?
32 Kt—Kt5!	....

(see diagram next page)

32	R—Kt2
33 P x Kt	R x P
34 Q—K3	R—K2
35 Kt—K6	R—KB1
36 Q—K5	Q x Q

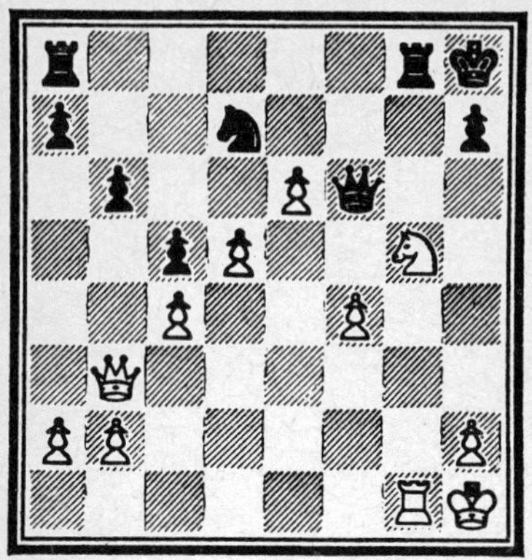

37 P x Q	R—B4
38 R—K1	P—KR3
39 Kt—Q8!	R—B7
40 P—K6	R—Q7
41 Kt—B6	R—K1
42 P—K7	P—Kt4
43 Kt—Q8	K—Kt2
44 Kt—Kt7	K—B3
45 R—K6ch	K—Kt4
46 Kt—Q6	R x KP
47 Kt—K4ch	Resigns

---

272. Philadelphia, 1936.

A far-sighted combination wins for Black.

RETI OPENING

I. KASHDAN	I. A. HOROWITZ
White	Black
1 Kt—KB3	P—Q4
2 P—B4	P—Q5
3 P—KKt3	P—QB4
4 B—Kt2	Kt—QB3
5 O—O	P—K4
6 P—K4	B—Kt5
7 P—KR3	B—K3
8 P—Q3	P—B3
9 Kt—R3	Q—Q2
10 K—R2	P—KKt4
11 Kt—B2	P—KR4
12 Kt—Kt1	KKt—K2
13 B—Q2	Kt—Kt3
14 P—R3	B—Kt5!
15 P x B	P x P dis. ch.
16 Kt—R3	Kt—B5!!

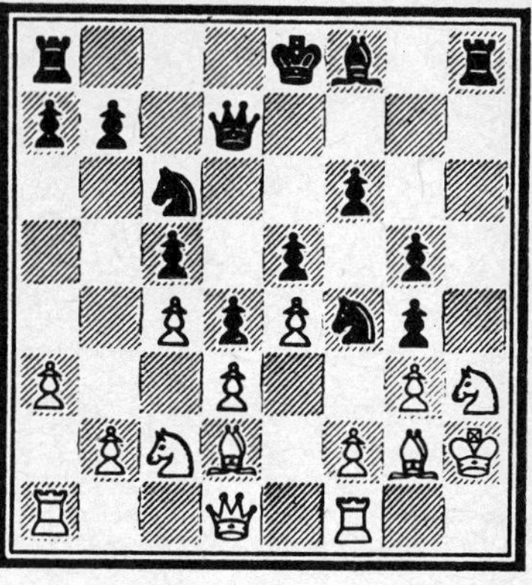

17 P x Kt	KP x P
18 P—B3	P x Kt
19 B—R1	Kt—K4
20 Q—K2	B—Q3
21 R—KKt1	O—O—O
22 P—Kt4	P—Kt3
23 P—R4	R—R5
24 B—K1	R—R2
25 B—Q2	R—R5
26 B—K1	KR—R1
27 B—Q2	QR—Kt1
28 P—R5	P—Kt5!
29 B x P	Kt x Pch
30 B x Kt	B x Bch
31 K—R1	P—Kt6!
32 R x P	R x R
33 RP x P	KR—Kt1!
34 P x RP	Q x P!
35 B—Kt4ch	KR x B
36 Q x Rch	R x Q
37 R x Q	R—Kt7
38 Kt—K1	R—KB7!
39 K—Kt1	P—R7ch
40 K x R	P—R8 (Q)
41 Resigns	

273. Nottingham, 1936.

White's game collapses with surprising suddenness.

QUEEN'S GAMBIT

DR. E. LASKER White	S. RESHEVSKY Black
1 P—Q4	P—Q4
2 P—QB4	P x P
3 Kt—KB3	Kt—KB3
4 P—K3	P—K3
5 B x P	P—B4
6 Kt—B3	P—QR3
7 O—O	P—QKt4
8 B—Q3	P x P
9 P x P	B—Kt2
10 B—Kt5	B—K2
11 Q—K2	O—O
12 QR—Q1	QKt—Q2
13 Kt—K5	Kt—Q4!
14 B—B1	KKt x Kt
15 P x Kt	Kt—B3
16 P—QR4	Q—Q4!
17 Kt—B3	KR—B1!
18 B—Kt2	Kt—K5!
19 R—B1	Kt—Kt4!
20 P x P	P x P
21 B x P	....

21	Kt x Ktch
22 P x Kt	Q—Kt4ch
23 K—R1	Q—Kt5!
Resigns	

274. Nottingham, 1936.

Brilliancy Prize

INDIAN DEFENSE

M. BOTVINNIK White	DR. S. TARTAKOWER Black
1 Kt—KB3	Kt—KB3
2 P—B4	P—Q3
3 P—Q4	QKt—Q2
4 P—KKt3	P—K4
5 B—Kt2	B—K2
6 O—O	O—O
7 Kt—B3	P—B3
8 P—K4	Q—B2
9 P—KR3	R—K1
10 B—K3	Kt—B1?
11 R—B1	P—KR3
12 P—Q5	B—Q2
13 Kt—Q2	P—KKt4?
14 P—B4	KtP x P
15 KtP x P	K—Kt2
16•P x KP	P x KP
17 P—B5	P x P
18 Kt x P	Q—B3
19 Kt—QB4	Kt—Kt3
20 Kt—Q6	B—K3
21 Kt x B	Kt x Kt
22 R x Kt!!	K x R
23 Q—R5	Kt—Kt3
24 Kt—B5!	R—KKt1
25 Q x P	B x P
26 R—Q1	QR—Q1
27 Q—Kt5ch	K—K3
28 R x R	P—B3
29 R x R	Kt—B5
30 Q—Kt7	Resigns

---

275. Belgian National Tourney, 1936.

Brilliancy Prize

Shades of Dr. Lasker!

QUEEN'S PAWN OPENING

G. KOLTANOWSKY White	M. DEFOSSE Black
1 P—Q4	Kt—KB3
2 Kt—KB3	P—K3
3 P—K3	P—Q4
4 B—Q3	P—B4
5 P—B3	Kt—B3
6 QKt—Q2	B—K2
7 O—O	O—O
8 P x P	B x P
9 P—K4	Q—B2
10 Q—K2	B—Q3
11 R—K1	Kt—KKt5
12 P—KR3	KKt—K4
13 Kt x Kt	Kt x Kt
14 P x P	P x P
15 Kt—B3	Kt x Ktch
16 Q x Kt	B—K3
17 B—K3	QR—Q1
18 B—B2	P—QKt4
19 B—Q4	B—QB4
20 QR—Q1	P—Kt5
21 B—K5	B—Q3

22 B x Pch!	K x B
23 Q—R5ch	K—Kt1
24 B x P!	K x B
25 Q—Kt5ch	K—R2
26 R—Q4	B—R7ch
27 K—R1	Q—KB5
28 R x Q	B x R
29 Q x B	R—KKt1
30 R—K5	Resigns

The double sacrifice of the bishop came as a surprise, and was as pleasing as it was decisive.

---

276. U. S. Championship Tournament, New York, 1936.

Reshevsky is not often beaten in this fashion.

CARO-KANN DEFENSE

I. A. HOROWITZ White	S. RESHEVSKY Black
1 P—K4	P—QB3
2 P—Q4	P—Q4
3 Kt—QB3	P x P
4 Kt x P	Kt—B3
5 Kt—Kt3	P—KR4
6 Q—Q3	P—R5
7 Kt—K4	Kt x Kt
8 Q x Kt	Kt—Q2
9 B—KKt5!	Q—Kt3
10 O—O—O	Q—R4
11 Kt—B3	Q x P
12 B—Q3	Q—R8ch
13 K—Q2	Q—R4ch
14 P—B3	P—R6
15 KR—K1	Kt—B3
16 Q—B4	Kt—Q4
17 Q—Kt3	P x P
18 P—R4	P—Kt8 (Q)
19 Q x Q	P—Kt4
20 R—R1	Q—Kt3
21 Kt—K5	P—Kt5
22 QR—B1	P x Pch
23 P x P	P—K3
24 Q—Kt4	B—Q3
25 P—R5	B x Kt
26 R x B	R—QKt1
27 B—R4	K—B1

28	Q—Kt3	P—B3
29	R x Kt!	P—K4
30	R x P!	B—R3
31	R—QKt1	Q—Q1
32	R x R	Q x R
33	R—QB5	Q—Kt7ch
34	B—B2	Resigns

---

277. Zandvoort, 1936.

Brilliancy Prize.

QUEEN'S GAMBIT DECLINED

	DR. M. EUWE White	G. MAROCZY Black
1	P—Q4	P—Q4
2	P—QB4	P—K3
3	Kt—QB3	Kt—KB3
4	B—Kt5	B—K2
5	P—K3	O—O
6	Kt—B3	QKt—Q2
7	R—B1	P—B3
8	P—QR3	P—KR3
9	B—B4	P—R3
10	P—R3	P x P
11	B x BP	P—QKt4
12	B—QR2	B—Kt2
13	O—O	P—B4
14	Kt—K5	P—B5
15	B—Kt1	R—K1
16	Q—K2	Kt x Kt
17	P x Kt	Kt—R2
18	Q—R5	Kt—B1
19	QR—Q1	Q—B2
20	B x P!	P x B
21	R—Q4!	P—B4
22	P x P e.p.	B x BP
23	R—Kt4ch	B—Kt2
24	Q x RP	QR—Q1
25	Kt—K2!	P—K4
26	Kt—Kt3	R—K3
27	Q—R4	R—Q6
28	Kt—B5	Kt—Kt3
29	Q—R5	Q—B2
30	P—KR4!	B—KB1
31	Kt—R6ch	B x Kt
32	Q x B	Q—R2
33	Q—Kt5	K—B2
34	B x R	P x B
35	Q—B5ch	Resigns

---

278. Ostend, 1937.

Keres made a brilliant start by winning this game from Fine.

QUEEN'S GAMBIT DECLINED

	P. KERES White	R. FINE Black
1	Kt—KB3	P—Q4
2	P—Q4	Kt—KB3
3	P—B4	P—K3
4	Kt—B3	P—B4
5	BP x P	Kt x P
6	P—K4	Kt x Kt
7	P x Kt	P x P
8	P x P	B—Kt5ch
9	B—Q2	B x Bch
10	Q x B	O—O
11	B—B4	Kt—Q2
12	O—O	P—QKt3
13	QR—Q1	B—Kt2
14	KR—K1	R—B1
15	B—Kt3	Kt—B3
16	Q—B4	Q—B2
17	Q—R4	KR—Q1
18	R—K3	P—QKt4
19	QR—K1	P—QR4
20	P—QR4	P—Kt5?
21	P—Q5!	P x P
22	P—K5	Kt—Q2
23	Kt—Kt5	Kt—B1
24	Kt x RP!	Kt x Kt
25	R—R3	Q—B8

26 Q x Ktch	K—B1
27 R—K3	P—Q5
28 Q—R8ch	K—K2
29 Q x P!	R—B1
30 Q—B6ch	K—K1
31 P—K6!	Resigns

---

279. Margate, 1937.

Black's weak opening play leads to a catastrophe.

INDIAN DEFENSE

P. KERES	C. ALEXANDER
White	Black
1 P—Q4	Kt—KB3
2 P—QB4	P—K3
3 Kt—QB3	B—Kt5
4 Kt—B3	P—QKt3
5 P—KKt3	B—Kt2
6 B—Kt2	Q—B1
7 O—O	P—B4?
8 Kt—QKt5!	P x P
9 B—B4!	Kt—R3
10 B—Q6!	Q x P
11 Q—R4	B—B3
12 KKt x P	B x KB
13 Q x Kt	B x R
14 R x B	Q x KKt
15 Kt x Q	B x B
16 Kt—Kt5	K—K2
17 R—Q1	B—B4
18 P—QR3	Kt—K5
19 R x Pch!	K—B3
20 Q—Kt7	Resigns

---

280. Kemeri, June, 1937.

The mating attack is very pretty.

ALEKHINE'S DEFENSE

A. ALEKHINE	S. RESHEVSKY
White	Black
1 P—K4	Kt—KB3
2 P—K5	Kt—Q4
3 Kt—KB3	P—Q3
4 P—Q4	B—Kt5
5 P—B4	Kt—Kt3
6 B—K2	P x P
7 Kt x P	B x B
8 Q x B	Q x P
9 O—O	QKt—Q2
10 Kt x Kt	Kt x Kt?
11 Kt—B3	P—QB3
12 B—K3	Q—K4
13 QR—Q1	P—K3
14 Q—B3!	O—O—O
15 B x P	Q—QR4
16 B—Q4	Q—KB4
17 Q—Kt3	P—K4
18 B—K3	B—Kt5
19 Kt—R4	B—R4!
20 P—B4!	B—B2
21 P—Kt3	P—B3
22 P x P	Q—K3
23 P—KR3!	KR—Kt1
24 B—Q4	Kt x P
25 Q—QB3!	Kt—Q2
26 P—B5!	KR—K1
27 P—QKt4!	Kt—Kt1
28 Kt—Kt6ch	B x Kt
29 P x B	Q x QRP
30 Q—KKt3!	R—Q2
31 B—B5	Q—B2
32 R—R1	Q—Kt3
33 Q—R2!	R—K4
34 R—R8	R—Q7
35 R x Ktch	K x R
36 Q x Rch	

and mate in three moves.

---

281. Kemeri, June, 1937.

Position play of the highest order.

QUEEN'S GAMBIT

A. ALEKHINE	R. FINE

	White	Black
1	P—Q4	P—Q4
2	P—QB4	P x P
3	Kt—KB3	Kt—KB3
4	Q—R4ch	Q—Q2
5	Q x BP	Q—B3
6	Kt—R3	Q x Q
7	Kt x Q	P—K3
8	P—QR3	P—B4?
9	B—B4	Kt—B3
10	P x P	B x P
11	P—QKt4	B—K2
12	P—Kt5	Kt—QKt1
13	Kt—Q6ch	B x Kt
14	B x B	Kt—K5
15	B—B7!	Kt—Q2
16	Kt—Q4!	Kt—Kt3
17	P—B3	Kt—Q4
18	B—R5	Kt(K5)—B3
19	Kt—B2!	B—Q2
20	P—K4	R—QB1
21	K—Q2!	Kt—Kt3
22	Kt—K3	O—O
23	P—QR4!	KR—Q1
24	B—Q3	P—K4
25	KR—QB1	B—K3
26	R x R	R x R
27	B—Kt4	Kt—K1
28	P—R5	Kt—Q2
29	Kt—Q5!	B x Kt
30	P x B	Kt—B4
31	B—B5!	R—Q1
32	K—B3!	P—QKt3
33	P x P	P x P
34	B x Kt!	P x B
35	P—Kt6	Kt—Q3
36	B—Q7!	R x B
37	R—R8ch	

and mate in two.

---

282. Semmering-Baden, 1937.

The modern gambit style.

SICILIAN DEFENSE

	P. KERES White	E. ELISKASES Black
1	P—K4	P—QB4
2	Kt—KB3	P—Q3
3	P—QKt4	P x P
4	P—Q4	Kt—KB3
5	B—Q3	P—Q4
6	QKt—Q2	P x P
7	Kt x P	QKt—Q2
8	Kt(4)—Kt5!	Q—B2
9	P—B4!	P—KR3
10	Kt—R3	P—KKt4
11	Kt(R3)—Kt1	B—Kt2
12	Kt—K2	P—K4
13	Kt—Kt3	O—O
14	O—O	P—K5
15	Kt x KP	Kt x Kt
16	B x Kt	Q x P
17	B—Q3	Q—Q4
18	R—K1	P—Kt5
19	Kt—R4	Kt—Kt3
20	R—Kt1	B—Q2
21	R—K4	KR—K1
22	R—B4	Q—Q3
23	B—Q2	Kt—Q4
24	R x KKtP!	B x R
25	Q x B	Q—KB3
26	Kt—B5	K—B1
27	Kt x B	Q x Kt
28	Q—R5	Kt—B3
29	Q—R4	P—KR4
30	R x P	QR—B1
31	P—KR3	R—B2
32	R—Kt5	R—K3
33	R x RP!	Resigns

For, if 33 . . . Kt x R; 34 Q—Q8ch, R—K1; 35 B—Kt4ch!

---

283. Played in U.S.S.R. Championship, 1939.

Keres' favorite move still continues to pay dividends.

FALKBEER COUNTER GAMBIT

P. KERES	V. PETROV
White	Black
1 P—K4	P—K4
2 P—KB4	P—Q4
3 KP x P	P—K5
4 P—Q3!	Kt—KB3
5 QKt—Q2	P x P
6 B x P	Q x P
7 KKt—KB3	B—QB4
8 Q—K2ch	Q—K3
9 Kt—K5!	O—O
10 Kt—K4	Kt x Kt
11 Q x Kt	P—KKt3
12 P—QKt4	B—K2
13 B—Kt2	B—B3
14 O—O—O	Kt—B3
15 P—KR4	P—KR4
16 P—Kt4	B x Kt
17 P x B	Q x KtP
18 Q—K3	Kt x KtP
19 P—K6!	Kt—Q4
20 P x Pch	R x P
21 B—B4	P—B3
22 R x Kt!	Q x B
23 Q—K8ch	Resigns

---

284. Los Angeles, 1940.

Simultaneous Exhibition: Brevity is the soul of wit.

VIENNA GAME

I. A. HOROWITZ	AMATEUR
White	Black
1 P—K4	P—K4
2 Kt—QB3	Kt—QB3
3 B—B4	B—B4
4 Q—Kt4!	Q—B3?
5 Kt—Q5	Q x Pch
6 K—Q1	K—B1
7 Kt—R3	Q—Q5
8 P—Q3	B—Kt3
9 R—B1	Kt—B3
10 R x Kt!	P—Q3

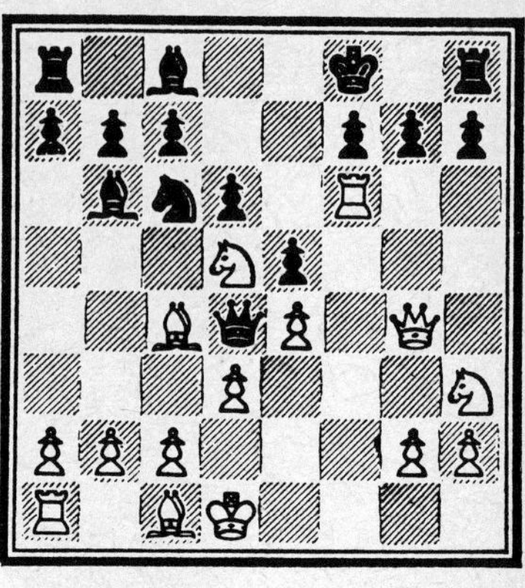

11 Q x Pch!!	K x Q
12 B—R6ch	K—Kt1
13 R—Kt6ch!	RP x P
14 Kt—B6 mate	

---

285. New York, 1940.

Brilliancy Prize

QUEEN'S GAMBIT DECLINED

DR. J. PLATZ	E. J. KORPANTY
White	Black
1 P—Q4	Kt—KB3
2 P—QB4	P—K3
3 Kt—QB3	P—Q4
4 B—Kt5	QKt—Q2
5 P—K3	B—K2
6 Kt—B3	P—B3
7 Q—B2	P—QR3
8 R—Q1	O—O
9 P—QR3	P—KR3
10 P—KR4	Kt—Kt5
11 B—B4	P—KB4
12 B—Q3	P x P?
13 B x QBP	Kt—Kt3
14 B—QR2	Kt—Q4
15 P—KKt3	K—R1
16 Kt—K5	KKt x Kt
17 B x Kt	B—Q3

18	Kt—K2	B x B
19	P x B	Q—K2
20	B—Kt1	Q—KB2
21	R—Q4	P—KKt3
22	P—KKt4	B—Q2
23	Kt—B4	QR—Q1
24	R—Kt1	B—B1
25	Q—Q1	P—B4
26	P x P!	P x R
27	Kt x Pch	K—R2
28	Kt x Rch	Q x Kt
29	P x Pch	K—R1
30	Q—Q3	Q—K2
31	Q—Kt6	Resigns

---

286. Summer, 1941.
New York State Championship

A brilliant young player defeats a famous veteran.

RUY LOPEZ

	H. SEIDMAN White	EDWARD LASKER Black
1	P—K4	P—K4
2	Kt—KB3	Kt—QB3
3	B—Kt5	P—QR3
4	B—R4	Kt—B3
5	O—O	B—K2
6	Q—K2	P—QKt4
7	B—Kt3	O—O
8	P—QR4	R—Kt1
9	P x P	P x P
10	P—B3	P—Q4
11	P—Q3	B—K3
12	Kt—Kt5	B—KKt5
13	P—B3	B—B1
14	P x P	Kt x P
15	Kt x RP	R—K1
16	Kt—Kt5	B x Kt
17	B x B	Kt x P
18	P x Kt	Q x B
19	P—KB4	Q—Kt3
20	Kt—Q2	B—Kt5
21	P—B5!	B x P
22	R x B!	Q x R
23	R—KB1	Q—Kt4
24	B x Pch	K—R1
25	R—B3!	P—Kt3
26	R—Kt3	Q—B3
27	B x P	Q—R5
28	R—R3	Q x R
29	P x Q	R—K2
30	Q—R5ch	K—Kt1
31	Kt—B3	R—KB1
32	Kt—Kt5	R—B3
33	Q—R6	Resigns

---

287. U. S. Chess Championship,
New York, 1942.

Dynamic play by the champion!

RUY LOPEZ

	H. SEIDMAN White	S. RESHEVSKY Black
1	P—K4	P—K4
2	Kt—KB3	Kt—QB3
3	B—Kt5	P—QR3
4	B—R4	Kt—B3
5	O—O	B—K2
6	Q—K2	P—QKt4
7	B—Kt3	P—Q3
8	P—QR4	B—Kt5
9	P—B3	O—O
10	P—R3	B—R4
11	R—Q1	P—Kt5
12	P—Q4	KtP x P!
13	P—Kt4	Q—Kt1!
14	B—Q5	Kt x B!
15	P x Kt	B—Kt3
16	KtP x P	Kt—R4
17	QKt—Q2	P x P!!
18	Q x B	R—K1
19	Q—Kt5	P x P
20	Kt—R4	P—KB3!
21	Q—B4	B—B7!
22	Kt—B5	B x R
23	Kt—K4	R x Kt!
24	Q x R	Q—K1!!

25	Q—Kt4!	Kt—Kt6
26	R—Kt1	Kt x B
27	R x Kt	P—B7
28	Q—Kt7	Q—Q1
29	Q—Kt3	R—Kt1
30	Q—R2	P—KR4!
31	Kt—Q4	P x P
32	P x P	Q—K1
33	Kt x P	Q—K7
34	P—Kt5	P x P
35	Q—R3	B x Kt
36	Q—QB3	B—K5
37	Q x P	Q—Kt5ch
	Resigns	

---

288. U. S. Championship Tournament, New York, 1942.

An old-fashioned slugging match.

ALEKHINE'S DEFENSE

	I. A. HOROWITZ White	H. SEIDMAN Black
1	P—K4	Kt—KB3
2	P—K5	Kt—Q4
3	P—QB4	Kt—Kt3
4	P—Q4	P—Q3
5	P—B4	P—Kt3
6	Kt—QB3	B—Kt2
7	Kt—B3	P x P
8	BP x P	B—Kt5
9	P—B5	Kt—Q4
10	Q—Kt3	B x Kt
11	P x B	P—K3
12	Kt x Kt	Q—R5ch
13	K—K2	P x Kt
14	Q x KtP	Q x QP
15	Q—B8ch	K—K2
16	B—Kt5ch	P—B3
17	Q x Pch	Kt—Q2
18	P x Pch	B x P
19	Q—Q6ch	K—K1
20	R—Q1!!	Q x Pch
21	R—Q2	Q—B6
22	Q x P	B x B
23	Q x Rch	K—K2
24	Q—K4ch	K—Q1
25	R—B2	Q—B3
26	P—B6	R—K1
27	P—B7ch	Resigns

---

289. New York, 1942.

Brilliant ten-second chess.

EVANS GAMBIT DECLINED

	H. HELMS White	O. TENNER Black
1	P—K4	P—K4
2	Kt—KB3	Kt—QB3
3	B—B4	B—B4
4	P—QKt4	B—Kt3
5	P—QR4	P—QR3
6	P—R5	B—R2
7	P—Kt5	P x P
8	B x P	Kt—B3
9	B—R3	Kt x KP
10	Q—K2	Kt x BP
11	Kt x P	Kt—Q5

12	Kt x QPch!	Kt x Q
13	Kt—B6 mate	

---

289. Blindfold, 1942.

A delightful finish.

DANISH GAMBIT

A. ALEKHINE	A. SUPICO
White	Black
1 P—K4	P—K4
2 P—Q4	P x P
3 P—QB3	P x P
4 Kt x P	B—Kt5
5 B—QB4	Q—K2
6 Kt—K2	Kt—KB3
7 O—O	O—O
8 B—KKt5	Q—K4?
9 B x Kt	Q x B
10 Kt—Q5	Q—Q3
11 P—K5	Q—B4
12 R—B1	Q—R4
13 P—QR3	B x P
14 P x B	P—QB3
15 Kt—K7ch	K—R1
16 Q—Q6!	Q—Q1
17 Kt—Q4	P—QKt3
18 R—B3!	P—QB4
19 Kt(4)—B5	B—R3
20 Q—Kt6!	Resigns

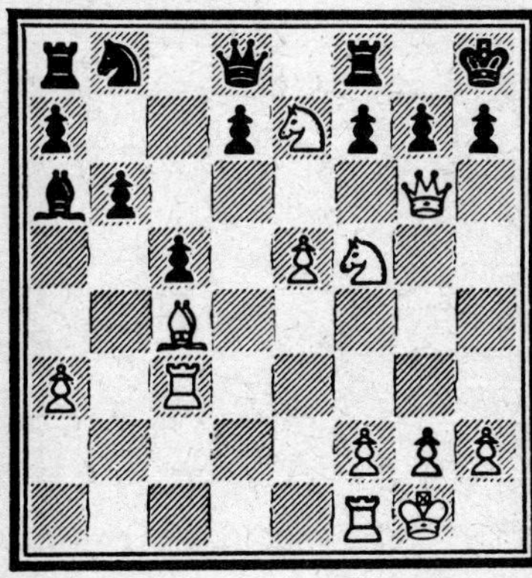

290. Ventnor City, 1942.

The same game in a handsome edition.

RUY LOPEZ

J. F. DONOVAN	S. N. BERNSTEIN
White	Black
1 P—K4	P—K4
2 Kt—KB3	Kt—QB3
3 B—Kt5	P—QR3
4 B—R4	Kt—B3
5 O—O	B—K2
6 Q—K2	P—QKt4
7 B—Kt3	O—O
8 P—B3	P—Q4
9 P—Q3	P—Q5
10 P x P	B—KKt5!
11 P—Q5	Kt—Q5
12 Q—Q1	Kt—R4
13 B—K3	Kt x Ktch
14 P x Kt	B—KR6
15 R—K1	B—Kt4
16 K—R1	B—B5
17 B x B	Kt x B
18 R—Kt1	Q—R5
19 Q—Q2	QR—Q1
20 Kt—B3	R—Q3
21 Kt—Q1	B—Q2
22 Kt—K3	Q x Pch!
Resigns	

PART VII

The Period of Russian Hegemony

For the past twenty odd years, the Russian players have been dominating the field. The Russian government, acting as sponsors, promoted a vast program of chess activity, subsidized and professionalized its top flight talent. Because no other country engaged in this practice on a comparable basis, Soviet victories have been many, and masses of grandmasters have flourished. Botvinnik, Smyslov, Bronstein, Keres, Geller, and Tal are only a few of the names.

Under the circumstances, Russian chess has reached a peak of technical perfection. One feature of this period is the great emphasis on openings. Hordes of analysts fine-comb existing ideas extensively and occasionally produce interesting innovations.

Chess talent knows no boundaries. In most countries, however, the talented chessplayers are gainfully employed in other pursuits. Not so in Russia. For the present we are living in a period of Russian hegemony.

291. Salzburg, 1943.

Typical of Keres at his best.

SICILIAN DEFENSE

P. KERES	E. BOGOLYUBOV
White	Black
1 P—K4	P—QB4
2 Kt—K2	P—K3
3 P—Q4	P x P
4 Kt x P	Kt—KB3
5 Kt—QB3	P—Q3
6 P—KKt4	Kt—B3
7 P—Kt5	Kt x Kt??
8 Q x Kt	Kt—Q2
9 B—K3	P—QR3
10 B—K2	Q—B2
11 P—B4!	P—QKt3
12 P—B5!	Kt—K4
13 P x P	P x P
14 P—QR4!	B—K2
15 P—R4!	Q—B4
16 Q—Q2	Q—B2?
17 R—KB1	B—Kt2
18 B—Q4!	R—KB1
19 O—O—O	R x R
20 R x R	B—Q1
21 Q—B4	Kt—Kt3
22 Q—Kt4	Q—K2
23 Q—R5!	. . . .

23	P—K4
24 B—K3	B—B2
25 Q x P	Kt—B5
26 B x Kt	P x B
27 B—R5ch	K—Q2
28 B—Kt4ch	K—B3
29 Q—B5!	P—Kt4
30 Q—Q5ch	K—Kt3
31 Q—Q4ch	K—B3
32 Kt—Q5	Resigns

---

292. Kiev, 1944.

One of the most amazing winning moves on record.

FRENCH DEFENSE

BRONSTEIN	GOLDENOV
White	Black
1 P—K4	P—K3
2 P—Q4	P—Q4
3 Kt—QB3	Kt—KB3
4 B—Kt5	B—Kt5
5 P—K5	P—KR3
6 B—Q2	B x Kt
7 P x B	Kt—K5
8 Q—Kt4	P—KKt3
9 B—B1!?	P—QB4
10 B—Q3	P x P?
11 Kt—K2	Kt—B4
12 P x P	Kt x Bch
13 P x Kt	P—QKt3
14 P—KR4	P—KR4
15 Q—B3	Kt—B3
16 B—Kt5	Kt—K2
17 O—O	B—R3
18 QR—B1	Q—Q2
19 Q—B6	KR—Kt1
20 R—B3	Kt—B4
21 Kt—Kt3	Kt x QP
22 KR—B1	Kt—Kt4
23 R(3)—B2	Q—Q1
24 R—B8!!!	. . . .

24 . . . . Resigns

Mate cannot be averted!

---

293. Groningen, 1946.

"A very pretty game."—Reinfeld

SICILIAN DEFENSE

V. SMYSLOV	C. KOTTNAUER
White	Black
1 P—K4	P—QB4
2 Kt—KB3	P—Q3
3 P—Q4	P x P
4 Kt x P	Kt—KB3
5 Kt—QB3	P—QR3
6 B—K2	P—K3
7 O—O	P—QKt4?
8 B—B3!	R—R2
9 Q—K2	R—B2
10 R—Q1	QKt—Q2
11 P—QR4	P x P
12 Kt x RP	B—Kt2
13 P—K5!	Kt x P
14 B x B	R x B
15 Q x P	Q—Kt1
16 Kt—B6	Kt x Kt
17 Q x Ktch	Kt—Q2

(see diagram next column)

18 Kt—B5!!	P x Kt
19 B—B4!	B—Q3

20 B x B	R—Kt3
21 Q x Ktch!	Resigns

---

294. Surrey, 1947.

Black's game seems safe enough — but Alexander lashes out with two powerful moves!

QUEEN'S INDIAN DEFENSE

C. H. ALEXANDER	E. CORDINGLY
White	Black
1 P—Q4	Kt—KB3
2 P—QB4	P—K3
3 Kt—KB3	P—QKt3
4 P—KKt3	B—Kt2
5 B—Kt2	P—B4
6 P—Q5	P x P
7 Kt—R4	P—Q3
8 Kt—QB3	Q—Q2
9 Kt x P	Kt x Kt
10 B x Kt	B—K2
11 Kt—B5!	O—O
12 B x B!!	Q x B
13 Q—Q5!!!	Resigns

(see diagram next page)

295. Vina del Mar, 1947.

Some of the most exciting games have ended in a draw.

FRENCH DEFENSE

H. ROSETTO	G. STAHLBERG
White	Black
1 P—K4	P—K3
2 P—Q4	P—Q4
3 Kt—QB3	Kt—KB3
4 B—Kt5	B—K2
5 P—K5	KKt—Q2
6 P—KR4	P—QB4
7 Kt—Kt5!?	P—B3
8 B—Q3!	P—QR3!

9 Q—R5ch!	K—B1
10 R—R3!	P x Kt
11 B—R6!!	Q—R4ch
12 B—Q2	Q—B2
13 R—Kt3!	P x QP!
14 Kt—B3!	Kt x P
15 RxP!	P—R3!!
16 B—R7!!	K x R
17 Q x Pch	Drawn

---

296. Baltimore, 1948.

(U. S. Open Championship)

Bisguier's teen-age masterpiece.

QUEEN'S GAMBIT ACCEPTED

A. MENGARINI	A. BISGUIER
White	Black
1 P—Q4	P—Q4
2 P—QB4	P x P
3 Kt—KB3	P—QR3
4 P—K3	Kt—KB3
5 B x P	P—K3
6 O—O	P—B4
7 Q—K2	Kt—B3
8 R—Q1	P—QKt4
9 B—Kt3	P—B5
10 B—B2	Kt—QKt5
11 P—QR4	Kt x B
12 Q x Kt	B—Kt2
13 P—QKt3	BP x P
14 Q x KtP	B—Q4
15 Q—Kt2	P—Kt5
16 P—R5	Q—B2
17 B—Q2	Q—Kt2
18 Kt—K1	Q—Kt4
19 P—B3	Q—K7
20 R—B1	P—R4
21 P—K4	Kt—Kt5
22 P x Kt	P x P
23 Q—B2	P—QKt6
24 Q—Q3	Q x Q
25 Kt x Q	B x P
26 Kt—Kt2	B—Q3
27 P—Kt3	K—Q2

28 Kt—B3	B—B6
29 Kt(3)—R4	R x P

30 Kt—Kt6ch	K—K2
31 B—Kt5ch	P—B3
32 K x R	R—R1ch
33 K—Kt1	B x P
34 R—B7ch	B x R
35 K—B2	R—R7ch
36 K—K3	R x Kt
37 B—R4	R—K7ch
38 K—Q3	P—Kt7
39 R—QKt1	B—K5ch
40 K x R	B x R
41 Kt—B4	B—Q6ch
Resigns	

---

297. Bad Gastein, 1948

An incisive rebuttal of lackadaisical opening play.

SICILIAN DEFENSE

N. Rossolimo	Hans Mueller
White	Black
1 P—K4	P—QB4
2 Kt—KB3	P—Q3
3 B—Kt5ch	B—Q2
4 B x Bch	Q x B
5 O—O	Kt—QB3
6 Q—K2	P—K3
7 R—Q1	P—Q4
8 P x P	Q x P
9 Kt—B3	Q—Q2
10 P—Q4	N x P
11 Kt x Kt	P x Kt
12 B—K3	Q—B3
13 R x P	R—B1
14 QR—Q1	P—QR3
15 Q—Q2	B—K2
16 Kt—K4	K—B1
17 Q—R5	P—B4
18 Kt—Q6	B x Kt
19 R x B	Q x P
20 Q—K5	R—K1
21 R—Q7	Kt—K2
22 B—R6	R—KKt1
23 Q—B6 mate	

---

298. Budapest, 1950.

(Challengers' Tournament)

"A diabolic combination."

—Kmoch

QUEEN'S GAMBIT

D Bronstein	A. Kotov
White	Black
1 P—Q4	P—Q4
2 P—QB4	P—K3
3 Kt—QB3	P—QB3
4 P—K4	P x KP
5 Kt x P	B—Kt5ch
6 B—Q2	Q x P
7 B x B	Q x Ktch
8 B—K2	Kt—QR3
9 B—B3	Kt—K2
10 B x P!!	R—KKt1
11 B—QB3	Q x KtP
12 Q—Q2!!	Q x R
13 O—O—O	Kt—Q4
14 Kt—B3!	Q x Rch
15 B x Q	Kt x B
16 Q x Kt	K—K2

17 Kt—K5! B—Q2
18 Q—QR3ch . . . .

18 . . . . P—QB4
19 Q—KB3! QR—Q1
20 Q x Pch K—Q3
21 Q—B4 QR—KB1
22 Kt—B7ch K—K2
23 B—R5 B—B3
24 Q—Q6ch K—B3
25 Kt—R6! R—Kt8ch
26 K—Q2 K—Kt2
27 Kt—Kt4! R x Kt
28 Q—K7ch K—R3
29 B x R R x Pch
30 K—K3 R—B8
31 P—KR4 K—Kt3
32 B—R5ch! Resigns

---

299. Leningrad, 1950.

A little-known player conducts a magnificent attack.

SICILIAN DEFENSE

SHAPIRO SOMOV
White Black

1 P—K4 P—QB4
2 Kt—KB3 P—Q3
3 P—Q4 P x P
4 Kt x P Kt—KB3
5 Kt—QB3 P—KKt3
6 P—B4 B—Kt2
7 P—K5 P x P
8 P x P Kt—Q4
9 B—Kt5ch K—B1
10 O—O B x P
11 Kt x Kt Q x Kt
12 Kt—B5! Q—B4ch
13 B—K3 Q—B2
14 B—R6ch K—Kt1
15 Kt x Pch Q x Kt

16 R x P! K x R
17 Q—Q5ch Q—K3
18 R—B1ch B—B3
19 R x Bch! K x R
20 Q—Q4ch K—K2
21 B—Kt5ch K—B2
22 B—QB4 R—K1
23 Q—B6ch K—Kt1
24 B—KR6 Resigns

---

300. Bled, 1950.

Najdorf called this the most brilliant game that he had seen in years.

RUY LOPEZ

A. FUDERER S. TARTAKOWER
White Black

1 P—K4 P—K4
2 KKt—B3 QKt—B3
3 B—Kt5 P—QR3
4 B—R4 B—Kt5
5 O—O KKt—K2
6 P—B3 B—R4
7 P—Q4 P x P
8 P—QKt4 B—Kt3

9	P x P	O—O
10	P—Q5	Kt—R2
11	Kt—R3	P—QB4
12	P—Q6	Kt—Kt3
13	Kt—B4	P x P
14	QB—Kt5	P—B3
15	Kt x B	Q x Kt
16	B—K3	Q—Q1

17	P—K5!!	Kt x P
18	Kt x Kt	P x Kt
19	P—B4!!	P—K5
20	P—B5!	Kt—B3
21	Q—Q5ch	K—R1
22	P—B6!!	P x P
23	B—Kt3	P—Kt4
24	R—B4	B—Kt2
25	R—R4	P—B4
26	R—R6	K—Kt2
27	R—KB1	R—B3
28	R x BP	R x R(3)
29	B x Rch	K—R1
30	Q—B7	Q—Kt3ch
31	K—R1	Q—Q5
32	Q—B8ch	Resigns

---

301. Amsterdam, 1951.

Najdorf's tactical mastery reaches a supreme high. Seldom has so brilliant an attack been created out of almost nothing!

CATALAN SYSTEM

	M. NAJDORF White	HAJE KRAMER Black
1	P—Q4	Kt—KB3
2	P—QB4	P—K3
3	P—KKt3	P—Q4
4	B—Kt2	P x P
5	Kt—KB3	QKt—Q2
6	QKt—Q2	Kt—Kt3
7	O—O	P—B4
8	Kt x P	Kt x Kt
9	Q—R4ch	B—Q2
10	Q x Kt	Q—Kt3
11	P—Kt3	B—Kt4
12	Q—B2	P x P
13	B—Kt2	P—Q6
14	P x P	B—K2
15	Kt—K5!	O—O
16	QR—B1	KR—Q1
17	KR—K1	Kt—Q4
18	Q—K2	B—KB3
19	Q—R5!	B—K1
20	B—K4!	P—Kt3
21	Q—K2	QR—B1
22	Kt—Kt4	B—Q5
23	R x R!	R x R
24	B x Kt!	P x B
25	Kt—R6ch!	K—B1
26	Q—K7ch	K—Kt2
27	R—K6!!	. . . .
27	. . . .	B x B
28	R x Q	P x R
29	Kt—Kt4	B—QB3

30 Kt—K5	B x Kt
31 Q x Bch	K—Kt1
32 P—QR4	R—K1
33 Q—Q4	P—QKt4
34 P—R5!	R—K3
35 P—B4	P—R3
36 K—B2	K—R2
37 P—KKt4	P—B3
38 Q—Kt6	Resigns

---

302. Neuhausen, 1953.

(Challengers' Tournament)

In for a penny Euwe goes in for a pound.

KING'S INDIAN DEFENSE

M. EUWE	M. NAJDORF
White	Black
1 P—Q4	Kt—KB3
2 P—QB4	P—KKt3
3 P—KKt3	B—Kt2
4 B—Kt2	O—O
5 Kt—QB3	P—B4
6 P—Q5	P—K4
7 B—Kt5	P—KR3
8 B x Kt	Q x B
9 P—Q6!	Kt—B3
10 P—K3	P—Kt3
11 B—Q5	K—R1
12 Kt—K4	Q—Q1
13 P—KR4	P—B4
14 Kt—Kt5	B—Kt2!
15 P—KKt4	P—K5
16 Kt—K2	B x P
17 Kt—B4	Q—B3
18 P x P	B x R
19 Kt x Pch	K—Kt2
20 Kt x P	B—B6ch
21 K—B1	Q x BP
22 Kt—B4!	K—R1

(see diagram next column)

23 Kt x B	QR—K1
24 Kt(3)—K2	R—KKt1
25 P—R5	R—Kt4
26 Kt—Kt3	R x Kt
27 P x R	R x P
28 K—B2	R—K1
29 R—K1	R x R
30 Q x R	K—Kt2
31 Q—K8	Q—B7ch
32 K—Kt1	Q—Q8ch
33 K—R2	Q—B7ch
34 Kt—Kt2	Q—B4
35 Q—Kt8ch	K—B3
36 Q—R8ch	K—Kt4
37 Q—Kt7ch	Resigns

---

303. Milwaukee, 1953.

(U. S. Open)

White's conception shows imagination. His opponent's tough resistance notwithstanding, he is able to carry it out with admirable elan.

NIMZO-INDIAN DEFENSE

DONALD BYRNE	R. PITSCHAK
White	Black
1 P—Q4	Kt—KB3
2 P—QB4	P—K3
3 Kt—QB3	B—Kt5
4 P—QR3	B x Ktch
5 P x B	P—QKt3

6	P—B3	B—Kt2
7	B—Kt5	P—Q3
8	P—K4	QKt—Q2
9	B—Q3	P—K4
10	Kt—K2	Kt—B1
11	O—O	Kt—K3
12	B x Kt!!	Q x B
13	Q—R4ch	P—B3
14	P—B5!	QP x P
15	P—KB4!!	KP x QP
16	P—K5!	Q—Q1
17	P—B5	Kt—B2
18	P x P!	P x P
19	B—K4	Kt—Kt4
20	P—B6	Q—Q2
21	QR—Q1	R—Q1
22	Q—B2!	P—Kt3
23	P—QR4	Kt—B2
24	Kt x P	Kt—Q4
25	P—K6!!	P x P

26	Kt x KP!!	Q x Kt
27	B x Kt	R x B
28	QR—K1	R—K4
29	Q—B3!	O—O
30	R x R	Q—B1
31	R—K7	R—B2
32	Q—QKt3	Q—B1
33	KR—K1	Resigns

---

304. Czecho-Slovakia, 1954.

White sets up and carries out a beautiful attack. He offers both his Rooks for sacrifice on the same square. Black cannot take either.

NIMZO-INDIAN DEFENSE

	L. PACHMAN White	DR. FILIP Black
1	P—Q4	Kt—KB3
2	P—QB4	P—K3
3	Kt—KB3	P—QKt3
4	P—K3	B—Kt2
5	Kt—B3	B—Kt5
6	B—Q3	O—O
7	O—O	P—B4
8	Kt—QR4	P x P
9	P—QR3	B—K2
10	P x P	Kt—K5
11	P—QKt3	P—B4
12	B—Kt2	B—KB3
13	Kt—B3	Kt x Kt
14	B x Kt	Q—K1
15	R—K1	Q—Kt3
16	B—B1	Kt—B3
17	R—B1	Kt—K2
18	P—Q5!	P x P
19	Kt—K5!	B x Kt
20	R x B	Q—Q3
21	R—K3!	R—B2
22	P x P	P—QR4
23	B—B4	Kt—Kt3
24	Q—Q4	P—B5
25	R—K6!!	. . . .

25	. . . .	Q x RP
26	B—Kt2	Q—B1

27 R x P	P—Q3
28 B—R3	R—Q1
29 R—K1	B—B1
30 R—K6!	R(2)—Q2
31 Q—K4	Q—B2
32 P—R3	P—B6
33 B x P	P x P
34 B—Kt3	K—R1
35 R x Kt!	P x R
36 Q—R4ch	Resigns

---

305. New York, 1954.

(USSR vs. USA)

When White comes rushing in, Black pulls the rug from under him.

KING'S INDIAN DEFENSE

M. TAIMONOV	L. EVANS
White	Black
1 P—QB4	Kt—KB3
2 Kt—KB3	P—KKt3
3 Kt—B3	B—Kt2
4 P—K4	O—O
5 P—Q4	P—Q3
6 B—K2	P—K4
7 O—O	Kt—B3
8 P—Q5	Kt—K2
9 Kt—K1	Kt—Q2
10 Kt—Q3	P—KB4
11 P—B3	P—B5
12 B—Q2	P—KKt4
13 R—B1	R—B3
14 P—B5	Kt x BP
15 Kt x Kt	P x Kt
16 Kt—R4	P—Kt3
17 P—QKt4	P x P
18 B x P	B—B1!
19 R x P?	. . . .
19	Kt—B4!!
20 B x B	Q x R
21 B—R3	Kt—K6

22 Q—B1	Q—KKt2!
23 R—B2	B—Q2
24 Kt—B3	P—Kt5
25 B—Kt2	P—Kt6
26 P x P	Q x P
27 B—B1	R—QB1
28 Q—K1	P—Kt4
29 Kt—K2	Q—R5
30 P—Kt3	P x P
31 Kt x P	Kt x B!
32 Kt—B5	R—Kt3ch
33 K x Kt	Q—R8ch
34 K—K2	R—B7ch
35 K—Q1	Q x Qch
36 K x Q	R—Kt8ch
Resigns	

---

306. New York, 1954.

Even Reshevsky sometimes falls into a trap.

KING'S INDIAN DEFENSE

A. BISGUIER	S. RESHEVSKY
White	Black
1 P—Q4	Kt—KB3
2 P—QB4	P—KKt3
3 Kt—QB3	B—Kt2
4 P—K4	P—Q3
5 B—Kt5	P—KR3
6 B—R4	O—O

7	P—B4	P—B4
8	P—Q5	P—QR3
9	Kt—B3	P—QKt4
10	B—Q3	P—Kt5
11	Kt—K2	B—Kt5
12	O—O	QKt—Q2
13	Q—Q2	Q—B2
14	QR—K1	QR—K1
15	P—KR3	B x Kt
16	R x B	P—K3
17	P x P	R x P
18	Kt—Kt3	Kt—R2
19	Kt—B1	QKt—B3
20	P—B5!	R—K2
21	P x P	P x P
22	P—K5!	R x P
23	R x R	P x R
24	B x P	P—K5
25	R—KKt3	Q—K4
26	Kt—K3!	Q—B5
27	Q—K1!	Kt—Kt4??

28	R x Kt!	P x R
29	B—Kt3!	Kt—R4
30	B x Q	Kt x B
31	B—B5	B—Q5
32	B—Kt4	Kt—Q6
33	Q—K2	R—B7
34	Q x R	Kt x Q
35	K x Kt	B x P
36	B—B5	P—R4

Reshevsky struggles hard, but the rest is only a formality.

37	B x P	P—R5
38	B—B2	P—Kt6
39	P x P	P—R6
40	B—Kt1 and wins.	

---

307. New York, 1955.

Stroke and counter-stroke! The errors help to make this game even more exciting.

KING'S INDIAN DEFENSE

	S. RESHEVSKY White	I. A. HOROWITZ Black
1	P—Q4	Kt—KB3
2	P—QB4	P—QB4
3	P—Q5	P—K4
4	Kt—QB3	P—Q3
5	P—K4	P—KKt3
6	B—Q3	B—Kt2
7	KKt—K2	O—O
8	P—KR3	Kt—R3
9	B—Kt5	Kt—B2
10	Q—Q2	Q—K1!
11	P—KKt4	P—QR3
12	Kt—Kt3	P—Kt4!
13	P—Kt3	R—Kt1
14	P—B3	Kt—Q2!
15	K—B2	Kt—Kt3
16	QR—QKt1	B—Q2
17	P—KR4	P—B3
18	B—K3	R—B2!
19	P—QR3	B—KB1
20	Kt—R2	B—K2
21	P—R5	P—Kt4
22	Kt—B5	B x Kt
23	KP x P	P—K5!
24	P x KP	Kt—Q2
25	B—K2	B—Q1
26	Kt—B3	Kt—K4
27	P—Kt4	BP x P
28	R x P	P—R4!
29	R—Kt3	P—Kt5
30	P x P	P x P
31	Q—B2	Kt—R3
32	Kt—Kt5	R—Q2
33	R—R1	Kt—B4!
34	Kt x P	. . . .

34	. . . .	Kt x KtPch!!
35	KB x Kt	Q—K4!
36	R—QB1	Kt x R
37	Q x Kt	Q x Kt?
38	P—B5	Q—K4
39	P—Q6ch	K—B1
40	Q—K6?	Q—R7ch
41	K—B3	R—R2
42	P—Q7	B—K2
43	P—B6	R(1)—R1!
44	P—B7	R x P
45	R x R	Q x R
46	P—R6	Q—Q3!
47	Q—B4	Q x P
48	B—R5	B—Q3
49	K—Kt4	R—B1
50	Q—Q5	Q—K2
51	B—Q4	R—Q1
52	K—R3	B—K4!
53	B—B5	R x Q
54	B x Qch	K x B
55	P x R	P—Kt6
56	B—B3	K—Q3
	Resigns	

---

308. Mar del Plata, 1955.

First Brilliancy Prize.

KING'S INDIAN DEFENSE

G. IDIGORAS		O. PANNO
White		Black
1	P—Q4	Kt—KB3
2	P—QB4	P—KKt3
3	Kt—KB3	B—Kt2
4	P—KKt3	O—O
5	B—Kt2	P—Q3
6	O—O	Kt—B3
7	Kt—B3	P—QR3
8	P—KR3	R—Kt1
9	P—Kt3	P—QKt4
10	P—K3!	Kt—QR4
11	P x P	P x P
12	B—Kt2	P—Kt5
13	Kt—K2	B—QR3
14	R—K1	Q—Q2
15	R—QB1	KR—B1
16	Kt—B4	P—B3
17	P—KR4!	Q—R2
18	R—B2	Kt—Kt2
19	P—R5!	P—B4
20	P x KtP	RP x P
21	B—KR3	R—B1
22	Kt—Kt5!	B—R3
23	Kt x KtP!!	. . . .

23	. . . .	P x Kt
24	B—K6ch	K—Kt2
25	P—B4	Kt—Q1
26	P—Q5	B—B1
27	R—R2	B x B
28	P x B	Q—R3
29	Q—Kt4	R—KR1
30	Kt—B3!	Q—Q6
31	P—K4	P—B5
32	P x P	Q x BP
33	P—B5	P—Kt4
34	Q—R5	K—B1
35	Q—Kt6	B—Kt2

36 R x Rch	B x R
37 Kt x P	B—Kt2
38 Kt—R7ch	K—Kt1
39 B x Kt	P x B
40 Kt x Pch	K—B1
41 Q—K8 mate	

---

309. Zagreb, 1956.

Beware the Knight Pawn.

QUEEN'S GAMBIT DECLINED

A. FUDERER	B. MILICH
White	Black
1 P—QB4	P—K3
2 Kt—QB3	P—Q4
3 P—Q4	Kt—KB3
4 B—Kt5	B—K2
5 P—K3	O—O
6 R—B1	P—KR3
7 B—R4	Kt—K5
8 B x B	Q x B
9 Q—B2	P—QB3
10 B—Q3	Kt x Kt
11 Q x Kt	Q—Kt4
12 Kt—B3!	Q x P
13 K—K2	Q—R6
14 QR—KKt1	P—KB4
15 R—Kt3	Q—R4
16 KR—KKt1	R—B2
17 Q—R3!	Kt—Q2
18 K—K1	P x P
19 B x QBP	P—B5
20 R x Pch!!	R x R
21 B x Pch	K—R1
22 R x R	K x R
23 Q—K7ch	K—R1
24 Kt—K5!	P x P
25 P—B4	Resigns

In the past four years, age has bowed to youth. On the international scene, Mikhail Tal, in his early twenties, defeated 49-year-old Mikhail Botvinnik for the chess championship of the world. At home, Bobby Fischer at 17 has annexed the U. S. Championship ahead of 49-year-old Samuel Reshevsky. Victory of an American students' team at Leningrad portends the trend of events to come.

310. United States Championship
New York, 1956

Dubbed the Game of the Century, the following is a stunning masterpiece of combination play performed by a boy of 13 against a formidable opponent. It matches the finest on record in the history of chess prodigies.

GRUENFELD DEFENSE

D. BYRNE	R. FISCHER
White	Black
1 Kt—KB3	Kt—KB3
2 P—QB4	P—KKt3
3 Kt—B3	B—Kt2
4 P—Q4	O—O
5 B—B4	P—Q4
6 Q—Kt3	PxP
7 Q x BP	P—B3
8 P—K4	QKt—Q2
9 R—Q1	Kt—Kt3
10 Q—B5	B—Kt5
11 B—KKt5	Kt—R5!
12 Q—R3	Kt x Kt
13 P x Kt	Kt x P
14 B x P	Q—Kt3
15 B—B4	Kt x QBP
16 B—B5	KR—K1ch
17 K—B1	. . . .
17	B—K3!
18 B x Q	B x Bch
19 K—Kt1	Kt—K7ch
20 K—B1	Kt x Pch
21 K—Kt1	Kt—K7ch
22 K—B1	Kt—B6ch
23 K—Kt1	PxB
24 Q—Kt4	R—R5
25 Q x P	Kt x R
26 P—KR3	R x P
27 K—R2	Kt x P
28 R—K1	R x R
29 Q—Q8ch	B—B1
30 Kt x R	B—Q4
31 Kt—B3	Kt—K5
32 Q—Kt8	P—QKt4
33 P—R4	P—R4
34 Kt—K5	K—Kt2
35 K—Kt1	B—B4ch
36 K—B1	Kt—Kt6ch
37 K—K1	B—Kt5ch
38 K—Q1	B—Kt6ch
39 K—B1	Kt—K7ch
40 K—Kt1	Kt—B6ch
41 K—B1	R—QB7 mate

311. World Team Championship, Leipzig, 1960

Mellow, then three-time U. S. champion, 17-year-old Bobby Fischer treats this game like a veteran pro. The tail-end sacrifice is stupendous and amusing.

KING'S INDIAN DEFENSE

R. LETELIER (Chile)	R. FISCHER (U.S.A.)
White	Black
1 P—Q4	Kt—KB3
2 P—QB4	P—KKt3
3 Kt—QB3	B—Kt2
4 P—K4	O—O
5 P—K5	Kt—K1
6 P—B4	P—Q3
7 B—K3	P—QB4
8 QP x P	Kt—QB3
9 BP x P	P x P
10 Kt—K4	B—B4
11 Kt—Kt3	B—K3
12 Kt—B3	Q—B2
13 Q—Kt1	P x P
14 P—KB5	P—K5
15 P x B	P x Kt
16 P x P	P—B4
17 P—B4	Kt—B3
18 B—K2	KR—K1
19 K—B2	R x P
20 R—K1	QR—K1
21 B—B3	R x B
22 R x R	R x R
23 K x R	....

23	Q x Pch
24 Resigns	

Through 1966, the Soviet steamroller has continued to dominate the field. The only threat to their almost vested retention of the title, at the present writing, is in the person of the American ace Bobby Fischer. Included in this new edition are six of his recent triumphs in important tournaments.

312. Varna, 1962

Fischer gives up the exchange for a bind.

SICILIAN DEFENSE

R. J. FISCHER	M. NAJDORF
White	Black
1 P—K4	P—QB4
2 Kt—KB3	P—Q3
3 P—Q4	P x P
4 Kt x P	Kt—KB3
5 Kt—QB3	P—QR3
6 P—KR3	P—QKt4
7 Kt—Q5	B—Kt2
8 Kt x Ktch	KtP x Kt
9 P—QB4	P x P
10 B x P	B x P
11 O—O	P—Q4
12 R—K1	P—K4

13 Q—R4ch	Kt—Q2
14 R x B	P x R
15 Kt—B5	B—B4
16 Kt—Kt7ch	K—K2
17 Kt—B5ch	K—K1
18 B—K3	B x B
19 P x B	Q—Kt3

20 R—Q1	R—R2
21 R—Q6	Q—Q1
22 Q—N3	Q—B2
23 B x Pch	K—Q1
24 B—K6	Resigns

313.

Varna, 1962

An incisive refutation of the double-edged Center Counter.

CENTER COUNTER DEFENSE

R. J. FISCHER	K. ROBATSCH
White	Black
1 P—K4	P—Q4
2 P x P	Q x P
3 Kt—QB3	Q—Q1
4 P—Q4	P—KKt3
5 B—KB4	B—Kt2
6 Q—Q2	Kt—KB3
7 O—O—O	P—B3
8 B—KR6	O—O
9 P—KR4	Q—R4
10 P—R5	P x P
11 B—Q3	QKt—Q2
12 KKt—K2	R—Q1
13 P—KKt4	Kt—B1
14 P x P	Kt—K3
15 QR—Kt1	K—R1
16 B x Bch	Kt x B
17 Q—R6	R—KKt1
18 R—Kt5	Q—Q1
19 R(1)—Kt1	Kt—B4
20 B x Kt	Resigns

314.

U. S. Championship
New York, 1963-1964

The astute sideline kibitzers were surprised at Byrne's final decision!

GRUENFELD DEFENSE

R. BYRNE	R. J. FISCHER
White	Black
1 P—Q4	Kt—KB3
2 P—QB4	P—KKt3
3 P—KKt3	P—B3
4 B—Kt2	P—Q4
5 P x P	P x P
6 Kt—QB3	B—Kt2
7 P—K3	O—O
8 KKt—K2	Kt—B3
9 O—O	P—Kt3
10 P—Kt3	B—QR3
11 B—QR3	R—K1
12 Q—Q2	P—K4
13 P x P	Kt x P
14 KR—Q1	Kt—Q6
15 Q—B2	Kt x P
16 K x Kt	Kt—Kt5ch
17 K—Kt1	Kt x KP
18 Q—Q2	Kt x B

(see diagram next page)

19	K x Kt	P—Q5
20	Kt x P	B—Kt2ch
21	K—B1	Q—Q2

Resigns

---

315. U. S. Championship
New York, 1963-1964

A quarter-back block clears the path to the post.

PIRC DEFENSE

R. J. FISCHER		PAL BENKO
White		Black
1	P—K4	P—KKt3
2	P—Q4	B—Kt2
3	Kt—QB3	P—Q3
4	P—B4	Kt—KB3
5	Kt—B3	O—O
6	B—Q3	B—Kt5
7	P—KR3	B x Kt
8	Q x B	Kt—B3
9	B—K3	P—K4
10	QP x P	P x P
11	P—B5	P x P
12	Q x P	Kt—Q5
13	Q—B2	Kt—K1
14	O—O	Kt—Q3
15	Q—Kt3	K—R1
16	Q—Kt4	P—QB3
17	Q—R5	Q—K1
18	B x Kt	P x B

19	R—B6	K—Kt1
20	P—K5	P—KR3
21	Kt—K2	Resigns

Fischer's brilliancy is par for the course — For Fischer of course

---

316.
Soviet Championship, 1964

A crosscheck and a quiet move and it's over.

CARO-KANN DEFENSE

N. BAKULIN		D. BRONSTEIN
White		Black
1	P—K4	P—QB3
2	P—Q4	P—Q4
3	Kt—QB3	P x P
4	Kt x P	Kt—B3
5	Kt x Ktch	KtP x Kt
6	B—K3	B—B4
7	Q—Q2	P—K3
8	Kt—K2	Kt—Q2
9	Kt—Kt3	B—Kt3
10	B—K2	Q—B2
11	O—O	P—KR4
12	KR—Q1	P—R5
13	Kt—B1	P—R6
14	P—KKt3	O—O—O
15	P—QB4	P—QB4
16	P—Q5	P—K4

17	QR—B1	P—B4
18	P—QKt4	B—Q3
19	P—B3	P—B5
20	B—B2	QR—K1
21	K—R1	KR—Kt1
22	R—K1	P—K5
23	B x P	Kt x B
24	P x Kt	Q x P
25	B—Q1	B—B2
26	KtP x P	P—K6
27	Q—K2	B—Q6
28	Q x B	R—Kt8ch
29	K x R	P—K7ch
30	Kt—K3	R x Kt
31	Q—B5ch	R—K3ch
32	K—R1	Q—B7
	Resigns	

---

317. Havana, 1965

The defense rests on a hairline.

SICILIAN DEFENSE

G. TRINGOFF		R. J. FISCHER
	White	Black
1	P—K4	P—QB4
2	Kt—KB3	P—Q3
3	P—Q4	P x P
4	Kt x P	Kt—KB3
5	Kt—QB3	P—QR3
6	B—Kt5	P—K3
7	P—B4	Q—Kt3
8	Q—Q2	Q x P
9	R—QKt1	Q—R6
10	P—K5	P x P
11	P x P	KKt—Q2
12	B—QB4	B—Kt5
13	R—Kt3	Q—R4
14	O—O	O—O
15	Kt x P	P x Kt
16	B x Pch	K—R1
17	R x Rch	B x R
18	Q—B4	Kt—QB3
19	Q—B7	Q—B4ch
20	K—R1	Kt—B3
21	B x B	Kt x P
22	Q—K6	Kt(4)—Kt5
	Resigns	

---

318. Havana, 1965

An amusing tail-end "combine" wraps up the point.

RUY LOPEZ

B. IVKOV		J. H. DONNER
	White	Black
1	P—K4	P—K4
2	Kt—KB3	Kt—QB3
3	B—Kt5	P—QR3
4	B—R4	Kt—B3
5	O—O	Kt x P
6	P—Q4	P—QKt4
7	B—Kt3	P—Q4
8	P x P	B—K3
9	Q—K2	Kt—B4
10	R—Q1	Kt x B
11	BP x Kt	B—K2
12	Kt—B3	O—O
13	B—K3	Kt—R4
14	QR—B1	Kt—Kt2
15	Kt—K4	B—KKt5
16	P—KR3	B x Kt

17	Q x B	P—QB3
18	Kt—Kt3	R—B1
19	Kt—B5	P—Kt3
20	R x QP	Q—K1

21 B—R6	Resigns

319.
Zagreb, 1965

Mate leaves no weaknesses in its wake.

ROBATSCH DEFENSE

A. BISGUIER — B. LARSEN

White	Black
1 P—Q4	P—KKt3
2 P—K4	B—Kt2
3 P—KB4	P—Q3
4 Kt—KB3	Kt—KB3
5 B—Q3	O—O
6 O—O	QKt—Q2
7 P—K5	Kt—K1
8 Q—K1	P—QB4
9 P—B5	P x KP
10 P x KtP	RP x P
11 Q—R4	KP x P
12 B—KR6	Kt (1)—B3
13 Kt—Kt5	Kt—K4
14 R x Kt	B—R1
15 R—B1	R—K1
16 B—B8	B—B3
17 R x B	P x R
18 Q—R6	R x B
19 Q—R7 mate	

320.
World Championship, 1966

Spassky wins the opening; Petrosian the end.

KING'S INDIAN DEFENSE

T. PETROSIAN — B. SPASSKY

White	Black
1 Kt—KB3	Kt—KB3
2 P—KKt3	P—KKt3
3 P—B4	B—Kt2
4 B—Kt2	O—O
5 O—O	Kt—B3
6 Kt—B3	P—Q3
7 P—Q4	P—QR3
8 P—Q5	Kt—QR4
9 Kt—Q2	P—B4
10 Q—B2	P—K4
11 P—Kt3	Kt—Kt5
12 P—K4	P—B4
13 P x P	P x P
14 Kt—Q1	P—Kt4
15 P—B3	P—K5
16 B—Kt2	KP x P
17 B x P	B x B
18 Q x B	Kt—K4
19 B—K2	P—B5
20 P x BP	B—R6
21 Kt—K3	B x R
22 R x B	Kt—Kt3
23 B—Kt4	KKt x P
24 R x Kt	R x R
25 B—K6ch	R—B2
26 Kt—K4	Q—R5
27 Kt x QP	Q—Kt4ch
28 K—R1	R—R2
29 BxRch	R x B

30 Q—R8ch	Resigns

---

321. Los Angeles, 1966

A modern immortal.

SICILIAN DEFENSE

B. LARSEN	T. PETROSYAN
White	Black
1 P—K4	P—QB4
2 Kt—KB3	Kt—QB3
3 P—Q4	P x P
4 Kt x P	P—KKt3
5 B—K3	B—Kt2
6 P—QB4	Kt—B3
7 Kt—QB3	Kt—KKt5
8 Q x Kt	Kt x Kt
9 Q—Q1	Kt—K3
10 Q—Q2	P—Q3
11 B—K2	B—Q2
12 O—O	O—O
13 QR—Q1	B—QB3
14 Kt—Q5	R—K1
15 P—B4	Kt—B2·
16 P—KB5	Kt—R3
17 B—Kt4	Kt—B4
18 P x P	RP x P
19 Q—KB2	R—KB1
20 P—K5	B x P
21 Q—R4	B x Kt
22 R x B	Kt—K3
23 R—B3	B—B3
24 Q—R6	B—Kt2

25 Q x P	Kt—B5
26 R x Kt	P x Q
27 B—K6ch	R—B2
28 R x R	K—R1
29 R—KKt5	P—Kt4
30 R—Kt3	Resigns

322. Los Angeles, 1966

Black's innocuous queen-side play leaves the other flank vulnerable.

SICILIAN DEFENSE

R. J. FISCHER	B. IVKOV
White	Black
1 P—K4	P—QB4
2 Kt—KB3	P—K3
3 P—Q3	Kt—QB3
4 P—KKt3	P—Q4
5 QKt—Q2	B—Q3
6 B—Kt2	KKt—K2
7 O—O	O—O
8 Kt—R4	P—QKt3
9 P—KB4	PxP
10 P x P	B—R3
11 R—K1	P—B5
12 P—B3	B—B4ch
13 K—R1	Kt—R4
14 P—K5	Kt—Q4
15 Kt—K4	B—Kt2
16 Q—R5	Kt—K2
17 P—KKt4	B x Kt
18 B x B	P—Kt3
19 Q—R6	Kt—Q4
20 P—B5	R—K1
21 P x KtP	BP x P
22 Kt x P	Q—Q2
23 Kt—B4	QR—Q1
24 Kt—R5	K—R1
25 Kt—B6	Kt x Kt
26 P x Kt	R—KKt1
27 B—B4	R x P
28 QR—Q1	QR—KKt1
29 P—B7	Resigns

Index of Players

— Y —

— Z —